ISSUES
IN CHILDREN'S
BOOK SELECTION

ISSUES IN CHILDREN'S BOOK SELECTION

A School Library Journal/ Library Journal Anthology

With an Introduction by
Lillian Gerhardt

R.R. BOWKER COMPANY
New York & London, 1973
A Xerox Education Company

XEROX

Published by R. R. Bowker Co. (A Xerox Education Company)
1180 Avenue of the Americas, New York, N.Y. 10036
Copyright © 1973 by Xerox Corporation
All rights reserved.
Printed and bound in the United States of America

Library of Congress Cataloging in Publication Data
Main entry under title:
Issues in children's book selection.
   A collection of articles reprinted from School
library journal.
 · 1. Book selection—Addresses, essays, lectures.
2. Children's literature—Addresses, essays,
lectures. I. School library journal.
Z1037.A1185   028.52   73-13553
ISBN 0-8352-0688-2

Contents

v

Part IV: THEMES AND GENRES

Part V: PAST, PRESENT, AND FUTURE

Introduction

The 29 articles on aspects of current book selection that are collected here are reprinted exactly as they were first published in *School Library Journal*. Each article reprinted carries the date of the article's publication and readers are advised to use these dates in order to check following issues of their volumes of *SLJ* for the critical correspondence most of the articles attracted. When each of these articles was first published, the children's books cited were all in print, unless otherwise indicated in the article's text or in its bibliography. Readers can establish the current availability of these titles by checking the citations against the latest edition of *Children's Books In Print* (Bowker) and they can measure the growth in new children's books on any of the topics discussed in these articles by checking under the topic in the latest edition of *Subject Guide to Children's Books In Print* (Bowker).

School Library Journal has always been generous to other publishers in granting permission to reprint *SLJ*'s articles on aspects of book selection for children and young people. When such collections are published, *SLJ*'s editors usually receive courtesy copies. Scanning them (without bias or prejudice, of course) the editors most often conclude that the primary articles on questions in

library book selection for minors were published first in our pages. It's high time then that our regular readers and students new to the subject of books for children had a collection from *SLJ*, unencumbered by lesser, lighter, and later articles from other periodicals. Bound issues of the back copies of our magazine are awkward to use and this expedient reprinting allows our readers to have it all, easily portable between two covers and without the eyestrain of hours over the indexes to library and education periodicals in which *SLJ*'s articles are cited.

Under "Perspectives on Selection" we've grouped six challenges to current book evaluation practices. Each of these articles examines an aspect of traditional book selection for children and each asks that readers measure the effectiveness of widely accepted practices against contemporary conditions and/or new knowledge.

"Intellectual Freedom or Censorship" is the broad heading that embraces five articles on the single most important issue that faces librarians serving every age level today. The Supreme Court's recent decision on pornography, which forces the question of permission to buy, sell, or circulate back on variant community standards, might have been forecast from the Court's refusal to hear the Piri Thomas case, the first school library censorship case ever taken to that level, a decision fully discussed and analyzed in "Impressionable Minds—Forbidden Subjects." Intellectual freedom for adults is constitutionally guaranteed; absolutists believe it should be granted without restriction or modification to children, too, and this view is propounded in "Acting for the Children." All of the articles in this section were intended to start continuing arguments, needed to help reveal the almost invisible line where library selection leaves off and official censorship begins.

"Images" might just as easily have been called "The Identification of Propaganda." The articles in this group analyze children's books for the biases and prejudices that can subtly affect children's developing reactions on such subjects as race, religion, and male/female roles. Such analytical articles have intensified the concerns of librarians, teachers and parents with the always problematic question of how children can be guided to conclusions about what is right and what is wrong through their entertainment reading.

"Themes and Genres" offers eight articles criticizing some of the most popular subjects in children's books at this time—forms of writing most popular with children, topics currently favored by children's book publishers, and selection questions most often raised by librarians serving children. Despite the fact that the popularity of the subjects with all three groups are certain to change in time, the articles are excellent guides to modes and methods in children's book criticism.

"Past, Present, and Future" presents three articles that outline and debate the implications of three long-term problems in children's book evaluation: the international exchange, through translation, of books for children; the impact of mass media reviews on nonspecialist book buyers and their effect on the climate of general opinion about books for children; and the marshalling of children's book collections as resources for scholars in every discipline.

A perusal of this collection of articles on children's book selection shows not only what *SLJ* has published within the past ten years on the many questions and concerns generated by this subject, but the gaps too—the articles that are *not* being written, *not* being published by this or any other magazine.

Each year relatively few critical essays appear on book selection for children in the United States. The annual volume of publishing for children in this country has, for many years, been so great that practicing children's librarians have, perforce, become reviewers without the time to become critics—forever caught in the endless task of considering new acquisitions for their collections on a book-by-book basis. In other countries, where the annual production of new general trade children's books comes nowhere near our yearly records of 2,000 titles and more, specialists in library work with children can compass all (or nearly all) of their country's new juvenile book production, spot the trends and gaps more easily, hone their critical expertise within narrower boundaries. Our new books for children get put through an initial mesh of written and oral reviews by librarians who seldom have the time to go back, reevaluate and discuss at length the changing conditions and tastes that make a children's book viable in its time, reveal a society's attitudes at a given point, or to trace the influences on changing modes of writing from decade to decade. The greatest deterrent to effective criticism in any art form is continuous over-supply.

Another striking reason for the dearth in current critical writing about books for children is the status accorded teachers of children's literature. The publish-or-perish system that so affects the faculties in other subject specialties has hardly any effect in this field. Few teachers of children's literature teach their subject full-time with full faculty rank. Of the 2,500 teachers of children's literature on the R. R. Bowker Company's mailing list for this group, a mere handful make their livings in schools of library service or education; most are teaching their courses once a week and are busy practicing librarians the rest of the time. They are effectively removed from the time to write and the pressure to produce at the pace and scholarly level essential to the expansion of any graduate or undergraduate study.

These facts are in no sense offered as an alibi for the difficulties of supplying the type and amount of criticism this field should have at hand after over 50 years of specialized publishing for children. Rather, they pinpoint the present conditions, under which criticism is produced mostly by working librarians who have taken fire from current problems in selection and by some of the authors who write books for children—authors with the critical capacity to look past their own books to the questions theirs and all other books raise. *SLJ* and its readers have every reason to be grateful for those who write in the face of the twin pressures of over-supply and too little time for the gaps they've helped to fill. Yet, there are still areas where the field needs much more—and soon.

The questions of school library selection that never reach the public hearing or courtroom stage are rife in every state. Case histories documenting the school library selection cases that go no further than boards of education and the policy solutions—or restrictions—that result are badly needed for a clearer picture of the selection conditions under which school librarians practice, seldom afforded the full control and freedom exercised by librarians in public libraries.

Another school library selection question without the heat of censorship charges but needing just as much light concerns the practical factors and steps in reorganizing school library collections for those schools in the states that are shifting to K–3 and middle grade separation.

Public libraries have been laggard in reporting their experiences with school-housed branches. Proposals to turn public library services to minors over to the schools have much tax-payer appeal despite the vocal reluctance of both school and public librarians. Selection conditions in school-housed public library branches are of first importance to considering these proposals.

Fifteen or twenty years ago, a collection such as this would undoubtedly have had a hefty section on the literary merits of various authors and genres. While current concerns center on the analysis of racism, sexism, or ethnic images, as a glance at the table of contents clearly shows, much—nearly everything—remains to be done in examining the techniques employed in writing fiction for children, its literary merits and the standards for discerning those merits. Questions of the degree and weight of the positive/negative suasions or propaganda in fiction for children will, and should, always be with us, but lately they have dominated the questions of excellence that are central to the consideration of any art form. There are prolific and/or stellar authors of children's books whose bodies of work offer a seemingly endless possibility for critical discussions that have never yet been written or published.

Nonfiction for children at every reading level has yet to receive its due, although every topic and method in juvenile nonfiction offers even the most inexperienced librarians a wide-open field for analysis—in terms of coverage, comparison to standard adult titles, measures of accuracy, effectiveness of presentation.

No magazine is ever complete; there is always the next issue for which plans must be made. The closest analogous experience is that of librarians, because the selection of collections for successive generations of children is never completed, must always be planned ahead. It is *SLJ*'s hope in offering this spectrum of recent articles on pressing aspects of book selection for children that readers at every level of library service will rethink the questions that affect their book selection and plan ahead to supply the primary criticism the subject requires. Librarians have always been the first and best suppliers of such criticism and *SLJ* will continue to be the first to find and publish it.

LILLIAN N. GERHARDT
Editor-in-Chief
School Library Journal

I

Perspectives on Selection

If That Don't Do No Good, That Won't Do No Harm: The Uses and Dangers of Mediocrity in Children's Reading

Sheila Egoff

MY TITLE, despite its very modern flavour (it is becomingly ungrammatical), is actually taken from an ancient English folk tale, *Tom Tit Tot*. Some of you may know the story better from its Germanic counterpart, *Rumpelstiltskin*. In the English version, the key phrase— "if that don't do no good, that won't do no harm," resounds throughout the story as the policy whereby the heroine, a greedy and witless girl, guides herself into one predicament after another. In the end, of course, she lives happily ever after, but anyone over six years of age is left wondering whether this successful outcome is because of, or in spite of, the heroine's laissez-faire philosophy.

And what has this to do with the current state of children's reading? I suggest, and you'll realize now how very artful indeed my title is, that the dilemma represented in *Tom Tit Tot* is the crucial issue in current writing for children. All of us concerned with children's reading—writers, publishers, editors, teachers, booksellers, librarians, parents—all of us must decide whether to stake out our ground on the basis of careful planning or laissez faire, of principles versus expediency, of guidance as compared to permissiveness. "If that don't do no good, that won't do no harm," is there perhaps merit in mediocrity?

This dilemma, of course, is by no means new. A friend of mine used to claim that it was the compelling interest of football players' exploits as recounted on cornflakes boxes that started him on his reading career and that it was by a purely simple and natural progression from this point that he ended up by taking Schopenhauer and James Joyce to bed with him.

Now, to extrapolate from the particular to the general is a widely practiced, if somewhat suspect, form of reasoning. My friend, the cornflakes man, maintains that what he did anyone else can do— that, in short, the road to Dostoevsky always begins with *Dick and Jane*. And, you know, up to a certain point, he is right. He is a compulsive reader—as indeed, I would guess, are many of you right here in this audience. Compulsive readers are like termites—they devour any book in their path, telephone directories and government publications included, and they have serious withdrawal symptoms when their bookish diet is somehow denied to them. There are even, I may add, specializations in compulsion—people who are perfectly normal about reading except when they are in a hammock or a bathroom. My prize for the most interesting variant in obsessional reading goes to the one book man, as exemplified by old Gabriel Betteredge in Wilkie Collins's *The Moonstone*. Betteredge made a lifetime's preoccupation with *Robinson Crusoe*: "When my spirits are bad—*Robinson Crusoe*. When I want advice—*Robinson Crusoe*. In past times, when my wife plagued me; in present times, when I have had a drop too much—*Robinson Crusoe*. I have worn out six stout *Robinson Crusoe's* with hard work in my service."

Well, this kind of addiction is a bit unusual all right, but it helps to make my point: the book addict *is* unusual and little purpose is served in generalizing from his case. The reader who begins with "cornflakes" boxes is, I'm afraid, more apt to move on to "super sugar crisp" boxes than to anything else.

Let me go on then to the more typical situation. The average child reads, outside of school books, perhaps a book a week, assuming of course, that he has a conscientious mother and that his father watches enough football games to prevent junior from monopolizing the set. For the eight years between ages six and 14, that makes a total of about 400 books. (If you are questioning my mathematics, I've given the child a week off each year for measles, mumps, etc.) Currently there are about 6000 children's books published yearly in the English language, give or take a few hundred for reprints, different versions, etc. Many of the previously published books, of course, are still available, so the child has, according to *Children's Books in Print*, perhaps 41,000 titles to choose from. Of this number two and one half percent are excellent, 35 percent are perceptibly sludge and dross, and the rest are in between, that is, mediocre. (The percentages, by the way, are purely of my own derivation, but I can vouch for their accuracy on the basis of my own infallible emotional reactions. A fine book sends me rushing to share it, with anyone I can find, child or adult; a mediocre book sets my teeth on edge, and a poor one makes me laugh). So, and here's the grand summation: if the number of mediocre children's books

extant is 62 1/2 percent of 41,000 or 27,000, and if the child reads 400 books overall, he has a very good chance of having spent his childhood in reading nothing but mediocre books.

Does this matter? There will be many who say that it doesn't and despite my personal prepossessions—you'll see that I'm already giving away my ending—I will admit that they have a considerable case.

They point out, first of all, that reading is a basic operation, and a child needs print simply for practice, if nothing else. Demosthenes practiced too. He practiced orations in order to eliminate his speech defect. But it was the pebble in his mouth, not the noble rhetoric that really did the trick. Similarly, reading for utilitarian purpose need have little concern for style and content. Yes, I concede, it is practice that makes the perfectly skilled reader and it doesn't make much difference what he practices on.

Along with reading for practice goes reading for progress. Most of us here today have advanced in life because we can absorb reading material quickly. We can take courses, retrain ourselves, write reports and briefs, and so on. I think it is safe to deduce that reading has always been deemed useful and if it weren't, I doubt that the technologically backward nations would be spending so much time and money on literacy programs.

The reverse is also true. Reading for pure pleasure can be just as artless as reading to develop literacy. We listen to the radio, watch TV, swim, ski, sail, or gossip just for the fun of it and do not berate ourselves for doing so. If a girl wants to spend a good deal of her time reading nurse stories, is it any different? Is it any worse? Reading for recreation needs little content and no defense, or at least, so say the esteemed scholars on the University of British Columbia faculty from whom I borrow my murder mysteries.

Then of course, there is also the argument that goes this way. "How can anyone discover what a good book is who has not experienced the bad?" I love this line of reasoning because it is so comforting. It enables me to overeat, come late, sleep in, and give poor classes for how else whould I know the right thing to do? Still, rationalizations aside, there *is* something to this line of reasoning. Good judgement derives ultimately from experience in comparison, and it is no accident that some of our finest works of art juxtapose the beautiful and the grotesque.

But these are all classical arguments; do they still hold true for our own time? More so than ever, I'm afraid. You have merely to examine the Report of the President's Commission on Obscenity to realize that the rights of the individual are now fiercely defended, even if it is only the right to do something foolish or repugnant. In the present atmosphere of "doing one's own thing," there is noticeable hesitancy for anyone to make a qualitative decision for another person. I met with considerable opposition a couple of years ago in my classes in children's literature when I stated that the Bobbsey Twins and their like were not worth acquiring by a public or school library. (And I gave some pretty good reasons, I assure you). However, my view was interpreted as an infringement of a child's freedom to read and I was roundly abused by my class. Now four or five years ago not only would the students have been more afraid of me as a teacher, but they would also have almost automatically conceded the right of a person in charge of public funds to have a very definite say about what materials are put into a public institution. What the students were arguing for is called in librarianship "the demand theory of book selection" which is to be translated as "give people what they want." "Let's be truly democratic," they tell me, which means, I suppose, that one person's literary taste should carry no more weight than one person's vote.

In many cases this attitude has induced fear in those who should be in a guidance role. Fear of not being popular; fear of taking issue where one's authority could be rejected; fear of one's judgments being judged and found in error. A person in this position tends to withdraw from the difficulty and adopt the principle "Safety first." How frequent is such yielding to popular pressure? No one can supply precise statistics, of course, but we have a clue of sorts in the somewhat similar situation that prevails regarding censorship of so-called "controversial books." Marjorie Fiske's study of California librarians showed that a *majority* were guilty of self-censorship—that is, they refused to buy or, having bought, hid away, those books which they feared might arouse public outcry. And perhaps the saddest aspect of the whole affair is that many of these fearful librarians managed to deceive themselves into believing that they were merely following community standards!

Fiske's study was conducted in the 1950's when the pressures came from the right. Nowadays the potent pressure comes from the left. It calls itself, in library circles at least, the movement for "social responsibility" and the reasoning is not without some considerable validity. It goes this way. Our society has disadvantaged groups. They are in a desperate situation that will call for desperate remedies, in matters of reading as well as in matters of economics. Worry not therefore about the maintenance of standards but find something, anything, that will bring them inside the library: cartoon movies, rock concerts and "easy books."

I have a good deal of sympathy for this point of view. It may well be that the tastes of middle-class librarians are not appropriate for the needs of slum children. What troubles me, though, is the strong element of condescension which I see implied in this attitude when it equates "easy" with "inferior." What the disadvantaged don't need surely is disadvantaged materials. When you can offer them *Sounder* (William Armstrong, Harper, 1969)—which is a poignant, believable story of a black family that has meaning for readers of every colour—why give them *Tessie*? (Jesse Jackson, Harper, 1968) (which has no relationship to reality). If *Pennington's Seventeenth Summer* (Maureen Daly, Dodd, 1948) is available, why read *Count Me Gone* (Annabel and Edgar Johnson, S. & S., 1968)? (While Pennington derives its plot from the nature of the hero's character, *Count Me Gone* is simply a piling up of rather lurid incidents).

However, I will admit that finding books that have both simplicity and substance is no small task. And this, of course, is *exactly* the virtue of mediocrity—if you can persuade yourself that almost any book will do, you avoid the large and nervous-making labor of selection. No blood, no sweat, no tears, Ché sera sera and let the blurb be my guide! This, of course, is *exactly* why I am suspicious of this philosophy. Hesiod, back in the eighth century B.C., already recognized the problem when he said: "Badness you can get easily, in quantity; the road is smooth and it lies close by. But in front of excellence the immortal gods have put sweat, and long and steep is the way to it, and rough at first. But when you come to the top, then it is easy, even though it is hard."

It takes some considerable hard training to be able to run a mile, to weld metal, to split the atom, to write *Crime and Punishment*, to read the *Bible*. Once the skills are mastered, then the results seem effortless. Working on skills should in no way preclude the effort to reach a goal of excellence, nor should the method of reaching it preclude the exercise of excellence. James Ryan did not run the mile in 3:51.1 after mediocre training.

Unfortunately, many writers and reviewers for children advocate almost the opposite approach. They concentrate on the age and the reading ability of a child as defined by tests and grades. For instance, have you noticed how many children's books of the 60's begin by giving us the actual age of the hero or heroine as if only the reader who is actually that age will enjoy it? The publishers, in their blurbs, hasten to categorize the book by age or grade, in case the author hasn't made this clear. And, of course, reviewers compound it all. For examples, I quote: "*children* may find this book touching, but to an old skeptic it is banal and unrealistic—highly compressed sentimentality." Or "as a serious work of art this novel has little to offer, but for *young people* whose understanding of this period has been clouded by the confused rhetoric of our own times it has an undeniable value." I suggest it is the reviewer who is confused. This confusion may be understandable, however. Since so many children's books are written for extraliterary purposes it is not surprising that they are reviewed with condescension. Anything is good enough for the young. A reviewer of an adult book might well say "this is a scholarly study of Lord Byron" or "this is a readable biography of Lord Byron," but they wouldn't say, "this isn't a very good book on Lord Byron, but it might be enjoyed by a truck driver with a grade 12 education," or "this is a great book, but only for a mature university graduate in English".

Well, let me ask my main question: "Does it matter what children read as long as they do read?" The answers are curiously mixed. Many people would balk at deliberately giving a child a poor book; others would balk at a controversial book. Relatively few, I fear, worry about giving a child something which is simply less than the best.

"If that won't do no good, that won't do no harm." Reading something is better than reading nothing.

Put in that way, such an approach is hard to controvert. But why put it that way? The choice is not really between something and nothing but between various kinds of something—between something so-so and something wow!

As I see it, there are two major facts about children's reading. The first is that whatever mediocre books do, good books can also do—and much better. The second is that mediocre content and style in a very real sense subvert the essential role of children's books. In effect, they deny the medium itself—the book—the opportunity to work its own special kind of magic, to make the kind of particular contribution that the book alone can make.

Let me explain. A book is often a vehicle for recreation and entertainment, but it is doubtful whether it is particularly well suited to such a purpose. Unless the writer is very skillful, the effort required in reading may be more trouble than the entertainment is worth. In any case, reading as pure recreation has no special claims. Is there really any more virtue in reading Earle Stanley Gardner than in watching TV's Perry Mason? However, make the content not one of entertainment value only but also one of depth of thought and emotion and the book wins hands down. No other medium is so fitted for the development of complex ideas and characters, to the building up of the rich texture of life. This is the contribution which is preeminently the book's alone to make and I am distressed when it is used for a much lesser role.

It is obviously valuable to work to improve reading skills, and there are many ways of doing this, but there is another saying besides "practice makes perfect" and that is that "you can keep on practicing your mistakes." There is a difference between literacy and literature.

The role of literature is to help develop the individual and it takes a good book to do this. A poor book takes a child and puts him back a step or two, a mediocre book takes a child and leaves him where he is. A good book promotes an awareness of the possibilities of life, the universality of life, the awakening of response.

And yet, some of us expect this to be done by the mediocre. We say we want the best for our children—in housing, education, medical care. But, when we have a choice, we are quite willing to abrogate any responsibility when it comes to putting things into their minds. Content doesn't matter to us, nor does style or characterization or any of the other indeterminate qualities that make up a fine book. Those of us who are li-brarians talk a great deal about enticing children into libraries, and of starting "at their level." This is as about a ludicrous idea as that old 19th Century one that libraries would wean the workers from the gin palaces.

What do we do when we deliberately provide the mediocre? (We do a lot of it accidentally and inadvertently anyway). My point is over deliberate provision, that is, to do it when we know better. First of all we underestimate children. And we should remember that slow learners and poor readers may be just as interested in *ideas* as quick readers. As a matter of fact, they may have more original ideas and minds because they haven't been clobbered by mediocre ideas picked up in mediocre books. And why is it assumed that the reluctant reader is also potentially a social deviant, particularly in need of moral lectures?

Secondly, the mediocre rarely gets challenged by adults. And if children are constantly presented with mediocre books, how will they know a *good* book when they run into one? You remember, I hope, the argument that children won't be able to judge the good if they are not exposed to the poor. My question is, if they get only mediocrity, how can they judge the good?

Thirdly, the mediocre builds laziness into children. At an age when they are best prepared for challenge it is unjust to deny it to them. Is it because some of us adults don't want to disturb ourselves with challenges that we find it easier to direct children away from them? So often we all find it easier to settle for second best. As far back as 1924, Alice Jordan, then supervisor of Work With Children at the Boston Public Library, recognized this problem when she said, "mediocrity in books for children is more universal and more baffling to combat than sensationalism."

We speak eloquently about the world commonality of children. Most of us as student teachers and librarians have read Paul Hazard's *Books, Children and Men* (Horn Bk., 1960) and have believed it. That is, we have seen a vision of children around the world being linked by their reading—African children, American children, Finnish children, and Turkish children being linked by common reading experiences—in translation, I'll admit. We have wanted the best children's books of each nation to cross boundaries to speak to the children of other nations. Well, if we settle for mediocrity we must give up this vision. Mediocrity is antithetical to commonality. Mediocre books, because they inevitably present a narrower view of life, will simply not translate well, nor will they carry well into another culture. More importantly, perhaps, as far as North America is concerned, the very abundance of the mediocre will prevent the best from rising to the top.

We give in to mediocrity in another sense when we are hipped on format as opposed to content. We look for a book with a sturdy binding, wide margins, large type, and lots of pictures. On one hand we want children to read, for all the reasons I have indicated, and on the other hand we judge books by their closeness to the pictorial media. Print itself, it seems to me, is the last thing some of us want in children's books. The result has been that we have a generation of children who shy away from a page of solid type.

There are no perfect books in the world, and certainly not every book deemed outstanding appeals to everyone. Not every so-called "good" children's book appeals to every child. And there is no reason why it should. But throughout the years and including our own time, the small percentage of children's books that have something to say to a child and say it well would still run into several thousands of books. Surely they are enough for any one childhood.

I'm sure you have noticed how respected the people are in our society who deal with the physical and emotional needs of children: child psychiatrists, pediatricians, social workers, dentists who specialize in children's teeth. (Come to think of it, orthodontists may be respected most of all because they charge so much!) These people are deemed spe-

cialists and we assume that they know what they're doing. Teachers and librarians who deal with children are less apt to be put in the specialist category by parents. The reason may be that many think the material we deal with is *childish*. When we ourselves fail to distinguish between what is "childish" and what is "childlike," I feel that this criticism is generally correct. Perhaps our own reading has failed to convince us of the difference; many adult books are childish; a good children's book is childlike. But if we haven't had a good dose ourselves of the best in literature, we are unable to make the distinction.

Many parents begin by not caring about the preschool child. A little book from Woolworth's is good enough. And second-rate picture books are even bought for our schools and public libraries. Quite a few people have warned us against this approach. *Proverbs* XXII, 6, says, "Train up a child in the way that he should go: and when he is old he will not depart from it." Well, the Jesuits also made a maxim out of this idea: "Give me a child for the first seven years, and you may do what you like with him afterwards." And Lenin believed this. Speaking to the Council of Education in Moscow in 1928, he said, "Give us a child for the first eight years, and it will be a Bolshevist forever."

I think we have also trapped ourselves into another false premise—that it is easier to read a mediocre book than a good book. Literature—to be good—doesn't need to be heavy. As a matter of fact, it is a safe guess that any children's book that requires inordinate effort on the part of the reader is not excellent. Sheer readability is a prime criterion of excellence in children's books as it is in adult books. Take the first words of *Moby Dick* "Call me Ishmael." And the first line of Leon Garfield's thriller *Smith* (Pantheon, 1967). "He was called Smith." You simply can't wait to read the next sentence in either book—and both sentences are simple enough. A child interested in horse stories surely doesn't need a whole string of the me-

diocre such as Hazel Peel's *Easter the
Show Jumper* (1965) in which a bad rider
ends by winning the Horse of the Year
Show, with the horse out of control most
of the time. Two excellent horse stories
K. M. Peyton's *Fly-By Night* (World,
1968) and Vian Smith's *The Horses of
Petrock* (Doubleday, 1965) are most exciting, fast-paced stories with a genuine
sense of reality to them. Good old *National Velvet* is surely still worthy of a
child's attention.

I also think we should have a little
more respect for children in regard to the
books of information we give them.
Many surely induce sloppy thinking,
again because we think that anything is
good enough for a child. Here is a quotation from V. M. Hillyer's *A Child's
History of the World* (Childrens, 1951),
"After Queen Elizabeth had died,
Raleigh was put in prison...." Actually
he was imprisoned by Elizabeth for about
five weeks, which fact intimates a lot
about Queen Elizabeth as well as
Raleigh.

And in 1970 a book was published on
the voyage of the Manhattan by Bern
Keating called *The Northwest Passage*
(Rand). The blurb reads: "but not until
man reached the moon did his earth-
bound contemporaries sail through the
ice-choked Northwest Passage and
bring to reality the dream of transpolar
commercial shipping." The publisher
may think he has avoided criticism by the
use of the word "commercial." But the
facts should be straight. The Royal
Canadian Mounted Police ship made
the voyage both ways in the 1940's. This
book gives it 4 1/2 lines with the dates
wrong. The Norwegian ship which made
the voyage first rates a line and a half.

By this time you may have realized
that I want to promote excellence in
books for children, but you may be confused on my stand on the bad versus the
mediocre. Well, let me say this—as long
as I have the excellent I prefer to cope
with the bad rather than the mediocre.
The bad is easily recognizable and therefore more combatable. The bad also has
its amusing side and who wants to be

without a joke. It's no accident that
Batman, Mrs. Miller, and Tiny Tim were
fads several years ago. Bad taste somehow has its own peculiar charm.
Nowadays we are in the counter-culture
of the granny gown, the grotesque an-
tiques, and the fringed buckskins. But
we all recognize that this is more or less
antiestablishment and a bit of a "put-
on."

But it's that great gray area between
the good and the bad that is so stultify-
ing. Generally speaking, the bad stuff in
reading—the commercialized series, the
sensational mysteries, the sickening romances—are at least not pretentious and
a position on them can easily be explained or discussed with a child. What I
principally object to are all our dreary,
smug books about growing up and coming to terms with oneself, that purport to
be "with it" and are merely another
brand of conformity; all the books on
race relations that are little more than a
condescending, inverse form of racism;
all our books of dull facts that take the
excitement out of science, or history, or
other countries. It's really hard to explain
one's stand on this "ho-hum" stuff unless
you take each book individually and put
a better book up beside it. Tolkien rather
than Frank Baum, Sendak rather than
Nan Agle, O'Dell rather than Wojiec-
kowska, Patricia Wrightson instead of
Jean Little.

Excellence is surely our goal in all that
we try to achieve in life. Why eliminate
children's books? Are children's books
and so therefore children too *humble*, too
insignificant to be taken seriously? The
words of John W. Gardner can be applied
to children's reading: "The society which
scorns excellence in plumbing because
plumbing is a humble activity, and
tolerates shoddiness in philosophy because philosophy is an exalted activity,
will have neither good plumbing nor
good philosophy. Neither its pipes nor its
theories will hold water."

It's the mediocre that drags us all
down to a common denominator; common is fine but does it have to be the
lowest? It's mediocrity that deprives us of

judgement; it's mediocrity that closes our minds to new ideas; it's mediocrity that particularly deprives us of a sense of humour.

So—I suggest in conclusion—let kids have the good stuff. Let them have the controversial. If a book is controversial there are strong opinions about it pro and con, and this is exactly the area where the young should have a chance to make up their own minds. The bad they will find around them and will recognize, having had a dose of the good. But let's give up mediocrity. I can't say that it doesn't work; the problem is that it works all too well. "If that don't do no good, that won't do no harm." Perhaps this is right—mediocre books do no harm in the sense of actual damage. But they do do harm in the sense of deprivation—the subtraction of opportunity to know and experience the best. Slum children are not the only ones who are deprived. Lacking genuine nutrition, you can starve on a full stomach.

Like the girl in Tom Tit Tot, a child, with a little bit of luck, may climb out of a distressing situation. But unless we can guarantee that the children in our care have long golden hair and are also able to uncover the secret of magic names, I would suggest that we teachers and librarians abandon the principle of "if that don't do no good, well that won't do no harm." Instead we should take our cue from Matthew Arnold: "I am bound by my own definition of criticism: a disinterested endeavour to learn and propagate the best that is known and thought in the world."

Innocent Children
or
Innocent Librarians

Ann Kalkhoff

WHEN I was first contacted by the ALA-CBC Joint Committee in regards to my participation in this preconference, my primary concern was my hatred of public speaking to groups above the age of 11. The idea of speaking on the topic that children's books should reflect what children are into at the expense of high quality literature frightened me not at all, for it is a viewpoint I hold to be true though I sincerely believe that good books and high quality literature can go hand in hand. I soon realized that I was in deep water when warned that my stand and comments could well incite fellow colleagues. Never one to let fear of retribution influence my expressions of concerns and beliefs, I agreed to address this assembly. After all it is my hope that a few of you will be converted, others will start thinking about the idea, and still others are simply interested in what some children's librarians are doing. Unfortunately, later I remembered one thing and discovered another. I remembered Atlantic City in June 1969 when I was shocked to hear fellow librarians boo a panel of teenagers whose ideas did not match theirs. I discovered once I began to reexamine library periodicals from the past couple of years that no one had come forth as a spokesman for those of us who feel that high standards of litera-

ture must be secondary. You might well ask why I was unaware of this before. Frankly, I have been too busy these last four-and-a-half years working with children to devote a great deal of time to reading what the so-called experts claim they need or desire. Few of the children I have worked with have been hesitant in expressing their interests and wants. It would appear that many of us who contend that children are not innocent and therefore do not warrant protection are too involved in the exciting world of children to have time to write articles or give speeches.

What are today's children like? What do the statistics say, the experts say, and most importantly the children say? Trying to pigeonhole children into the molds that have proven satisfactory in the past just won't do. Try it and they will be lost permanently. Granted, there are still scores of innocents around, but they are more and more in the minority and are the ones who will find something on the shelves regardless of its relevance to today's world. Our real concern rests with the other type of child.

This is the age of Sesame Street. Alan Caruba in his *Publishers Weekly* article, "Marshall McLuhan Lives on Sesame Street," says that the average pre-schooler watches about 30 hours of

11

television per week (twice the amount of time spent before the set in 1961). It is estimated that 4000 hours have been devoted to TV viewing by the time that a child enters first grade. Sesame Street has a potential audience of 12 million between the ages of three and six. The ratings indicate that 2.2 million homes watch at least a portion of the show on a daily basis. Most everyone of the preschoolers who attend my weekly story time are ardent fans of the program. As a result of the TV show, even the three-year-olds know their alphabet, but all enjoy new alphabet books. When Chwast's *Still Another Alphabet Book* (McGraw, 1969) first appeared, I tried it out on them despite the feeling that some of the concepts portrayed were above their comprehension. I was quite surprised when a few immediately grasped that the gradual eating of the letter D stood for disappear. Even at their young age realism is important, as evident by the fact that their favorite alphabet book is Matthieson's *ABC* (Platt, 1968)—for photographs are preferred to drawings. Two-and-a-half years of working closely with the three to five age bracket has enlightened me as to just how aware they are of real life and the grown up world despite their love of fantastic stories. Several of the four and five-year olds demand a true book to take home besides the picture books. When told by Christine, age five, that her mother was going to have a baby, I asked her if she wanted a brother or a sister. I was informed that "you have to take what they give you." Recently a three-year-old was told by a four-year-old that he was wrong about buying babies—mothers get them at hospitals. These children are alive and vibrant—always full of questions and answers. It is hard to believe that within a few short years they have the potential of joining the ranks of the so-called non-reader. Maybe it is because they have gone far beyond the point that kindergartners and first graders are expected to be—I really don't know, for formal education and its theories are out of my realm.

On April 18, 1972, CBS News Special presented "What's New at School." Some of the statistics and comments were interesting and a little frightening. Of the 63 million children who attend school daily, half are in elementary school. Two thirds of American parents believe that maintaining discipline is more essential than student educational interest. Children are soon taught that the best answer, regardless of the number of correct ones, is the one the teacher wants. By the fourth grade this is so firmly instilled that all are aware of how to please the teacher. In the traditional school, as opposed to the open class-room, the teacher talks 80 percent of the time. Here's the point that applies to us: it is hoped that love of reading will bring the child to better literature. As the commentator said, first we better get the children reading. That goes right along with a quotation from the August 1970 *Horn Book* where educators and psychologists were reported to say, "Children's books are condescending, out of touch with the reality of children's life, superficially optimistic." Unfortunately, the *Horn Book* writer pretty much felt that educators and psychologists were out of their own field when they dared to attack children's books. I suppose much the same reaction would be given to Toffler, whose comments about education in *Future Shock* (Random, 1970) could well be applied to libraries and librarians.

> The present curriculum and its division into airtight compartments is not based on any well thought out conception of contemporary human needs. . . . Still less is it based on any grasp of the future, any understanding of what skills Johnny will require to live in the hurricane's eye of change. . . . Education must shift into the future tense.

All hope is not lost, for innumerable books have been written by teachers who are concerned and fearful of the educational process that exists today. I cannot help but wonder how many children's librarians have bothered to read such books as Decker's *The Empty Spoon*

(Harper, 1970), Fader's *The Naked Children* (Macmillan, 1971), Haskins' *Diary of a Harlem Schoolteacher* (Grove, 1970), Hentoff's *Our Children Are Dying* (Viking, 1966), or any of John Holt's books. If so, could they forget the boy in *The Empty Spoon* who said, "I like books because they are the only things that don't tell you you're stupid." Cleo, Wentworth, Snapper, and Rubbergut in *The Naked Children*; the frustrations of a black teacher in *Diary of a Harlem Schoolteacher*; Hentoff's explanation that our children are dying because their brain cells have never been fully brought to life; or Holt's story about a boy whose love of reading was stopped for years because he was forced to read and understand *The Deerslayer*. These books are as meaningful to our reading lists as the Newbery-Caldecott winners, the notable books, and professional journals. Why? Because in them we can read the conditions under which the children we are involved with a few hours each afternoon spend the majority of their time. The apathy and disinterest expressed in these books can be found in any school, regardless of its location. The most positive action has been undertaken by the Teachers and Writers Collaborative. It proposes to:

> Bring together writers, teachers, and students for the purpose of creating a curriculum which is relevant to the lives of children today and which can therefore make the study of language a living process. We believe that writers and teachers working together can encourage children to create their own literature from their own language, experience, and imagination.

The results of this collaboration is printed in their newsletter.

Isn't it time that we come down out of our ivory towers and wake up to the fact that we idealize early childhood. Lanes in her *Down the Rabbit Hole* (Atheneum, 1971) calls it the Peter Pan Principle—we are reluctant to ruffle the blanket of primal innocence with which all children enter the world. Why should we be so protective—look around at the world in which the children live. On the nightly news they can watch killing in Vietnam, learn about the slaying of another policeman, hear statistics on the rise of drug abuse in elementary schools, and witness how adults permit animal-like conditions to exist in hospitals for the retarded. How many witnessed the assassination attempt on Governor George Wallace? Walk into any toy department and examine what is offered. Read Troy's article "Little TV Doll, Who Made You? (And What Exactly Did He Have in Mind?)" From it you can learn there is a teenage culture, not a kiddie culture. Little girls are growing up having no idea what it is like to be a child. Listen to what the children themselves have to say. In the Summer 1970 issue of *Youth* (a publication of the New York State Division for Youth) a third grader wrote:

> Why everybody dying
> stop war
> Make every man even
> Black people can't get jobs
> People are starving
> Pollution from factories
> Why were cigarettes ever made.

In that same issue a 16-year-old says, "Today's youth is growing up faster and getting involved in the adult world sooner. We are living today's problems and worrying about tomorrow's." Wendy in Kingman's *The Peter Pan Bag* (Dell, 1971) says "15 in your youth, Mother, is equivalent to about age 11 today. Absolutely unformed and inept." (Think about the ever popular Cavanna and Stolz books if you do not agree with Wendy. While obviously written for the teenager, the current audience are in fifth and sixth grade). Joan Bodger Mercer obviously would put the age even lower, for in her editorial comments in the October 1971 *Wilson Library Bulletin* she states:

> Eleven-year-olds are better able to dig sex, drugs, out of wedlock pregnancies, and bumbling parents than are their escapist elders.

Durham in "Children's Literature for Today's World; Where Will It Lead" comments on hearing a child say *IF* I grow up not *WHEN* I grow up. Children want the answer to who I am in relation to background, other children, and the hidden self. In May, a group of 11-year-olds marched in protest to the war. Several months ago I had a six-year-old refuse to help me throw out the paint water from a painting session until I explained it was water colors and that it would break down easily and not cause pollution. No wonder Lloyd Alexander claims young people are finding it less acceptable to use parental models as a means to find one's identity. Look at the nightly news and think about it.

Despite all the problems and lamentings that can be expressed, here we are, a group of 200 attending a one day conference. It is an important step forward, but I cannot help but question its impact, as I fear too many of those present are coordinators or editors that no longer work directly with children and therefore have lost touch with the reality of the situation. The ones who might most benefit or provide supportive evidence are not here, nor will they be here for the regular conference—they are back in the children's rooms answering the questions and attempting to handle the needs and demands. It seems inconceivable that so few children's specialists are devoting so few hours to a problem that first appeared in the 1950s. The concept of pursuing one's identity so one knows who he is gentically, historically, and realistically was sparked by the entire civil rights movement. Then there were the 1960s when the *real thing* literature began with the discovery of minorities, the drug problem, and the idea that war is evil. It is now the 1970s and still you can read:

Children's interests are as broad as the horizon. They are interested in practically everything—with the exception of sexual love, which bores them, being beyond their experience. They know that grownups fall in love and marry, but it is a convention they accept without caring about details.

Granted the person goes on to say:

As for all the problems related to life (including death), it is impossible to overestimate the capacity of children to feel, suffer, understand, and share them all if properly presented.

Obviously the author has not seen a fifth grade girl seven months pregnant, nor had a sixth grade boy offer to explain all aspects of sex to him. Robbie Branscum in *Me and Jim Luke* (Doubleday, 1971) wrote a passage about a ten-year-old and his 12-year-old uncle discussing the latter's penis size and how he wishes it was long like a snake so it could sneak inside a particular girl without her noticing. I use this example for the boys experience other problems related to life (their life that is)—a body hidden in a tree, the Klu Klux Klan, and attempts on their lives.

Fortunately there are others who see things in a different light.

I like to think that we respect our children's intelligence enough to suppose that the world need be presented to them in no rosy right ... The world has not spared children hunger, cold, sorrow, pain, fear, loneliness, disease, death, war, famine, or madness. Why should we hesitate to make use of this knowledge when writing for them?

John Neufeld expressed his viewpoint in the October 1971 *WLB* when he said that he wanted books that presented the whole child—a girl curious about sex yet fearful of the pain; a boy afraid he cannot perform as he thinks he should. Dirty jokes and slanderous asides are a part of the child's life so why not reflect them in books. Mr. Neufeld provided two superior works: *Edgar Allen* (NAL, 1969), the story of the failure of a white family to adjust to their adoption of a black child, and *Lisa Bright and Dark* (NAL, 1970), the story of Lisa's mental breakdown and the failure of adults to heed the warning signs. Undoubtedly, Mr. Neufeld would be quite pleased with Blume's *Are You There God It's Me*

Margaret (Bradbury Pr., 1970) and *Then Again Maybe I Won't* (Bradbury Pr., 1971). Margaret is a sixth grader so anxious to grow up and menstruate that she practices with a kotex for months. Tony is a seventh grader full of sexual fears about erection and nocturnal emissions.

Our business is reading, yet somewhere along the line it would appear that we missed the boat. Library circulation figures are nose diving—in my branch we have lost 10,000 in one year—yet many go along attributing the problem to cutbacks in federal or local funding, the advent of the paperback, and television. All these do create difficulties, but it is time that we pull ourselves together and do a little self-examination. The times have changed, but not so children's librarians. Who cares what children are asking for and demanding, we have our high standards of literature to maintain. We have our Newbery winners which stand for "the most distinguished contribution to American literature" for the year they were published. Of the winners since 1960, my guess is that you would find every one sitting on the shelves in my branch except possibly *Summer of the Swans* (Betsy Byars, Viking, 1970), *From the Mixed Up Files of Mrs. Basil E. Frankweiler* (E. L. Konigsburg, Atheneum, 1967), or *A Wrinkle in Time* (Madeleine L'Engle, Farrar, 1962). Why these three—children are interested in the handicapped, mysteries, and science fiction. I do not deny that the award winners these past 50 years are not the best a particular year had to offer, I just think that the award should admit that it reflects the judgment of adults with little regard for what children are reading. If this would be pointed out, maybe parents, teachers, and librarians would not force the title on an unwitting child. I doubt if great numbers of adults will be rushing to read *The Collected Works of Flanery O'Connor* simply because it won the National Book Award for fiction, yet some of these same adults will purchase *Mrs. Frisby and the Rats of Nimh* (Robert O'Brien, Atheneum, 1971) despite the fact that little Gertrude gave up animal stories at age three and is another Madame Curie.

Remember how the *Interracial Books for Children* attacked *Sounder* (William H. Armstrong, Harper, 1969) saying it was white fundamentalist in its style and dehumanizing in its refusal to name any of the characters except the dog? What about the cries that while the committee has chosen black books never has a black author received either the Newbery or the Caldecott. Tom Feelings in his attack of *Sounder* states, "that a story of the black experience must come directly from one who has lived it." Locally I have heard heated attacks on d'Aulaire's *Abraham Lincoln* (Doubleday), the 1940 Caldecott winner, because the illustrations of the blacks are stereotyped. Upon examination of the book I wonder why someone has not attacked the picture of Lincoln where the rising sun behind him gives a halo effect worthy of the second coming. The Feminists on Children's Media have attacked the 1967 winner *Up a Road Slowly* (Irene Hunt, Follett, 1966) and the 1957 winner *Miracles on Maple Hill* (Virginia Sorensen, Harcourt, 1956) citing these passages:

Accept the fact that this is a man's world and learn how to play the game gracefully.

For the millionth time she was glad she wasn't a boy. It was alright for girls to be scared or silly or even ask dumb questions. Everybody just laughed and thought it was funny. But if anyone caught Joe asking a dumb question or thought he was the littlest bit scared, he went red and purple and white. Dad was even something like that, old as he was.

Laugh if you want but Howe reveals in her *Saturday Review* article that children know their sexual roles by 18 months and these are hard to change past the fifth grade.

The Feminists on Children's Media is the same group which compiled the *Little Miss Muffet Fights Back* bibliography, which received national coverage and initially appeared in *Women's Day* rather than any library periodical. They also did a study of the award winners and noted that boys outnumber the girls three to one in the Newbery and two to one in the notable books. Currently a study of the 1970 Notable Books is underway with plans for the 1971 list. This group is not going to fade away any more than the Council on Interracial Books for Children. In addition to the Feminists on Children's Media there are two groups currently writing and publishing their own titles. Granted the publications by the Feminists Press and Lollipop Power Inc. are second or even third rate, but they fill a need. At their low price and paperback format, we can purchase them as ephemeral and replace them as soon as superior works come along. My case for two four-year-old "lovers" and a skeptical five-year-old, all of whom denied there was any such thing as a woman doctor, much less a male nurse, would have succeeded had I been able to show them Danish's *The Dragon and the Doctor* or Heyn's *Challenge to Become a Doctor: the Story of Elizabeth Blackwell* (both from Feminists Press). The fact that sexism in children's literature has received coverage in such popular periodicals as *Redbook*, *Saturday Review*, and *Ms* should indicate something.

Maybe you think that I am too hard on the Newbery-Caldecott winners and those responsible for their selection. We are gathered here to discuss new criteria for evaluation so we best not have any sacred cows. John Rowe Townsend at the 1971 May Hill Arbuthot Honor Lecture spoke about "Standards of Criticism for Children's Literature." He prefers that these questions be asked:

Will this book be suitable for MY child, popular with MY class, will this be relevant for the children in the area served by MY library.

Try using that sentence when examining the Newbery-Caldecott winners. Also think about this one.

If a children's book is not popular with

children here and now, its lack of appeal may tell us something.

Remember that children will read only what they want to read and will immediately reject badly written, contrived books or ones that have outlived their usefulness. As Augusta Baker said in her open letter to juvenile editors, books must be *FOR* children not *ABOUT* children and present people who are individuals with character and life. Literary standards are not fixed forever, they only serve as a guide for the time. It is my contention that literary standards should either be greatly eased or merely take a back seat for a while. Putting standards before reading is like providing the book collection before the library is built.

Any discussion of evaluation must always take up the subject of reevaluation. I agree with Sara Fenwick that reevaluation is the most crucial aspect. Initial errors can be made but there is little excuse for retaining or replacing. It is not always the result of an error that a title should be withdrawn. Times quickly change and we must awaken to our past failure to achieve justice and quality of opportunity and make every attempt to eliminate prejudice, sexism, and racism from the books we offer children. All are a part of the realism I advocate, but librarians and books are teachers and should stride to provide material that teaches the common humanity of us all, not the hatred of a few. The reviewing and criticism of children's literature is the most complex and most capable of being misconceived. Fenwick is right, "Not all good books are good for all seasons." Such books as *Roosevelt Grady* (Louisa Shotwell, World, 1970), *Mary Jane* (Dorothy Sterling, Doubleday, 1959), and *The Empty School House* (Natalie Carlson, Harper, 1965) were good, but they have outlived their usefulness and should be shifted to the historical collection.

Many libraries have relegated *Little Black Sambo* to the historical collection, so why not Newbery-Caldecott books that have received similar attack. *The*

Story of Dr. Dolittle was removed fom Brooklyn Public Library before I joined the system, so that I had to inquire why. I was not surprised when I heard that Black Prince Bumpo daydreams, "if only I was a white prince" as he reads fairy tales. P. L. Travers' *Mary Poppins* refers to Africans as pickaninnies and has their speech full of dems and dose. *Travels with Babar* (Random, 1934) was recently suggested for possible withdrawal from our branch collections because of detrimental illustrations of Africans, yet Barbara Murphy's *Home Free* (Delacorte, 1970) is still with us. This latter book was published in 1970 and was highly recommended as an interracial friendship story. What a surprise to discover black intellectual inferiority referred to as is "that smell." Maybe there is some unwritten rule that states that only those titles whose authors are dead can be attacked and withdrawn. If true, then I must ask as did Isabelle Sahl after her study of Dr. Dolittle titles:

How many more generations of black children must be insulted by them and how many more white children allowed to be infected with their message of white superiority.

Change the wording and it can apply equally as well to sexist titles.

Anne Carroll Moore once wrote:

Writing for children, like daily living with them, requires a constant sharpening of all one's facilities, a fresh discovery of new heights and depths in one's own emotions.

The words still apply, though now children's books must keep pace with the realities of the world. Augusta Baker says, "people who write realistic fiction must be inside writing about life rather than outside looking at it." Authors should cease writing about topics they know solely through research or observation. Sensitivities of children, and hopefully in the near future librarians, spot a fraud very quickly.

The age of fantasy is over, though all sorts of books are still needed for "one man's realism is another man's science fiction." The escapist must always be provided for, but it is the seeker who is hardest to please, for often he is difficult to reach. The seeker will not accept distilled relevance—he wants books that offer life, not just orations about it. Lloyd Alexander was right when he wrote in "No Laughter in Heaven" (*Horn Book*, February 1970),

Occasionally, we all need to escape into a fantasy world, but perhaps it is good also to escape from our own real world into someone else's real world.

Maybe those contesting the inclusion of Piri Thomas' *Down These Mean Streets* (NAL, 1971) in a school district in Queens, N. Y., should listen to Mr. Alexander. One parent is reported to have said that while Thomas shows life in Spanish Harlem, she does not feel her child should experience such until old enough to understand. Understand what—that the pain and suffering is all right because Thomas is a Puerto Rican. The talk and ideas in Steptoes's *Uptown* (Harper, 1970) has frightened more than one librarian. It is a beautiful portrayal of street life for young black boys and deserves the attention of every library. For years minority children have been forced to leave their own real world and enter the white middle class world of Dick and Jane. It is time that the journey be reversed, for children need to be aware of the cultural heritage each race has to offer. Isn't it time that we quit buying books that state America was found by either Leif Erickson or Christopher Columbus—it never was lost. Isn't it time that English be seen as a second language for blacks as well as Puerto Ricans and Chicanos? Hopefully most of you were able to obtain a copy of the Western Electric recording. Recently I read a manuscript copy of Dr. Hugh Butts' and James Haskins' *Psychology of Black Language*, to be published by Barnes and Noble. It is the authors' belief that "black language perpetuates the ghetto" for nonstandard black language is not seen as legitimate. Public education is a means to raise the child's social mobility and vocational success, yet no ways have been developed to teach standard English to blacks. Maybe we as librarians should start thinking about seeking black language books just as we have Spanish, French, and Hebrew ones.

No book is for every child and no book should be made to appeal to every child. A book is made to be loved and cherished by the child it is right for and rejected by those who prefer others.—Jean Karl

We have a good number of realistic books, but we always need more. Besides, the turnover in older fiction titles is far greater than it ever has been before. This was really brought home recently because of my appointment to a special BPL committee to make preliminary decisions on which of the uniquely held YA titles (seventh and eighth graders) should be recommended for nonreplacement and which ones for juvenile or adult consideration. Close to 60 percent were deemed unworthy of replacement, with the majority of those to be retained being reconsidered by juvenile. Growing up never was a ball; but authors, editors, parents, and librarians did not want to admit the pain or reveal the mess the world is in, so they chose to shelter the child. Television ended the dream. The problems of drugs, sex, race, and growing up are not new—today's child is just more aware of them and willing to discuss them. Remember what the 16-year-old wrote in *Youth*. The young teenager in Harrison's *Journey All Alone* (Dial, 1971) is not the first black Harlem girl to be sexually attacked by a gang of boys, but it is the first time it has been written about. The boys in Donovan's *I'll Get There: It Better Be Worth the Trip* (Dell, 1971) and Holland's *The Man Without a Face* (Lippincott, 1972) are not the first boys to have to contend with divorced mothers and homosexual ex-

periences. The Cleavers devote much of their writing skills to life in Appalachia in *Where The Lillies Bloom* (Lippincott, 1969) or problems faced by the people in a metropolis in *The Mimosa Tree* (Lippincott, 1970) but it's not a new phenomenon. Other boys have faced internal conflicts after smoking grass long before Coles wrote *The Grass Pipe* (Little, 1969). Girls have had sexual attractions for their stepfathers before *The Phaedra Complex* (Lippincott, 1971) appeared. Interracial dating existed before *Anything for a Friend* (Russell, Davis, Crown, 1963). Teenagers found themselves forced into marriage before *Mr. & Mrs. Bo Jo Jones* (1967) and girls were unwed mothers before *My Darling My Hamburger* (Paul Zindel, Harper, 1969). I'm sure the couple in *His Own Where* (June Jordan, Crowell, 1971) are not the first to face family alienation and see the creation of their own child as an answer to their problems. The list could go on and on. The dehumanization of the child has finally ceased so now maybe the traumatic years of childhood will not be such a mystery.

Most of you here can probably cope with the idea of realism in children's books, though I suspect many would temper it. Besides realism, I said I believed in providing the child with what he wants so that reading occurs. How many could accept Nancy Drew and Hardy Boys into your collections? After much debate and weighing, Brooklyn Public finally decided to purchase those titles in the series that withstand a staff review. To my mind they are no more escapist than the Mary C. Jane titles or Encyclopedia Brown stories. Sure Nancy and the Hardy brothers transcend their age, but so do Claudia and Jamie in *From the Mixed Up Files of Mrs. Basil E. Frankweiler*, (E. L. Konigsburg, Atheneum, 1967) the young soldier in *Across Five Aprils*, (Irene Hunt, Follett, 1964), and the boys in *Pirate Rock* (David Walker, Houghton, 1969). Other books have been purchased in a desire to gain library users—*Partridge Family* (Michael

Avallone, Curtis, 1970), *Marcus Welby*, (Bruce Cassiday, Ace, 1971), *It Takes a Thief* (Ace), *Hawaii Five 0* (Michael Avallone, NAL, 1969), *TV Stars 1971* (Scholastic, 1972), *Pop Rock Lyrics* (Jerry Walker, Scholastic, 1970), not to mention *Peanuts* (Fawcett), *Dennis the Menace* (Fawcett), *Beetle Bailey* (Tempo), *Letters from Camp* (Signet). My purchase of books that they want seems to make the children more willing to seek my recommendations and accept my suggestions. Earlier I commented on a 10,000 drop in circulation. I should add that that figure is basically lower than it should be because juvenile has either had an increase in circulation or held its own for most of the year. If only my budget wasn't so low. Let me add that the award winners and notable books are still on the shelves, but they usually are still there at closing unless a teacher drags out a yellowed reading list. I feel it is better to take the children's "walking slow" so they don't end up being described as Cameron did their elders "the most inarticulate group of college students ever." They are the second generation television child. We failed with their parents, let's not repeat the performance.

As long as I am begging librarians to come down out of their ivory towers let me issue the invitation to a few authors, editors, library school professors, reviewers, and most importantly, writers of articles in library periodicals that discuss the ever lasting glory of good literature. In self defense I read Cameron's *The Green and Burning Tree* (Little, 1969). I cannot argue her love of words and beautiful style, but there is more to children's books than fantasy, classics, and historical fiction. Children still love to hear nursery rhymes and the Beatrix Potter tales, but heaven help them if they use Miss Potter as a model. She was a virtual prisoner as a child and a recluse as an adult. Ms. Cameron claims to agree that "nothing that happens after we are 12 matters very much." How can she believe that in today's society? Besides leaving their ivory towers I suggest that all arrange to spend a week with me at my branch. I'd like to introduce them to today's child with their love of life and realistic approach to the ills we adults have created as their heritage.

Kids, Kulture and Us

Frank McLauglin

RARELY a month goes by that one of my three sons doesn't find a way of revising my perceptions. Several years ago, when my oldest boy was three, he provided such an opportunity.

It was a bright, sunny morning. I had just spanked my three-year-old and sent him to his room. For the umpteenth time, he had run out in the street, and he had repeated a variation that especially upset me . . . he challenged a passing car! When I had retrieved him from the street, my eye caught the body of a dead squirrel lying in front of our driveway.

Within minutes a plan occurred to me. I was puffed with pride. The great teacher would work his wiles. A.S. Neill and John Dewey would be proud of me. Quickly gathering my son in my arms, I carried him out to the street.

"See the dead squirrel, Frankie, he didn't do what his father told him. He ran out in the street, and the car smashed him." I paused, letting the finality of the squirrel's death make its impact on him.

We returned to the house in silence. A half hour later, Frankie ran into the kitchen, tugged on my pant leg, and excitedly pulled.

"C'mon dad, let's get the car and go and SMASH squirrels!"

Just last week, it was my second son's turn. I was driving a VW busfull of kids to the playground. I was irritated because Paul was again resorting to phrases I didn't feel a seven year old should be spouting. "Jerk off! Faggot!" he yelled at his brother Matt, for some reason. I called him up beside me.

"Paul, how many times do I have to tell you not to use those words. They're not nice . . . if you knew what the words meant, you wouldn't use them."

"I know what faggot means, you don't!" Paul retorted.

"I *do* know what it means, Paul, but you tell me what you think it means."

"Faggots are a bundle of sticks," he responded with absolute confidence.

I drove on in silence for the next five minutes.

As I think about my children and my students growing up today, I can't help but feel that Marshall McLuhan was correct in suggesting that today's young person must be the hardest working in history if he intends to survive and master his environment. I would add that he also stands to have his sanity tested in trying to make sense of things.

As a starting point, let's reflect about the confusion a child faces in the conflicting views of life presented by his school and the media outside school. Schools ignore the culture he is living in, and nearly all instruction is centered

20

around the past. The school itself re-wards the following virtues:

—doing homework and generally working hard;
—obeying teachers and other adults;
—being neat and orderly;
—*consuming* the knowledge dished out.

On the other hand, TV, radio, records, billboards sing a different song:

—relax and get away from it all;
—leisure is the time that counts;
—do your own thing;
—be casual, be cool, be hip;
—above all, *consume* the products being advertised.

What schools and the living room king, TV, have in common is treatment of their audience as consumers.

Vicarious experiences are an area we need to give more attention. For the most part, children, whether seven or 17, are fed stories in school that are full of nice, good things. The seven-year-old probably reads many sterile stories about an insip-id postman, policeman, doctor, or fire-man who is always smiling and appears only to exist to do good things. The 17-year-old gets a steady diet of the "good books" too. These, of course, are called classics, which for at least 60 percent of the students serve only to bore, irritate, or intimidate them. My personal bias is that the main psychological outcome of studying Shakespeare is making a large percentage of high school students feel inferior about their own taste. We have also destroyed our chance for sensitizing students through literature.

Frequently teachers in the various humanistic disciplines are responsible for reversing or inhibiting the very con-sciousness-raising they prate so much about. Rather than explore life with stu-dents using the ethnicity of appropriate media experiences, the media experiences themselves become packages to be studied, memorized, and tested. This approach trivializes Art as product and renders the works of great authors, painters, etc. to being cultural objects to be consumed. The super-serious, pon-derous mis-efforts of educators in this fashion has prompted movie critic Pauline Kael to comment that Art is what ladies, gentlemen, and foundations like.

At home much of the adult approved and selected stories for younger children have about the same reality level as "TV family comedies" such as *The Partridge Family* and *The Brady Bunch*. I wonder how much weight these stories carry after the child hears or sees nightly reports about the U.S. trying to set Vietnamese forests on fire, Catholics killing Prot-estants or vice versa in Northern Ireland, the latest Mafia hit, or police corruption indictment. One thing I feel certain about is that there is incredible dis-sonance in the communication a child confronts every day.

Jules Feiffer, I know, feels much the same way. In *The Great Comic Book Heroes* (Dial, 1965) he describes how children react to the pressure of parents and schools:

Children hungry for reasons, are seldom given convincing ones. They are bombarded with hard work, labelled education—not seen therefore as child labor. They rise for school at the same time as or earlier than their fathers, start work without office chatter, go till noon without coffee breaks, have waxed milk for lunch instead of dry martinis, then back at the desk till three o'clock. Facing greater threats and riskier decisions than their fathers have had to meet since their day in school.

And always at someone else's conveni-ence. Someone else dictates when to rise, what's to be good for breakfast, what's to be learned in school, what's to be good for lunch, what're to be play hours, what're to be homework hours, what's to be delicious for dinner and what's to be suddenly, bedtime. This goes on until summer—when there is, once again, a "leisure problem." "What," the child asks, "am I going to do with myself?" Millions of things, as it turns out, but no sooner have they been discovered than it is time to go back to school.

It should come as no surprise, then, that within this shifting hodgepodge of external pressures, a child, simply to save his sanity, must go underground. Have a place to hide where he cannot be got at by grownups. A place that implies if only obliquely, that they're not so much; that they don't know everything; that they can't fly the way some people can, or let bullets bounce harmlessly off their chests, or beat up whoever picks on them, or—oh, joy of joys!—even become invisible! A no-man's land. A relief zone. And the basic sustenance for this relief was, in my day, comic books.

With them we were able to roam free, disguised in costume, committing the greatest of feats—and the worst of sins. And, in every instance, getting away with them. For a little while, at least, it was our show. For a little while, at least, we were the bosses. Psychically renewed, we could then return above ground and put up with another couple of days of victimization. Comic books were our booze.

This viewpoint was reinforced by Ray Bradbury, one of our great science fiction writers, author of *The Martian Chronicles* (Bantam, 1950) and *Fahrenheit 451* (Ballantine, 1961). In a talk this past summer with teachers in San Diego, California, Bradbury recalled his own childhood and his love of Edgar Rice Burroughs' books. Without pretension, Bradbury spoke of his infatuation with Flash Gordon, Buck Rogers, and popular culture heroes. He feels children need to adventure far and wide vicariously, let their imaginations roam free, and he disapproves of censoring their reading and film choices. While doing a story for *Life*, Bradbury found that many of the astronauts and scientists he met in Houston found similar childhood delight in Burroughs and other "popular" writers such as Haggard, Stevenson, and Wells. Thirty years ago teachers and librarians were not favorably inclined toward such writers, and ordinarily attempted to channel a youngster's atten-

tion to more sanitized and "academically approved" authors.

Five years ago, in the old *Saturday Evening Post* (March 11, 1967), Bruno Bettelheim, noted psychiatrist and educator, suggested that we "push" children to a competitive pitch, but deny them acquaintance with aggression. We prevent them from exploring violence even though our newspapers, TV, and magazines report on the violence at every level of our lives. Bettelheim wonders what "outlets" do parents and teachers provide. What do we teach them to do about their violent feelings? It seems to me that many of the horror films, comic books, and sci-fi thrillers that Bradbury and Feiffer managed to survive so gracefully, might at least vicariously present aggression in a manner with which the young can cope.

I remember a discussion Bettelheim had with a young mother who was disturbed with her child always turning on Dick Tracy-like cartoons instead of something she approved. Bettelheim helped the mother see that she was trying to impose her taste on the child. My own opinion is that as adults we have misdirected our efforts. Instead of spending so much time in monitoring what programs children watch, I'd prefer that we limited the *total* amount of a child's viewing time.

Let me return for a moment to the "content" of stories that we worry so much about. In our home, books play a prominent role. My wife and I read a great deal, and our children are becoming readers. But I've noticed a curious phenomena—children read in very definite patterns and these patterns can tell us much about them if we are simply attentive.

For example, I've noticed that the majority of children's books that we have accumulated simply sit on book shelves. The same few books keep getting read and the same few are requested for bedtime stories read by my wife or me. My second son, Paul, keeps requesting *The Bible in Picture for Little Eyes*, and then returns over and over again to the same few stories. He loves the David and Goliath story and the story about Joseph and his brothers. Think about those stories for a moment. How many "kiddie stories" can you remember that contain action such as a small boy overcoming a giant of a man, or a favorite son being sold into bondage by his brothers. Both stories allowed him to vicariously work out his own aggression; both when discussed in the context in which they took place, allowed me to clarify experiences with him.

As I think about my own children and look at the young people I work with and then at adults my own age, I am increasingly concerned with a person's dependence on a medium such as television. In my estimation, television addiction is nearly as serious as drug addiction, and both point to the same condition—the inability of individuals to create meaning for themselves and cope with the pressure of their lives.

In closing, let me outline a few of the changes I would like to see take place:

—We need to stop trying to change people or impose our tastes on them; our time would be better spent on changing ourselves; we can do this by becoming attentive to ourselves and our relationships. Krishnamurti in *Think on These Things* has talked of this process with profound eloquence.

—We need to pay attention to children; become sensitive to the pressures and fears that beset them, and help clarify their perplexities.

—Encourage kids to explore on their own and be alive to materials that will "touch" them. In one junior high in Manhattan, the reading teacher and librarian work hand in glove. We need much more interaction between school people, not the usual-alienated-everyone-keeps - to - his - own - function - and - cubicle-approach.

—Librarians must not be passive educators. They are in excellent position to conduct media research that could better inform us of "transactions" between books, films, tapes, and students. Furthermore, they need to actively create and promote programs that attract a larger community, especially the nearly invisible disadvantaged who can be found everywhere.

—All of us must become media ecologists. With so much of our lives dominated by man-made tools, we must begin to undertand how our perceptions and life styles are being changed, and begin to regain control over the forces that contribute to our confusion and unhappiness.

The Double Image: Language as the Perimeter of Culture

Elaine Konigsburg

A SHORT WHILE ago a certain distant relative of mine told me that I ought to buy an electric typewriter. She said, "Just think how much better you could write if you had an electric typewriter. In your line of work, darling, you ought to have the best tools." She suggested that even a reconditioned electric typewriter would be better than what I'm using.

With some relatives you just can't explain anything that isn't tax deductible. But you understand. What I use in my line of work, darling, is not a machine at all. I use what you use—language, sometimes fresh and sometimes electric and sometimes reconditioned. Language is my tool. It is also a weapon, a set of symbols, a key. And it is a perimeter. It is a perimeter because it does what perimeters do: it shows the shape of and defines the limits of something. In this case, culture.

Language shows the shape of culture by reflection. When one is grown up, he finds that the language plunges deep and comes up with a double image: it not only reflects the culture of now but also the culture of then. A grown-up's *now* is made up of a lot of *then*, a lot of past, his own special past

and an accumulation of the past of his culture.

Let me show you what I mean about language as a perimeter showing the shape of culture present as well as culture past. Listen with me. Listen to language reflect a double image in the tattersall of suburbs that I have lived in. A tattersall that spreads across a horizontal of time and a North to South vertical of geography.

Listen first to the talk that bounces out of my first suburb, a neighborhood of three-bedroom, ranch-type homes in a new subdivision of medium-priced houses three miles from the city bus stop in Jacksonville, Florida. The time is early marriage, early familyhood, and time itself is limited, for there are so many language imperatives to be obeyed.

Imperative One: Recognize your child's needs.

Imperative Two: Respect your child's individuality.

Listen to a young mother obey One and Two as she explains the laws of physics to a two and a half year old who is runny-nosed from crying:

I'm sorry, Gregory, but you cannot take your wagon *through* the tree. You

see, don't you. Gregory, that the tree will
not move. Daddy always takes his wagons
around trees. To the right or to the left.
But *around*. Around the tree, Gregory.
Why don't you try that? . . . No, Mother
cannot move the tree right now. She has
to feed your baby sister.

Only a demand greater than Gregory's, *demand feeding*, keeps her from
axing down the tree.

Or listen to this conversation between a young husband and wife, and
see if it, too, doesn't show the shape
of a culture.

Ronald, why don't you call the Harrises
and tell them that we'll be late. About an
hour late. I still have to bathe Stevie and
put a load of his things in the washer. You
know that if he doesn't get his bath just
before bed, he'll be restless all night. And
we both know what that will mean.

That will mean they have failed
Imperative Number Three: Adjust to
your child's schedule.

There are other imperatives in this
Spockled suburb. Discover your child's
creativity. Provide your child with the
companionship of others his age. Adjust to him.

And there, in that three-mile outer
limit from the city bus stop, you can
observe all the nice young middle-class
ladies and all the nice young middle-
class men adjusting. The conversation
of an afternoon among the young
mothers or the conversation of the evening among the mixed couples changes
little. Sitting in any living room in the
whole of that suburban subdivision
and listening to the talk, one becomes
overwhelmed with a feeling of *déjà vu*,
a feeling that you've heard it all before.
That the language is reflecting not only
life in this culture, perhaps, but in some
other life once upon a time.

Once upon a time.

That phrase is the clue.

Listen to James Thurber tell it:

Once upon a time, in a kingdom by the

sea, there lived a Little Princess named
Lenore. One day Lenore fell ill of a surfeit
of raspberry tarts and took to her bed.

The Royal Physician sent for the King,
Lenore's father, and the King came to see
her.

"I will get you anything your heart desires," the King said. "Is there anything
your heart desires?"

"Yes," said the Princess. "I want the
moon. If I can have the moon, I will be
well again."

Now, the King had a great many wise
men who always got for him anything he
wanted, so he told his daughter she could
have the moon.

Or listen to George MacDonald's
King as he asks his daughter, the Light
Princess:

"Is there nothing you wish for?"

"Oh, you dear Papa! Yes," answered
she. "I have been longing for it—Oh such
a time! Ever since last night."

"Tell me what it is."

"Will you promise to let me have it?"

"Tell me what it is first," said he.

"No, no. Promise first."

"I dare not. . . . What is it?"

"Mind, I hold you to your promise. It
is—to be tied to the end of a string—a
very long string indeed, and be flown like
a kite. Oh, such fun!"

Oh, such fun!

Oh, such fun for whom?

I had dreamed about such a fun land
when I was THE CHILD, but it existed
only in fairy tales then. The fairy tale
land of Sleeping Beauty where the environment adjusts to the princess. A
land where I, the princess, wouldn't
have to learn to recognize spinning
wheels or ever have to take my red
wagon *around* trees. A land where the
spinning wheels would all be removed
so that I would never prick my finger.
At last I was living in that land. But *I*
was the one moving the spinning
wheels. Isn't that ridiculous? To at last
be living in a fairy tale land but at the
wrong end of it? To be moving spinning wheels out of the way of perfectly

normal, middle-class children—without all the king's men or even one fairy godmother to help with demand feeding?

We left the sounds of those suburbs a half dozen years ago, but before we left, we had added yet another sound to them. Laughter. Laughter at ourselves.

We moved to new suburbs, and the language of our new neighborhood sounded strange until I located it in Ruth Benedict's *Patterns of Culture*. Listen to this chant of a Kwakiutl Indian Chief from Vancouver Island. The chief was host at a great potlatch feast, and as he sang, his song reflected his culture as well as my new one. Listen:

I am the first of the tribes.
I am the only one of the tribes.
The chiefs of the tribes are only local
    chiefs.
I am the only one among the tribes.
I search among all the invited chiefs
    for greatness like mine.
I cannot find one chief among the
    guests.

That was his chant at a potlatch feast. The purpose of the feast was simple: to outdo all the other chiefs by showing how much property he could afford to burn up. And if they didn't believe his greatness, his chant kept reminding them of it as they watched. Blankets and oil and even canoes were added to his bonfire. Conspicuous consumption is the name of that game, and the song of the chief as he watches the great bonfire is a clear reflection of what was important in his culture. Uncomfortably clear. Here was a culture that was built upon an ample supply of goods, inexhaustible, and obtained without excessive expenditure of labor. A culture that could only happen in a land where the living was easy. A land where life's necessities were provided without a huge expenditure of energy, so all the leftover ambi-

tion went into accumulating property and showing it off. Such a culture existed years ago on the Northwest coast of the United States.

Such a culture exists now on the North*east* coast of the United States. The affluent suburbs of New York. That was our new neighborhood. Here is a culture that is also built upon an ample supply of goods, inexhaustible, and obtained without excessive expenditure of labor—a 35-hour work week, maybe. A culture where leftover energy goes into accumulating property.

For the Kwakiutl there was only one thing better than collecting property, and that was to show how much of it could be given away or destroyed. It was important to always give away more or destroy more than the other chiefs. Thus, the great potlatch feasts which could use up a year's savings. Sort of like a wedding in the bedroom suburbs. Vancouver Island could be Long Island. Listen:

I don't know what to get Edna and Bill. They gave us a $25 bond. That's $18.75. I figure that if we get them a $25 gift certificate from Saks, we'll be safe.

The Kwakiutl's language was only a little more direct; *I search among all the invited chiefs for greatness like mine.*

The Kwakiutl were always pursuing those experiences which they most dreaded. Dancing with glowing coals held in their hands, self-inflicted torture, starving in isolation to bring on frenzy, always striving for an experience outside of the day to day, something at an acute angle from the middle road.

Pursuit of the dreadful is reflected in the language of the affluent suburbs, too. Here it is an attenuated pursuit. It is often talk of experience instead of experience. Talk of meaningful experiences, exciting experiences, enriching experiences, *an* experience, *quite an* experience. Listen to this conversating bouncing back from the walls of a chic room in which a dinner party is going on:

Jonathan dreads going to camp, but we feel that it is something he really needs. We think that he must be made to try it. At least for one session.

Do you think, Jane, that four weeks is a fair trial? You really should send him for the full eight weeks. Otherwise, I'm afraid, it will be nothing but an aborted experience.

Thus, parents in this civilzation often plan safe, dreadful experiences for their children. They also plan group play experiences, and making Jello becomes a science experience. Here is a passage from an article in the *New York Times Magazine*. See what culture this language reflects:

A nursery school administrator feels most earnestly that mothers cannot begin to provide as valuable an experience as nursery schools can. "Nursery education is so extremely important and so complicated that it requires all the training and experience a teacher can acquire."

He was talking about middle-class children, ages three to five, children from homes having refrigerators and stoves and books and mothers with bachelor degrees. Does his statement not sing, does it not chant of the Kwakiutl need to experience that which is outside the home? Outside of the mother's range? Outside of the norm?

In his pursuit of the exotic experience, the Kwakiutl would eat human flesh. Cannibalism was regarded with horror by them, and yet the most highly honored society among the Kwakiutl was the Cannibal Society; an initiate would take bites out of the arms of bystanders while a chorus of onlookers would count the mouthfuls

of skin he had taken. The Kwakiutl was not a epicurean cannibal; he took emetics immediately afterwards and tried not to swallow the bits of skin at all.

Listen to Ruth Benedict describe how it was done on the Northwest Coast before that civilzation died:

. . . the final thing they strove for was ecstasy. The chief dancer at least at the high point of his performance, should lose normal control of himself and be rapt into another state of existence. He should froth at the mouth, tremble violently and abnormally, do deeds which would be terrible in a normal state.

Now hear *Life* magazine describe how it is done in a newer civilization:

She had taken LSD twice before. . . . This time she "went up" slowly at first, wandering about the room, savoring her heightened perception. Then she began to turn nervous and furtive, and started rubbing her face with her fingers. Sucking her thumb, she rolled out of her chair and onto the floor, then bit down on her whole hand. For a while she lay silent, but soon began to sob, pushing herself about the floor as if trying to escape something that was biting her from within.

That was written in March of 1966; it reflects a culture that reincarnates the Kwakiutl.

Language shows the shape of my newest suburb, too. A city on the Southeast coast of the U.S., a city remote from others, bound by the sea on the east, a wasteland on the north, and country all around. A city that is a speck of downtown, a little urb, completely surrounded by suburbs. Jacksonville again. But the time is different. The time is now upper middle-class, and the suburb fits the time. Four bedrooms, two and a half baths, a family room, and a formal dining room. Living is easy. Warm. The isolation of the people has bred a certain closeness to each other. A refined closeness, where manners are more minuet than rock and roll. The lack of availability of high culture has left the land as one of the few remaining places where conversation is a principal form of entertainment. The usual place of entertainment is the home, and the ready availability of household help makes partying much easier than in northern suburbs. There is a lot of language to reflect culture when conversation is a form of entertainment.

One evening in a traditionally furnished brand new living room, one of a guest couple said to one of a host couple that she longed for some good French food, and she went on to complain about the lack of good French restaurants in town. The hostess wife mentioned that her maid was from New Orleans and made a terrific onion soup, and that she, herself, had a recipe for chocolate mousse, somewhere. As a matter of fact, having the first and the last of a great meal, all it would take would be someone who could fix the in-betweens, and she knew that Sally Jo Hazen had a wonderful recipe for beef burgundy. A thought was born, and the hostess wife continued:

"We can have a regular Gourmet Club. Take turns having a different menu every month. The hostess decides the menu. No fussing, though. No extra work for the hostess. The food will be the thing."

"I think," said the guest wife, "that when it is my turn, I'll serve Mexican food. World Bazaar up at the shopping center has the cutest Mexican tin plates and place mats."

"When you serve Mexican style," added the hostess, "I'll make the tacos. I happen to have a package of taco mix that I bought when we were down there. And I'll wear my poncho."

One of the husbands suggested, "Why don't we all just fly down to Mexico. It sounds simpler."

And his wife answered, "C'mon now, George, don't be a party poop."

You've heard that before. Doesn't that sound echoes from another suburban culture? Another gentle, remote culture? Another culture where if we can't go to the restaurant, we'll bring the restaurant to us. Or would you believe, theater? Hear Jane Austen tell about it in *Mansfield Park,* somewhere outside London at the beginning of the 19th century.

Tom Bertram says, "Yates, I think we must raise a little theater at Mansfield and ask you to be our manager."

This, though the thought of the moment, did not end with the moment; for the inclination to act was awakened.

Henry Crawford said, "I really believe that I could at this moment undertake any character that ever was written. Let us be doing something. Be it only half a play, an act, a scene; what should prevent us? And for a theater? Any room in this house might suffice."

"We must have a curtain," said Tom Bertram; "a few yards of green baize for a curtain, and perhaps that may be enough."

"Oh, quite enough!" cried Mr. Yates, "with only just a side wing or two run up, doors in flat, and three or four scenes to be let down; nothing more would be necessary. For mere amusement among ourselves we should want nothing more."

"I believe we must be satisfied with less," said Maria.

"Nay," said Edmund. "Let us do nothing by halves. If we are to act, let it be in a theater completely fitted up with pit, boxes, and gallery . . . let it be a play with good tricking, shifting afterpiece, and a figure-dance, and a hornpipe, and a song between the acts . . ."

"Now, Edmund, do not be disagreeable. . . ."

In this soft, Southern land of friendly persuasion, hear this telephone conversation:

"It started out just being a get-together for a few of our friends after the Florida-Georgia football game, but I decided that it would also be a wonderful opportunity to pay back some of our social obligations, too. Now, it turns out that we're expecting 35 couples."

Here is Jane Austen's *Persuasion:*

It was but a card party, it was but a mixture of those who had never met before, and those who met too often—a commonplace business, too numerous for intimacy, too small for variety.

Thus, language is a reflection of my specific cultural present, my now, and it is also a link to a broader cultural past, my then. Everyman's then. As an adult, writing for the future, and all writing for children is for the future. I must use my tool, language, honestly so that it will reflect a culture. So that kids reading my books know my neighborhood, a suburban one where fathers commute and mothers sometimes have to take over the management of Little League. They must know about my neighborhood, *About the B'nai Bagels,* just as I know the neighborhood of Jane Austen or Ruth Benedict's Kwakiutl or the fairy land of George MacDonald. I owe that to myself, and I owe it to the children that I write for. For my now is their tomorrow. Just as my now is Jane Austen's or the Kwakiutl's yesterday. And if language in my books is to mean anything, it should reflect a culture, and by that reflection show the shape of it.

Showing the shape of something is only one function of a perimeter; the other function is to define the limits of something. Sometimes those limits are a hard edge and are very visible. Like the time several years ago when my daughter was listening to a song being sung in French; she didn't understand a word of French, and she turned to me with a glowing smile and said, "I love to listen to songs in a foreign language; it's like a design." There she sat totally outside that design, the whole of which was abstract to her,

and because she was so far out of it, she saw its hard edge, the perimeter of which I speak.

If one understands French, he has moved inside that perimeter, and the elements of the design are no longer abstract but are representational. Any stranger to a language must be told what the designs mean, what the symbols mean, what the words mean, if they are to mean what society wants them to. For language is our guide to social reality.

A child is, in a sense, a stranger to even his own language. When an adult writes for children, he is writing as one who is living somewhere within the language pattern of culture, and he is writing for one who is standing on its perimeter, on its edge. I keep thinking about my daughter hearing the sounds of that French song and finding it an abstract design. And I realize that I want my words to do something else besides reflect a culture. I want the language in my books to be the tool that pokes holes in that perimeter. To let my daughter in. To let my readers in a little bit deeper into the pattern of culture. I want the pattern to be familiar, to be representational, to be reflecting a neighborhood, but not all of it. I also want to push out the limits of that edge a little.

Kids have to bump into something unfamilar. Let them meet the unfamiliar in words. Let them have language patterns of a social reality that they have not met yet. Let them use that language as a tool to poke holes with. Let them find enough familiar symbols so that they will feel at home, so that they can gather the words of an adult's now, an adult's social reality to use as a template for broader patterns of their own. Let them read about having a secret interior as the children in *From the Mixed-Up Files of Mrs. Basil E. Frankweiler* did, or let them read about how it is to be an outsider named Elizabeth who makes friends with another outsider named Jennifer.

Those are the holes that I hope I poke in that perimeter, and that I hope all my readers see through.

Our way of using language actually influences our views of both the physical and social worlds. Perhaps, if I give you an example where a lack of language served a positive purpose, I can make more clear this idea about language being a guide to social reality.

There once was a boy who could not begin a sentence without repeating the initial sound or syllable in it. This boy had a wise father who told everyone in the household to listen to the child as if he spoke as normally as they did. Friends were asked to cooperate, and when the youngster started kindergarten, the father went to the teacher and asked that she do the same. The teacher replied that the school had a speech therapy program that would help a stutterer.

And the father said, "No, thank you. I don't want him put in therapy; I don't want him called a stutterer. If he has no word for it, he can't think of himself as one."

And the teacher cooperated, and so did friends. Even relatives did. And the little boy is nine years old now, and he said to me the other day, "You know, Mom, I used to have trouble saying some sounds. Like at the beginning of a sentence, I would go I-I-I-I-I. That was a funny kind of baby talk."

That dumb kid still doesn't know that he was a stutterer. He never learned to fear being one. He could never adjust to the reality of being a stutterer because he didn't have the language tool to tell him so.

But what about some positive words?

Try to keep some out-of-sight problem in mind without thinking of it in terms of language. Try to think about buying groceries or finishing some assignment without language. Now try to think about privacy or loyalty or conformity without language. Try to think at all without language.

I bring all of my adulthood to my writing for children. I make an effort to help them hear the language of my culture, a culture that reaches into the past and spreads over the present. And I also make an effort to expand the perimeter of their language, to set a wider limit to it, to give them a vocabulary for alternatives, perhaps. Because language not only tells you the shape of a culture; it helps shape it.

Humpty Dumpty said to Alice, "When *I* use a word, it means just what I choose it to mean—neither more nor less."

"The question is," said Alice, "whether you *can* make words mean so many different things?"

"The question is," said Humpty Dumpty, "which is to be master, that's all."

Which is to be master, indeed!

Only a Humpty Dumpty can be master by proclamation. The rest of us are at the mercy of the particular language which has become the medium of expression for our society. Most kids are in the position of Alice listening to "Jabberwocky" or my daughter listening to the French song. That is, until Humpty Dumpty comes along to explain it.

Or until we help them learn to do it themselves.

Victim of Success?
A Closer Look at the
Newbery Award

Peggy Sullivan

HAS the Newbery Award become the victim of its own success and prestige? Was it meant to change the world of American children's books—and if so, has it? Whatever its effect on the book world, what has it done to children, librarians who work with them, and parents and teachers who are interested in the award?

It is hard to keep away from soap-opera questions like the ones just mentioned when discussing the Newbery Award. There can be little doubt of its success on the terms which Frederic Melcher, the first donor, and the American Library Association had in mind when the award was first instituted. To get proof of its prestige, one need only visit the typical book department of a large department store. There, along with a handful of the new season's offerings, a plethora of series and gimmick books, will be a fairly good representation of single copies of books that have won the award over the years. Their jackets may be less than fresh, but the Newbery Award symbol still flashes on them, and inevitably, all the salesperson knows about them is: "*This* book won the Newbery Award!" Yea, verily, that is all she knows and all she needs to know. That fact sells an occasional book and it dooms nearly all of the winners to a peculiar kind of unpopular bestsellerdom.

Librarians who work with children, whether in school or public libraries, perpetrate the same kind of special treatment. Let a new branch or a new school open, and there among the carefully selected titles in the collection will be a fair sampling of Newbery Award winners. In some instances, they will not even share shelves with their more mundane fellow-books; they will be set aside on other shelves carefully lettered and perhaps adorned with a poster to indicate they are the proper domicile of Newbery books. Back with the unchosen are *Harriet the Spy, Charlotte's Web, Across Five Aprils*, and dozens of others which just didn't make the grade.

Tradition

There are legends and customs which have grown up around the Award winners. And almost every legend and custom has its converse. There are those who believe that the chosen book every year is, without shadow of doubt, the most distinguished book of the year. There are those who believe it never is, just as there are the two camps who shout "Yes!" or "No!" to the question: "Has the Newbery Award committee ever made a mistake?" Some are convinced the award winning book loses something of its luster if it becomes popular. Most recently, that happened to *From the Mixed-Up Files of Mrs. Basil E. Frankweiler.* It may be saved from that fate of popularity by the fact that librarians will segregate it from the same author's equally distinguished titles and, by making it just that little bit more difficult to lay hands on, will keep it from falling into the too-eager hands of a readership that would cherish it. On the other side of the conviction about lusterless popularity is a fairly widely held opinion that the award should never go to a distinguished book that is not, at the same time, extremely popular. Librarians react with shock to the selection of a title that has not moved from the shelves since the day it was purchased—but then they hasten to publicize it. If chance and/or the wisdom of the Newbery Award committee achieves the selection of a winner they have not yet seen or, perhaps, reviewed and rejected for purchase, they blithely snap it up for the collection too and, without enthusiasm but also without embarrassment, they point out its values to the local press, the teachers, and parents who always want the winner the instant the decision is announced, and, eventually, they tell the few special children who may be conned into reading it because it is a Newbery Award winner: "Now, here's the best book of the year! Let me know what you think about it."

Selection and Use

Of course, there are librarians who disagree loudly and violently with what the committee has chosen for the award. And there are others who use the award effectively to highlight not only the winner but other notable books of their own choice from the same year. Some are even so bold as to suggest to teachers that "teaching the Newbery Awards" is not necessarily the most meaningful foray into literature that elementary or junior high students may take. But these bold few do so at their peril. One of the most convincing of them is Sally Fenwick, who was chairman of the Newbery Award committee in 1971. A few weeks after the award was announced, I invited her to speak to a workshop on language arts for teachers from the fourth through ninth grades of a school district in the Chicago suburbs. In the course of her talk, in which she highlighted the committee's method of selecting a winner, she made a strong statement to the effect that teachers might kill all interest in the Newbery books if they insisted that they be required for reading and exhaustive study. It may be that some accepted her suggestion, but one very enthusiastic teacher drew me aside the following week to say, "I was glad to know more about the Newbery Award committee, but I certainly disagree with Miss Fenwick about not teaching them. I require my students to read them. After all, they're the best books, aren't they?" So much for preaching to the convinced. I do wonder how the same teacher—or even a teacher of children's literature in a college or university who relies almost exclusively on Newbery Award winners in compiling a reading list—would react if American literature were taught by exhaustive study of the Pulitzer Award (or even the National Book Award or American Nobel Award) winners.

There is something ingenuous in the attitude that once a book has won the Newbery Award, it demands the allegiance and attention of all who are concerned about children's literature. Any attempt to review it fairly along with other titles is considered an effort to undermine the prestige of the award. Sadder yet, there really are people who think that knowing the award-winning books is the equivalent of knowing all materials for children. Several years ago, when I was teaching a course with a title something like Materials for Children, the head of the library school where I was teaching asked me how much my students would know about the Newbery Award books. I replied, "Very little. We refer to the award and if a book that's been read and discussed is one of the Newbery books, we mention that, but I don't teach the Newbery Award books." His response? "Then what the hell are you teaching in there?" The implication, of course, was that if the Newbery Award books weren't the heart and core of a course in materials for children, the students were being shortchanged. The possibility that they just might be getting a view of how to select books without being either dazzled or awed by their prestige did not seem to be very important.

There must be people reading this thinking: "So here's one more person who doesn't like the Newbery Award books!" I can see it now; I'll visit a school library, and the librarian will say, "I know *you* don't like the Newbery Award books, but *I* think they're important, and here they are." So I say, "I like them, too. Some of them I love. The idea is great, but as librarians, indeed as adults concerned with selection of books for children, we should not let the idea or the award overwhelm us. We should *use* the award." And how can it be used? Its announcement can be the occasion for calling attention to good children's books in general. In fact, ALA's Children's Services Division now has a memorandum on how to do that most effectively. We should not kid ourselves into believing that every award-winner belongs in every elementary school library. We should accept the fact that the committee is not always right, but that does not allow us to question their motives or their morals. Those of us entitled, by membership in the Children's Services Division, to vote in the membership straw vote, should do so after broad reading in the year's production of books. And, while giving the award prestige and attention, we should not treat the books in so special a manner that they become sacrosanct, even inaccessible, to the children who might just enjoy them as good books.

Straw Votes

In some communities, the straw vote

of the membership can provide a good time for librarians and teachers to discuss and defend their own choices. I can recall with great pleasure years when, as a children's librarian at the Enoch Pratt Free Library, I listened to Barbara Moody's impassioned championing of Gipson's *Old Yeller* and Doris Stotz's mirthful enthusiasm for Merrill's *The Push Cart War*. The books did not win, but all of us gained from the interchange of views and the exploration of tastes. Just incidentally, preparing for this kind of discussion means that the library system or school district has to have a selection process that allows librarians to get their hands on the books before the year is out. I know of another library system where the effort to get a good discussion of possible award winners is forever stymied by the fact that only a handful of librarians—those in the office and in the central children's room—have an opportunity to read children's books during the year when they are published. In another, a number of the librarians really believed that the purpose of the discussions was to instruct the supervisor in how to cast her vote in the Newbery ballotting. The link between CSD membership and the right to vote was never made. The number of CSD members who cast ballots in the straw vote is amazingly low. Perhaps, in addition to being concerned about what happens after the announcement, we should have some concern to encourage more participation in that voting.

A current charge made to the committee by a group of librarians was that the awards were going too often to books for older children. To my certain knowledge as a member of the Children's Services Division board, the board has not yet discussed this. My own view is that the only question is whether the books are children's books or not. If they are, they are eligible. It must be difficult to compare a simple, beautiful straightforward story for younger children with an involved, beautiful, complex novel for older children. But no one ever said that choosing a winner was easy.

There is another aspect, however, to the matter of grade levels of award winners. All of us have observed the phenomenon of having favorite books be read by children at progressively younger ages. We may like to believe that children are becoming better and better readers, as well as growing more and more sophisticated at younger ages. But might it not be that, just as we set aside the Newbery Award books for the special child, we overestimate the grade level of a book in the first place? One of the most interesting findings a student of mine made in comparing two editions, over a ten-year span, of a city school system's manual for librarians was that the same titles which were recommended in the 1950's appeared in the later edition as recommendations for grades two and three levels below the grades where they were recommended initially. Has the reading level of children changed that much? Or had librarians imposed an artificially high level in the first place, which was changed by the children's own enthusiasm? Among the Newbery Award winners, *It's Like This, Cat* is one that comes to mind as a title that librarians first introduced to boys in about the same early teen age bracket as the hero. Fortunately, wiser, younger heads prevailed, and it is the younger children who have taken it as their own.

Surely by this time, someone has noted that the Caldecott Awards have not even been mentioned. I do not consider them similar to the Newbery in terms of controversy, even in terms of prestige. Only when there was a fairly well organized flurry (if flurries are ever well organized) of support for Edwin Tunis as a Caldecott winner several years ago did the matter of age levels attract much attention. The Caldecott Award is younger, also, as an award, but perhaps one needs to mention it only to indicate that the Newbery-Caldecott Awards are not really a tandem, but two distinctive awards established for distinctive purposes.

Much has been written about the Newbery Awards; more will be written. Discussion and controversy only prove the prestige and success of the awards. One should, however, be qualified to discuss them, so I give my credentials: in 20 years of membership in the Children's Services Division, I have, as far as I can recall, never voted in the straw ballotting for a book which later won the award, but I have often realized that what was chosen was superior to my first choice. I have never served on a Newbery-Caldecott Committee, but I have been impressed with the expertise, enthusiasm, or at least with the honesty and sincerity of people whom I have known on the committee. Any of them would, I think, agree with me that one value of the awards has been the provision of opportunity at this national level for discussion of books, not in terms of expense, social relevance, or relation to the curriculum, but for that quality the Newbery Awards have assisted us in recognizing: excellence.

Moral Values and Children's Literature

Dorothy Broderick

ANY DISCUSSION of moral values can rapidly run astray and most do because they get hung-up on what Harvard psychologist Lawrence Kohlberg calls the "Boy Scout bag of virtues." Take honesty, for example. Most of us would agree that honesty is a virtue and we often describe someone as being "an honest man." Yet what does it mean? A man may pad his income tax form without ever dreaming of embezzling his business firm or robbing a bank. He is honest or isn't he? A child cheats on a test and, if caught, may be labeled dishonest on the records. However, as Kohlberg points out, the child may simply have absorbed the ethic of the classroom, namely that the grade is the all important thing and if one has to cheat to acquire it, then that is what is done.

Early researchers were very unhappy over the lack of correlation in their findings. Because a child cheated in one situation, it did not follow that he would cheat in another. Only in recent years have we been offered genuine insight into the fact that virtue-words "point to certain behaviors with approval, but give us no guide to understanding them." This insight comes to us through "The Theory of Moral Development in Children," as developed by the above mentioned Lawrence Kohlberg.

For 15 years Kohlberg has been conducting a longitudinal research study on the moral development of children. As an educational psychologist, Kohlberg is basically concerned with the possibilities of moral education within the schools, but his theory opens up many doors for all of us working with children in any situation. A most vital point about Kohlberg's theory is that it is not culturally limited to a particular society. It has been found valid in a Malaysian aboriginal village, in Taiwan, Mexico, Turkey, and Great Britain. The *rate* of development may differ within specific societies, but not the development itself.

Kohlberg's research technique consists of presenting the child with a dilemma situation that cannot be responded to by the use of virtue-words. Each dilemma poses a socio-moral conflict to which the child must explain *why* he selected his solution. Thus, the action itself does not determine a level of moral development but the reasons underlying the action.

A typical Kohlberg situation involves a man whose wife is dying. A druggist has discovered a drug that will cure her but he wants more money than the man can possibly raise and will not compromise about the price. What should the man do?

Analysis of the responses given to this and similar dilemmas has led Kohlberg to conclude that moral development consists of: 1) three levels, 2) six stages, and 3) 25 aspects. For obvious reasons, we cannot explore all the aspects Kohlberg covers, or even list them, but we can look in some detail at two aspects that have vast implications, the behavioral motivation and the value of a life.

Each of the three levels contain two of the stages. At level one, which Kohlberg calls "preconventional morality," stage one children have an obedience and punishment orientation. For example, the child at this stage says the man should steal the drug because he'll get in trouble if he lets his wife die. Another child responds that the man should not steal the drug because he will be put in jail. Either way, it is the threat of punishment that motivates the decision. The value of a human life at this stage has little meaning to the child. Moreover, he confuses the value of a life with the status of the person and with property. (When Mayor Daley told Chicago police to shoot looters, he was demonstrating the lowest level of moral development by equating the value of a man's life with a T.V. set.)

The second stage of level one is an ego-centered stage that Kohlberg calls "naive instrumental hedonism." Moving from the threat of physical punishment, the child begins to think of rewards. Thus, a child reasons that the man should steal the drug to save his wife's life because he needs her to take care of him, the children, and the house.

(When Kohlberg analyzed Eichmann's statements defending himself, he placed all but one of the rationalizations at these two stages—something we can all ponder.)

Level two is "conventional morality," and encompasses stages three and four. These require very little explanation except to note that they represent a growing recognition on the part of the child that there is a structure to society. Stage three is basically a role-playing response and can be summed up by the phrase, "good boys do this, good girls do that." Here, the man saves his wife's life because that is what a good husband would do.

Stage four is the respect for authority, whether secular or religious, and represents movement from the informal disapproval or approval of stage three to an institutionalized approval or disapproval. The value of a human life at this stage is seen as sacred within a "categorical moral or religious order" and intimately tied up with the society at this stage.

Level three constitutes "postconventional morality," and represents a movement from the appeal of authority to a growing recognition of the value of human life per se. The stage five person is very much the traditional liberal; he respects the authority inherent in stage four, but does recognize that there are such things as bad laws. He would work to change the law, but only rarely feel forced to break it. The stage six person, on the other hand, recognizes no law above the sanctity of human life. This person would steal the drug openly, fully expecting to be arrested, but willing to demonstrate the immorality of placing profit above a human life.

There are two other important points about Kohlberg's theory that we need to understand before moving on to how it might help us in our own field. The first has to do with an individual's ability to grasp the reasoning of stages other than his own. Once the individual has passed through a stage, he can understand the reasoning, but cannot accept it. On the other hand, it is rarely possible for an individual to grasp the reasoning more than one stage above his own. Thus, authority oriented people at stage four find it difficult to conceive of stage six reasoning being valid.

The second point is that when offered a choice of six possible reasons for an action, the child almost inevitably selects as "best" the one immediately above where he is actually functioning. Moreover, Kohlberg discovered that if you place children from two adjoining levels in an interaction situation, the higher level children help the lower level children move up more rapidly.

This theory has vast possibilities for use in both reader's guidance and book evaluation.

KOHLBERG's implications for reader guidance can be stated in briefer terms than those involving book evaluation, let us look at them first. Each of the three implications stated below are possibilities for research projects and hopefully someone with a background in educational psychology might develop a doctoral dissertation on the subject:

1) We can hypothesize that the books a child likes best are either at his own level of moral development or the one immediately above. For example, we know that Marjorie Flack's *The Story About Ping* has been a favorite with young children for four decades. Applying Kohlberg's stage one—fear of physical punishment—we can see that Ping initially does not return to the houseboat out of fear of being whacked as the last duck up the ramp. After his adventures of being on his own, he makes the decision that being whacked is a lesser form of punishment than ending up in a supper pot. Tentative analysis of other popular picture books shows that this theme in many guises—*Harry the Dirty Dog* and bath-taking, for example—permeates the most outstanding of the books.

2) We can hypothesize that books rejected by children (or adults for that matter) are operating at a stage more than one above where the reader is at, or are below his level. This implication will be discussed in more detail when it comes to the analysis of why a book labelled good by librarians may have extremely limited appeal for children.

3) Finally, we can see that if discussion groups containing children from two adjoining levels help the children at the lower stage move more rapidly into the upper stage, then the same might be true for books. That is, once we have determined the child's level and the book's level, we can offer him material above his own level and thus aid in his upward movement.

Evaluation

Since we all know that there aren't any better books in the world than Newbery winners, this past summer (1971) the children's literature class at the University of Wisconsin Library School read almost everything Kohlberg has written and applied his theory to analyzing the 50 winners. A large debt is owed these students but they should not be held responsible for this writer's interpretations of the results.

For years we have talked about character development as a criterion for evaluating a book but we have approached the problem with considerable subjectivity. In an attempt to make the phrase "character development" more meaningful, we asked the question, "At what level of moral development does the character make his decisions?"

First, I must report that there are a large number of books in which the characters appear to operate on a minus scale. It is truly astounding to discover the number of books for which it is impossible to identify a character's motivation.

Books are strong when a character makes real moral development in the course of a book. (At the adult level, *The Autobiography of Malcolm X* can be seen as the great book it is because Malcolm takes the reader and himself from stage one to stage six.) The attacks made by the feminist movement on *Caddie Woodlawn* as a cop-out book achieve validity when looked at in relationship to the Kohlberg scale. Early in the book, Caddie is seen operating at level five, at least, and maybe six when she is willing to risk all to save her Indian friends. At the end of the book, after father's little bedside chat with her about growing up into a lady, she has slipped to level three—the "good girls do this" syndrome.

The Witch of Blackbird Pond misses being a great book by a hair. Kit is a complete stage six person in her defense of Hannah, the Quaker. She recognizes that no law can take precedence over the human values of Hannah's life. Yet here again the emphasis on the proper role of a woman—getting married—takes her back to level three.

Johnny Tremain, by far the greatest of the Newbery titles, is great exactly because Johnny makes such fine progress in moving from the hedonistic stage two in the beginning of the book to level six at the end. While the reader himself may not operate at level six, or be within range of it, he does experience Johnny's growth vicariously. This point seems vital since a book cannot hold the reader's attention if it begins at too high a level for the reader to comprehend in the first place.

A great book with a limited audience demonstrates this point. The book is Coatsworth's *The Cat Who Went to Heaven*. Here, the problem would seem to be that the artist is seen at the beginning operating strongly at level four— respect for authority. His awe of the Buddhist priests who commission his painting is clear. In the end, his decision to paint the beloved cat into the picture is almost a classic case of Kohlberg's level six reasoning: he breaks the law of the religion openly, fully willing to accept the punishment that will attend the act, yet unwilling to sacrifice a beloved friend, cat though it may be, to the rigidity of the authorities.

Unfortunately, the book's potential audience is not at an age where such reasoning has any meaning. Thus we can see the importance of a book's moral level coinciding with its potential audience's level. A book that is far more popular for the same age group is *Rabbit ·Hill*. The highest level Georgie achieves is the "good rabbits do this" stage— which most ten-year-olds can easily grasp.

When we get into a hassle about a book, as we occasionally do, the progression of stages may help us understand what we are arguing about. A book that has always been unsatisfying to me

(which is not the same as not liking it— just that there is something elusive about it that bothers me) is *Shadow of a Bull*. Looked at in terms of moral development, the answer now seems clearer. There is too unreasonable a jump in the character's development. In *Shadow of a Bull*, Manolo is operating completely at stage three—he is role playing the part of the good boy as seen by his townsmen. Then, bang. At the end he has jumped to level six and a concern for the sanctity of human life without the intervening stages accounted for.

Movement from one level to another must be smooth if the book is to succeed. An example of another great Newbery is *And Now Miguel*. Throughout the major portion of the book Miguel is at level three, striving only to fulfill the expectations of what a good boy does. With the arrival of his brother's draft notice and the fulfillment of his prayer, Miguel is seen taking his first tentative steps toward level four and the recognition of authority as represented by both God and the government.

Problems

This initial exploration into the possibilities of Kohlberg's theory as applied to children's literature ran into two problems, one explicit, the other implicit.

Explicitly, there are too few books beyond stage three—the role playing of boys and girls is stressed even in the titles for older children who could at least comprehend stage four and maybe stage five. This may well account for the number of junior high students who are looking to adult titles for their reading satisfaction.

Implicitly, the question arises whether adults who are themselves fixated at lower stages can be of any help to children wishing to move up. I suspect that this, more than any other single factor, accounts for the large gap we keep talking about between adults and the youth of the counterculture. The most we may be able to do for the younger generation is to simply step out of its way as it seeks to establish a world where human beings—all human beings—are cherished.

Introduction to Kohlberg's
Theory of Moral Development*

Kohlberg, L. "The Development of Moral Character and Ideology" in M. Hoffman (ed.), *Review of Child Psychology*. Russell Sage Foundation, 1964.

_____. "Moral Development and Identification," ch. VII in H. W. Stevenson (ed.), *Child Psychology 62nd Year Book Nat. Soc. Stud. Ed. Part I*. Univ. of Chicago Pr., 1963.

_____. "Stage and Sequence: The Cognitive-Developmental Approach to Socialization," c. VI in David Goslin (ed.), *Handbook of Socialization Theory and Research*. Rand McNally, 1969.

_____. "The Child as a Moral Philosopher" in *Psychology Today*. No. 7, 1968. p. 25-30.

_____. "Moral Education in the School." *School Review*, 14. No. 1, 1966. p. 1-30.

_____. "Education for Justice: A Modern Statement of the Platonic View" in T. Sizer (ed.), *Moral Education*. Harvard Univ. Pr., 0000.

Rest, J., Turiel, E., & Kohlberg, L. "Level of Moral Development as a Determinant of Preference and Comprehension of Moral Judgements Made by Others." *J. of Pers.* June, 1969. p. 225-252.

Kohlberg, L. "The Development of Children's Orientations Toward a Moral Order: I. Sequence in the Development of Moral Thought." *Vita Humana (Human Development)*. Vol. 16. 1963. p. 11-33.

*For a full understanding of the evolution of Kohlberg's Theory, it is suggested that the articles be read in chronological order.

II
Intellectual Freedom
or Censorship?

The Grand Illusion

Eli M. Oboler

> *Except in rare and specific cases, infants are not isolated from the world. They are given shots which immunize them to the world. . . . It is not then, a germ-free world we seek; it is a strong, healthy population. . . . Parents who cannot clean up their children find a tempting satisfaction in cleaning up the book stalls." Robert F. Hogan, "Obscenity, the Law, and the English Teacher," National Council of Teachers of English, 1966*

IN 1951 a popular song had a line expressing the common plaint, "They tried to tell us we're too young." Who were "they"? "They," of course, were the ones the new generation seems to find especially annoying, the ones who are over 30, or 35, or 40. "They" are trying to tell kids that they are far too young to do what they're doing. Naturally, this leads to resentment on the part of teenagers, and in exasperation and natural reaction, they do even more of whatever it is that "they" try to tell them they are too young to do.

This problem of "the generation gap" ties in with reading and communication. Even Restif de la Bretonne, best known today as a pornographer, in his later years waxed most eloquent on the cause and effect relationship of "bad" books and youthful delinquencies. The Durants tell us in their most recent volume, *Rousseau and Revolution,* that de la Bretonne "berated Rousseau for having unleashed the passions of the young. . . ." He charged, "It is *Emile* that has brought us this arrogant generation, stubborn and insolent and willful, which speaks loudly, and silences the elderly."[1] Today's teenage generation may not be inspired by

Emile, but it certainly could be described by some of the same adjectives applied by de la Bretonne.

Common among the restrictions on our teenagers are those which, in the case of movies, tell them that particular movies are for those 18 and over only; or, in the case of books, tell them that they cannot buy particular paperbacks at the corner drugstore, or they cannot find in their public libraries the books that they would like to read, or even that, within those public libraries, if they can locate them, they may not *read* them unless they, again, are over the magic age of 18.

This matter of age as related to interest in sexual matters is often ignored in considering how best to give appropriate library services to those between 13 and 18. For many years we have known, on the basis of scientific proof, from Dr. Alfred Kinsey's famous studies and others, that adolescence, particularly for the male, is coincident with the high peak of sexual activity and interest.[2] So we have the interesting paradox that the very period in human life when the human animal is most interested and concerned with sexual activity is the period when he or she

43

is expressly barred from reading material directly concerned with his or her greatest interests. As might be expected, this often leads to difficulties.

To clarify further, the Kinsey report, discussing the adolescent boy, says that "the peak of *capacity* occurs in the fast-growing years prior to adolescence; the peak of actual performance is the middle or later teens."[3] In other words, the typical male high school student is much more preoccupied with sex than even the college student, whom conventional wisdom accepts as the leader in this respect. Kinsey comments on "an intensification of the struggle between the boy's biologic capacity and the sanctions imposed by the older male. . . ."[4] It is about these sanctions and the *realities* of adolescent life that I am writing.

Often, the mistaken impression exists that some kind of mysterious or magic change in brainpower and self-control occurs between the last day of the 17th year of an individual and the first day of his 18th year. This is not so. People mature at different rates, and, indeed, some never mature at all in the psychological or even the physical sense.

Intellectual Freedom for Teens

Our present library rules on access to books of a presumably sexual nature for adolescents are not only outdated; the rules themselves are almost obscene in the commonly accepted sense of being "offensive to . . . decency." What could be more indecent than what Browning, in his mid-Victorian way, referred to in *The Statue and the Bust* when he said:

> The sin I impute to each frustrate ghost
> Is in the unlit lamp and the ungirt loin.

Surely our modern psychology has verified this Victorian rebel's literary attempt to single out the sin of the loin which is girt, when the human physiology calls for the opposite.

Don't misunderstand me. I am advocating neither promiscuity nor the widespread reading of obscene and/or pornographic literature by teenage boys and girls; rather, I am asking that we face up to what our own experience, knowledge, and the scientific facts of life indicate to us.

The 1967 meeting of hundreds of librarians and others interested in the topic of "Intellectual Freedom and the Teenager," sponsored by the ALA Intellectual Freedom Committee, came to several rather interesting conclusions. Among these were that if any group of library users needs protection and a "bill of rights," it is certainly the teenager in America today. A prominent lawyer, Stanley Fleishman, discussing the legal aspects of censorship, asked librarians to check into why they were restricting access to certain books. He wondered if librarians are "truly interested in complete freedom for the young, or are they interested in controlling, directing, and shaping young people in the present cultural molds."[5]

The Supreme Court of the United States, on May 15, 1967, ruled that "neither the Fourteenth Amendment nor the Bill of Rights is for adults alone." Detailed evidence indicates that despite the fact that in many states and local communities adolescents have been denied their just rights, they are still entitled to them. This is certainly another step toward indicating that these days are different from the past, and that if the majority of the Supreme Court of the United States can agree that juveniles are entitled to the safeguards of the Bill of Rights and other parts of the Constitution, surely there should be no differentiation made between laws on censorship for adults and for adolescents.

The Case for Censorship

A prominent sociologist, Ernest van den Haag, writing in *Esquire Magazine* for May 1967, under the title *The Case for Pornography Is the Case for Censorship and Vice Versa,* has claimed that censorship on the whole is needed because "if pornography were allowed to proliferate unchecked it might influence both public and private attitudes and sensibilities, and, therefore, ultimate reactions." He says that "certainly books can follow the atmosphere so as to engender a support of abominable and criminal acts."[6] You will note that he gives no evidence to support this, but simply states that it is so. There have been many opinions to the contrary, held by equally prominent sociologists, psychologists, and other authorities, based on research and investigation.

Even if it were true that the reading of so-called "bad" books causes or contributes to socially undesirable behavior, "most believers in censorship apparently reject as too long-range or visionary the corollary that the answer to a bad book is a good one. Rather, their philosophy seems to be that the best answer to a so-called "bad" book is no book.

Let's face it. At this point, we really don't *know* for sure what the actual cause-and-effect relationship is between reading and behavior. As Bergen Evans has stated, "In the realm of sexual customs—the field in which censors are most industrious —the effect of books is very slight. Raping is a much older activity than reading, and men are rarely incited to it by the printed page."

Fortunately, something is being done about this facet of the censorship problem. At the ALA preconference I referred to, one of the major recommendations was that a truly scientific study in depth be made to ascertain the causal relationship, if any, between reading and deviant

social behavior. When funds become available, it seems fairly certain that this study will be made. Furthermore, the United States Congress has passed a bill to set up a study commission on the subject. And, most important, this fall the U. S. Supreme Court issued a judgment on a New York case involving the limits of what can be published and made available for teenagers.

But whatever the results of the studies and the verdicts, they cannot really affect the most important part of dealing with teenagers as far as libraries are concerned. Librarians are prone to follow the criteria their professional groups set up, and this is probably more true of those lax in standards than of any other type.

Loopholes in Selection Guides

The leaflet entitled *Selecting Materials for School Libraries: Guidelines and Selection Sources to Insure Quality Collections,* prepared by the American Association of School Librarians in 1965, states:

The individual school library collection should include all facets of the curriculum with materials which reflect different points of view on controversial subjects and which provide opportunities for pupils and teachers to range far and wide in their search for information and inspiration. . . . All materials selected for the school library, in whatever format, should meet high standards of excellence. Materials which deal with current topics should be up-to-date; those which reflect a biased point of view should make the prejudice recognizable.

Let us speculate on the possible effects of following these "guidelines." To begin with, there seems to be a pretty strong indication that school libraries must reflect whatever is in the curriculum: if there were to be no curricular matter connected with sex, surely the library would be obligated, under these guidelines, to bar materials on sex, since they would be unrelated to the particular courses taught.

Another reflection based on these guidelines might be that the injunction about the "up-to-dateness" of materials would imply a rather rigid weeding program. If one were to consider Vietnam, for example, as a "current" topic, then books and other reading materials dated before 1967 could possibly be considered out of date, and therefore not needed in the library, which certainly would hurt any historical study on this important subject.

Librarians have, to a great extent, begged the question of what to do about controversial and censorable materials. To say that "all materials . . . should meet high standards of excellence" is equivalent to saying that "God is good." What would be a *low* standard of excellence? What would be a standard of *less* than excellence? What, indeed, would be a standard? There is no indication in these guidelines to help any school librarian, or school board member, or principal, or even the people most directly concerned—the students.

Let us consult another official publication: *Standards for School Library Programs,* issued by the American Library Association in 1960. This is the latest available set of standards for this branch of the profession and it says that: "A wealth of excellent materials is available for children and young people, but there is no justification for the collections to contain materials that are mediocre in presentation of content." It also says, "Maintaining qualitative standards of selection of materials is essential. All materials are, therefore, carefully evaluated before purchase, and only materials of good quality are obtained."

This sounds very nice. But just what are these "qualitative standards"? Nothing is stated specifically; there is simply a reference to "the established criteria for the evaluation and selection of materials."

Let us try the School Library Bill of Rights. It says that:

It is the responsibility of the school library to . . . provide materials that will enrich and support the curriculum . . . ; to provide materials which stimulate growth in factual knowledge, literary appreciation, esthetic values, and ethical standards . . . ; to provide a background of information which will enable pupils to make intelligent judgments in their daily life; provide materials on opposing sides of controversial issues so that young citizens may develop under guidance the practice of critical reading and thinking; provide materials representative of the many religious, ethnic, and cultural groups and their contributions to our American heritage; . . . to place principle above personal opinion and reason above prejudice in selection of materials of the highest quality in order to assure a comprehensive collection appropriate for the uses of the library.

Once again, some questions are being begged or evaded here. What materials "provide growth in . . . ethical standards"? Would *Little Lord Fauntleroy* be of more value than *Studs Lonigan* to a teenager living in a slum area in one of America's large cities today? How far does one go in attempting to provide "materials on opposing sides of controversial issues"? Practically everything and anything is controversial, and budgets are, after all, limited. Would ten books on religion and one book on atheism be a fair balance? Or should no books on atheism be included in a school library? How far should the school library go in including materials "representative of the many religious, ethnic, and cultural groups" which make up America? If one lives in a town which is 40 percent or 60 percent of one particular religious faith, should 40 percent or 60 percent of the books on religion in that school or public library deal with that particular faith, and should all books which are inimical to that faith be excluded?

A Solution for the Librarian

After these somewhat negative reflections, here is what I recommend as a simple and constructive proposal: that the librarians, responsible for selecting books, and the trustees, responsible for preparing or approving book selection policies for libraries, should not, at any time, place books in a public or school library specifically for a particular age group. Either a book should be in a library or it should not. If a teenager—a boy or girl under 18, since that is the generally accepted legal age of maturity—has a library card and requests a book which is in the library and which follows the various criteria cited above, he or she should be given that book, regardless of his or her age and no matter what the possible censorable quality of the book may be. If it is good enough to be in the library, it is good enough to be read by anyone who can read it.

The last people in the world to be censors are librarians. Once the decision has been made to add a particular book or magazine to the library, there should be no further censorship or selection that will keep it from anyone wanting it.

Finally, it is clear that trying to solve as complex a problem as the appropriate amount of intellectual freedom to which a teenager is entitled these days is somewhat like giving a pat answer to the question, "How can the U. S. get out of Vietnam with honor and with safety?"

The *kind* of answer one gives to such questions as these, rather than the actual details of the answer, is what is important.

Here is a brief credo to which I hope all librarians can subscribe. The librarian should be on the side of the positive, the progressive, the one who seeks new answers rather than the one who goes along entirely with more of the same. What was earlier referred to as "the conventional wisdom" tells us that the older we are, the smarter we are. It also tells us that we must stop the young from finding out too soon what the world is really like. Librarians should disagree with both of these all-too-widely held judgments. The true librarian should be for freedom, for searching, for trying to find new and better answers to important questions, rather than relying on answers that have been given in the past. Getting down to the very basics in librarianship, librarians and library trustees are not, and *must not* try to improve or regulate the morals of today's teenager. The family, church and to some extent, the school, (outside of the library), are far better and far more appropriate institutions to see to it that American youth today becomes a mature, responsible, worthwhile, older generation. The library's function in this is to do whatever it can to make the wealth of fine books, so-called good literature, available, even if there are a few four-letter words or pictures of nudes included in the package.

FOOTNOTES

[1]Durant, Will and Ariel. *Rousseau and Revolution* (The Story of Civilization: Part X). Simon and Schuster, 1967. p. 919.
[2]Kinsey, Albert C. and others. *Sexual Behavior in the Human Male.* Saunders, 1948. p. 219.
[3]*Ibid.*

[4] *Ibid.*, p. 222.

[5] "Intellectual Freedom and the Teenager," *ALA Bulletin,* July, August 1967. p. 833.

[6] "The Case for Pornography Is the Case for Censorship and Vice Versa," *Esquire,* May, 1967. p. 134-135.

[7] Jennison, Peter. "Freedom to Read," *Public Affairs Pamphlet No. 344,* May, 1963. p. 17.

Impressionable Minds—
Forbidden Subjects

Alan H. Levine

"What else can the School Board now decide it does not like? How else will its sensibilities be offended? Are we sending children to school to be educated by the norms of the School Board or are we educating our youth to shed the prejudices of the past, to explore all forms of thought, and to find solutions to our world's problems?"
—United States Supreme Court Justice William O. Douglas (dissenting from the Supreme Court's refusal to hear President's Council, District 25 v. Community School Board No. 25)

IN MOST RESPECTS the drama was all too ordinary. It began, as it usually does, when a parent discovered that a school library was exposing students' impressionable minds to "forbidden" subjects. In this Queens, New York version, the book was *Down These Mean Streets* (Knopf, 1967), the highly acclaimed book autobiography by Piri Thomas portraying the process of growing up in the Puerto Rican ghetto of East Harlem in New York City. The book was on the shelves of three of the junior high school libraries in Community School District No. 25.

The parent complained to the school board and a stormy public meeting was held on April 19, 1971. On one side, civic, community, and education groups—including the New York Library Association—passionately warned against "censorship" and "book-burning." On the other side, the chief spokesman for those seeking to ban the book warned of psychological damage to young children, bolstering his argument by treating the audience—including some young children—to a rendering of the book's most sexually explicit passages. When the shouting died down, Community School Board No. 25, by a vote of 5 to 3, passed the following resolution:

"The Superintendent is hereby directed to remove *Down These Mean Streets* from all student libraries in the district."

For regular readers of *SLJ*, it may be an unpleasant story, but certainly not a new one. Book banning, is, in fact, rooted in a long and dishonorable tradition of American education. Over the past century, campaigns against school books have been waged by, among others, the American Legion and Veterans of Foreign Wars (texts were "unAmerican"), the Ku Klux Klan (books favored "papists and antiChristian Jews of the Bolshevik Socialist stripe"), the Daughters of the American Revolution (insufficient emphasis on military history), National Council for Prevention of War (insufficient emphasis on the peace-loving qualities of American heroes), organized labor, the Women's Christian Temperance Union, and the National Association of Manufacturers (books "laced with antibusiness sentiment and economic determinist and socialist theories").

As for the more recent past, a perusal of issues of *SLJ*, and the American Library Association's *Newsletter on Intellectual Freedom* for the past two years reveals attacks on libraries for shelving

49

books such as Cleaver, *Soul on Ice* (McGraw, 1968); Roth, *Goodbye Columbus* (Houghton, 1959); Brown, *Manchild in the Promised Land* (Macmillan, 1965); Griffin, *Black Like Me* (Houghton, 1961); Carmichael, *Black Power* (Random, 1968); Salinger, *Catcher in the Rye* (Bantam, 1970); and an anthology of modern literature because it contained such reputedly Communist authors as Langston Hughes, Richard Wright, Woody Guthrie, Martin Luther King, Malcolm X, and Dick Gregory. It is noteworthy that books by nonwhites appear to come under particular attack.

At the same time, the court battle was being fought over *Down These Mean Streets*, a school board in Connecticut ordered the book *Boss* (Dutton, 1971), a political biography of Chicago Mayor Richard Daley, removed from a high school reading list because, as one board member explained, it "slandered" local law enforcement officials and "doesn't tell the truth." A Roselle, New Jersey school board forbade its high school library from purchasing four books, including John Kenneth Galbraith's *The Affluent Society* (NAL, 1970), as reference materials for a federally funded American studies course. As the president of the Board of Education explained, "In my opinion, the books were too liberal and I disagree with their points of view."

A few weeks after the Queens School Board decision to ban *Down These Mean Streets*, the New York Civil Liberties Union filed in the United States District Court in Brooklyn a suit with the rather cumbersome caption of *President's Council, District 25 v. Community School Board No. 25*. Although to litigation-conscious civil-libertarians a lawsuit was the natural device for testing the constitutionality of an action that provoked cries of "censorship" and "book-burning," we soon learned, to our surprise, that no other school board had ever been sued for book-banning. The only similar challenge was an administrative appeal, not a lawsuit. The New York City Board of Education had banned *Nation* maga-

zine because of articles critical of the Catholic Church. The State Commission of Education upheld the ban as a valid exercise of educational discretion (*Matter of Kornblum*, 70 St. Dept. Rep. 19—1949).

The suit against Community School Board No. 25 was brought on behalf of a librarian, a principal, teachers, students, and parents of students at schools at District 25. The decision to file the suit was made even though the librarian had not been fired. It was, after all, the school board's order removing the book, and not the librarian's response, which implicated First Amendment values. We argued citing Supreme Court precedent that it should not be and was not the law that the librarian had to defy its ban and risk dismissal, with its attendant disruption of school functions, in order to challenge it.

Soon after we filed suit, the School Board passed a so-called "parent option plan" which permitted those schools which originally had the book to permit its direct loan to parents but not to students. Other schools in the district remained under the ban imposed by the Board's original resolution.

The Case for the Ban

The school board defended its action in affidavits submitted by school principals and teachers that spoke of the possible harm to children from reading such harsh and vivid language. The theme of their statements is illustrated by the affidavit of a psychologist:

"If youngsters are steeped in a literature of violence, lawlessness, sexual promiscuity and perversion at this time of life, it cannot but influence their development adversely, no matter how significant the underlying purpose of the book. . . ."

"Lately, it has become fashionable to sneer at middle-class values, but an indication of which ones should be eliminated and how our society would benefit thereby is not spelled out. Should we dispense with honesty, or self-control, conscientious performance of work and studies, ambition, family loyalty, marital fidelity, devotion to children, respect for parents, cleanliness, religious convictions, or observance of the law?"

The Case for the Book

In reply, several eminent psychologists and psychiatrists dismissed as simplistic and unsupportable the contention that the scenes depicted in *Down These Mean Streets* could have an adverse impact on the psychological development of children. Moreover, because children bring to the books they read their own special experiences and fantasies, it was impossible to anticipate how children would react to even seemingly benign literature. Or, as one judge had observed over 20 years earlier, "a moron could pervert to some sexual fantasy to which his mind is open the listings in a seed catalogue."

Our librarian-plaintiff noted first that several reviewing journals she had consulted all wrote favorably of the book. (*School Library Journal*, a publication which reviews more than 2000 children's and adolescent's books per year and offers guidance on book selection to a readership of more than 70,000 librarians, saw the book as an important adjunct to the social studies and civics curriculum of teaching today's problems. *SLJ* included it among its "Best Books of the Year" in the category of "Adult Books for Young Adults.") She recognized that the language was strong and the episodes vivid, but she thought the book would "reach" some students. As with all other library books, it would appeal to some students and not to others, and some students would understand it and others would not. But she believed that a school library must have books suited to all tastes and interests. For those students who were seeking to understand the people and conditions of the ghetto, the librarian said, she knew few books that were more suitable.

Several junior high school students submitted statements that made light of the suggestion that they would be shocked or led astray by the language or sex scenes in the book. Perhaps the most telling indictment of the ban was the sophistication of a 13-year-old's comment: "... Why are you banning this book? Doesn't this book tell you what it's like to live a life in Spanish Harlem? Are you afraid we will learn how hard it is to live there? Banning this book is like banning part of Harlem, which you can't do. If this book is so bad for us and it described how it is to live in such a place, then that place should be banned."

That same "impressionable" young mind formulated an ironic truth which has mocked the efforts of censors throughout history:

"To tell you the truth, I never heard of the book until this bit about banning it came about. Now everyone is trying to get the book. Have you ever wondered how many people took this book out of the library before this incident? Now there's a waiting list on the book. You know, the people who brought up the subject about this book really did just the opposite of what they wanted to do. I am sure no one would have said anything after reading about the homosexual and other acts in the book. But now all the kids are reading the book (because of the description of the homosexual acts? I don't know.) All I can say is, all you people who wanted to get the book banned shouldn't have made such a big deal about it, because by the time you get the book banned, many people will have already read the book."

To the parents and students of this Queens school district, the issue was of genuine urgency. School libraries are, after all, the only place in the school where students are generally free to read books and consider ideas of their own choosing. For many of the students, products of white middle class homes in a nearly all-white school district, the library would be a place to learn about the new worlds and new people that would greet them when they entered more racially-mixed high schools in the next year or two. Their parents, unable to describe those worlds from personal experience, wanted and expected the school and its library to fulfill that vital role.

The Legal Issues

Such were the factual issues. The legal issue was the authority of the school board against the provisions of the First Amendment.

The plaintiffs argued that the ban was unconstitutional, the librarian claiming an infringement of academic freedom, the students of their First Amendment "right to know," in this case, the right to read a book. The district court (its decision has not been reported) and later the Second Circuit Court of Appeals (the decision is reported at 457 F.2d 289) rejected this position. Said the district court: Since the school board by statute was given the power "to determine matters relating to the education of students," it followed that "the Board, acting pursuant to its statutory powers, had the discretion to order the book or refuse to do so, to put it on the school library shelves or remove it therefrom." Therefore, the decision to ban the book could not be reviewed by the courts. The Court of Appeals, affirming the decision of the district court, said matter-of-factly that someone, after all, has to make a determination as to what the library collection will be.

They are seductively logical statements. (They would, by the way, apply equally to book banning decisions of public library boards of trustees.) They ignore, however, some 50 years of constitutional law. To say, as do the courts here, that the school board has the statutory power to make educational decisions, affords those decisions no immunity from constitutional principles. A ban against teaching German in Nebraska (*Meyer v. Nebraska*, 262 U.S. 390), one against private schools in Iowa (*Bartels v. Iowa*, 262 U.S. 404), another against teaching Darwin in Arkansas (*Epperson v. Arkansas*, 393 U.S. 97), and one against student protest in Des Moines (*Tinker v. Des Moines Independent Community School District*, 393 U.S. 503), as well as a compulsory flag salute (*West Virginia State Board of Education v. Barnette*, 319 U.S. 624), were all defended as educational judgments by school officials. All were invalidated by the Supreme Court.

School boards do indeed have ultimate legal responsibility for courses of instruction and instructional materials. But, if as the Courts suggested in *President's Council*, their power over educational materials is unlimited, does that mean that school boards have the power to systematically purge their libraries of all books advocating peace or integration, or their curricula of all courses treating the United Nations? "What else," Justice Douglas pointedly inquires, "can the School Board now decide it does not like? How else will its sensibilities be offended?"

If school boards are permitted to take books found offensive to some and make them unavailable to all, they will encourage every pressure group, every self-appointed guardian of public morals to make known their own selection for banning. On the other side, every teacher and every librarian will be put on notice that they select at their peril any but the most benign and undistinguished materials.

How then to resolve the conflict, the over-all responsibility of school boards for instruction in the schools as against the constitutional rights of librarians and students? Two recent cases offer some guidance.

In *Keefe v. Geanakos*, 418 F.2d 359 (1st Cir. 1969), a high school teacher was dismissed for assigning the reading of an article containing the same "dirty" word most frequently employed in *Down These Mean Streets*. The teacher asserted a right to academic freedom, to be free to select, within reason, materials he considered educationally valuable; the school board asserted its obligation under state law to provide an education for students in the district.

The court conceded the proposition that "some measure of public regulation of classroom speech is inherent in every provision of public education." Nevertheless, the Court said: "[T]he question in this case is whether a teacher may, for demonstrated educational purposes, quote a 'dirty' word currently used . . . or whether the shock is too great for high school seniors to stand. If the answer were that the student must be protected from such exposure, we would fear for their future."

As to the fact that some parents may have been offended, the Court observed, "We do not question the good faith of the defendants in believing that some parents have been offended. With the greatest of respect to such parents, their sensibilities are not the full measure of what is proper education.

"We of course agree with defendants that what is to be said or read to students is not to be determined by obscenity standards for adult consumption . . .

[However], as in all other instances, the offensiveness of language and the particular propriety or impropriety is dependent on the circumstances of the utterance."

Similar issues were presented in *Parducci v. Rutland*, 316 F.Supp. 352 (M.D. Ala. 1970). A high school teacher, after assigning a short story by a noted author, Kurt Vonnegut, to her English class, was called into the principal's office and told by the principal and the school system's associate superintendent that the story was "literary garbage" and that she should not teach it in her class. She claimed, in reply, a "professional obligation to teach the story" and was subsequently dismissed. The court weighed her claim against what it acknowledged to be "the state's vital interest in protecting the impressionable minds of its young people from *any* form of extreme propagandism in the classroom." While observing that the story contained "several vulgar terms and a reference to an involuntary act of sexual intercourse," the court could "find nothing that would render it obscene."

Then, evaluating the school board's and teacher's competing interests, the court conceded "that 'school officials should be given wide discretion in administering their schools' and that 'courts should be reluctant to interfere with or place limits on that discretion.'

"Such legal platitudes should not, however, be allowed to become euphemisms for 'infringement upon' and 'deprivations of' constitutional rights. However wide the discretion of school officials, such discretion cannot be exercised so as to arbitrarily deprive teachers of their First Amendment rights."

The principle of *Keefe* and *Parducci* should have protected the librarian's selection of *Down These Mean Streets*. In fact, the competing interests were easier to resolve than in those cases. There the books were *assigned* as part of the classroom curriculum, precluding alternative instructional materials which the school board would argue were more educationally valuable. In *President's Council*, the judgment of the librarians conflicted with no conceivable educational interest of the school board. The book's retention in the library would exclude no other books considered more valuable, nor would its study take up any class time that could be put to better use. The book would simply be made available to interested students.

Just as there was no justification for denying the librarians' right of academic freedom, there was no justification for denying the students their constitutional rights. They did not claim, as the Court of Appeals mistakenly assumed, "an unqualified First Amendment right of access to books." Recognizing that schools inevitably choose some books and reject others, they did not argue that they have a right to have any books they want placed in the school library. Rather, they asserted three interrelated propositions: 1) that they no longer had access to a book previously available to them; 2) that their First Amendment "right to know" was to that extent, impaired; 3) that, in the words of the Supreme Court, no "compelling" or "substantial" state interest justified that impairment.

The school board did not even hint at any compelling state interests. The Second Circuit attempted to supply some—namely "financial and architectural realities," but such "realities" had nothing to do with this case. The school board had not been engaged in the process of selecting books for its libraries. If it had been, its decision to spend its limited dollars on books other than *Down These Mean Streets* would be defensible on educational grounds and beyond judicial review. Nor was there ever the suggestion that "architectural" considerations such as limited shelf space motivated the book's removal.

The Court of Appeals summed up its rejection of the plaintiffs' constitutional claims by pointing out that "discussion of the book or the problems which it encompasses or the ideas it espouses have not been prohibited by the Board's action . . .," a comment which prompted Justice Douglas to wryly observe, "they can do everything but read it." To permit school boards arbitrarily to deprive students of the opportunity to read books previously available in the school library offends what Justice Black once described as the principle that "government should leave the mind and spirit of man absolutely free . . . . [P]ublic officials cannot be constitutionally vested with powers to select the ideas people can think about. . . ."

If students are to be deprived of the opportunity to read books and are thus to be afforded diminished guarantees under the First Amendment, authority must, as the Court insisted in *Parducci*, be found in two recent Supreme Court cases treating the First Amendment rights of minors, *Tinker* v. *Des Moines Independent Community School District*, 393 U.S. 503 (1969) and *Ginsberg* v. *New York*, 390 U.S. 629 (1968).

In *Tinker*, the Court's broad affirmation of students' First Amendment rights was qualified only where their exercise "materially disrupts classwork or involves substantial disorder or invasion of the rights of others." The school board in *President's Council* made no attempt to defend their action by contending that students became disruptive or disorderly after reading the book. The District Court made no finding on the matter. At best, the reaction of students who have read the book seems to be some degree of enthusiasm. At worst, students seem to have been rather indifferent to the book's existence.

The other case treating the First Amendment rights of minors is *Ginsberg* v. *New York*, where the Court upheld the concept of "variable obscenity." The Court, however, did not give the state broad, roving authority to determine what was and was not "appropriate" for children. Rather it merely upheld a New York statute which restricted sale of material to minors, according to a specific standard adopted from *Roth* v. *United States*, 354 U.S. 476 (1957). The test required that the material, *taken as a whole*, be harmful to minors.

The comparison of *Down These Mean Streets* with the class of near-pornographic literature which has tested the legal limits of obscenity is possible only if, instead of reading the book, one has merely read selected passages.

Application of the *Ginsberg* test makes it clear that the state could not make unlawful the sale or loan of this book to minors. And if the state cannot totally prohibit the book, there is no legal basis for suggesting that the state can bar its school libraries from lending it.

On November 6, 1972, the Supreme Court declined to review the Court of Appeals decision. Justice Douglas and Stewart voted in favor of review (the votes of four Justices are necessary for a case to be heard).

But the refusal of the Court to hear the case by no means forecloses the possibility of successful court challenge in the future. The Second Circuit's decision is not binding on other circuits, which may be more alert to the dangers in school book-banning. The Supreme Court, itself, may be willing to consider the issue after hearing from some more of the lower federal courts. It is not unusual for the Court to decline to rule on novel constitutional controversies, then decide them later when they have been analyzed and debated by other judges and legal scholars. Also, when the Court does choose to resolve this controversy, it will almost undoubtedly prefer to decide the issue in its pristine form, that is, where the ban on the book is absolute, and not qualified by parent option plans.

If successful lawsuits are to be brought, both the public and the courts must be made aware of the real issues at stake in controversies like this. The Queens school board, like school boards everywhere, denied that it was engaged in censorship. They claimed instead only to be concerned about profanities and vulgar language, as if such a well-meaning undertaking could not be questioned. Supreme Court Justice Harland answered that argument in an earlier case:

"... We cannot indulge the facile assumption that one can forbid particular words without also running a substantial risk of suppressing ideas in the process." *Cohen* v. *California*, 403 U.S. 15 (1971).

Could one have written a portrait of the ghetto, eliminating the "words" to which the school board objected, and not change the entire "idea" of the ghetto that Piri Thomas sought to convey? It is safe to assume, I think, that Thomas would not, and could not, have written an honest book about his experiences in a way that would have satisfied the Queens school board.

And if some junior high school students choose to subject themselves to harsh descriptions of ghetto life, isn't that all to the good? How long must school boards remain unaware that, for better or worse, junior high school students use with each other the same words that Piri Thomas uses, that they exchange tales and fantasies about sex not very different from those Thomas describes, and that, through a combination of schoolyard gossip and the mass and underground media, they are daily exposed to images which are every bit as brutal and violent as those that are in the book?

It is important to remember that these are students who are about to enter high school. They have attended junior high schools which, together, have the third lowest percentage of minority group students of New York City's 31 school districts—about 15 percent as compared to more than 60 percent citywide. The percentage of nonwhite students in the Queens high schools to which these students would most likely go ranges up to about 35 percent. For many, it will be their first substantial encounter with blacks and Puerto Ricans, their first direct experience of the tensions and conflicts which are so frequently a part of mass urban education. What better way to ease those tensions, to anticipate those conflicts, than by reading a book about a culture never before experienced? That is, presumably, one of the purposes of the First Amendment.

In the final analysis, the school board's ban was little more than a symbolic protest against what their supporting psychologist described as a trend towards rejection of "middle class values." No other explanation accounts for an action which is so devoid of educational, or any other defensible, justification.

If the school board's concern was to protect chidren, they utterly failed because the book remains available for purchase and for loan outside of school. And the evidence is that more of that is going on as a result of the ban. As the student quoted above commented, "I never heard of the book until the bit about banning it came about. Now everyone is trying to get the book." Their action thus protects no one except those unable to borrow it or too poor to buy it.

If it is an "immoral" book for junior high school students, by proscribing it in the school, the school board has effectively precluded open discussion of the book under the guidance of professionals and concerned adults. Their public labeling of this as a "dirty" book has encouraged its being relegated to furtive readings behind locked doors.

If their concern was with the exposure of junior high school students to "dirty" words or sexual portrayals, they are grossly ignorant of what these students already know and understand.

If their concern was "harm" to their

students from reading an "immoral" book, they have totally failed to understand the book. They have allowed a few isolated passages to obsure the book's highly moral theme and its message of optimism.

If their concern was with the effect on their students' future development from reading sexually explicit scenes, then they have grossly oversimplified the process of adolescent growth and development, and the complex factors which influence that process.

No, the banning of a library book cannot be described as a rational act. But it must be challenged if its sinister consequences are not to destroy our schools. If school boards are permitted a free hand in what they claim are "educational decisions," to whom may parents, students and professionals look when their libraries and their curricula are stripped of books which happen to be in political disfavor with a shifting majority of the school board? Who will prevent our nation's schools from becoming instruments of majoritarian propaganda? If, as appears to be the case, school boards are especially responsive to demands that schools not carry books which honestly deal with race relations in America, will minorities ever be able to secure the promise of the school desegregation cases? If we concede to school boards the power to exclude all but the current orthodoxy from the classrooms and libraries of our schools, will we not be granting them awesome power over the minds of our future citizens?

I believe that neither the public nor, ultimately, the courts, will allow one agency of state such power.

The Courts and the Child

Tinker vs. Des Moines Decision

This statement, taken from the Supreme Court decision in Tinker vs. Des Moines Independent School District, vindicated the action of seven students who had worn black armbands to school in December 1965 to protest the Vietnam War. The students had the support of their parents and other adults and students in the community; on learning of the "armband plot," however, the Des Moines school principals had met December 14 and ruled that students wearing armbands would be dismissed. The reasoning: intruding this controversial issue into the school could disrupt the school's normal operations.

Among the five students who were suspended for defying the ruling were Paul Tinker, eight years old and in the second grade; Hope Tinker, 11 and in the fifth grade; Mary Beth Tinker, 13 and in the eighth grade; John Tinker, 15, and a high school junior; and Christopher Eckhardt, also a high school junior. Challenging the school officials and the school board, the fathers of these children filed suit in their names, asking for an injunction to restrain the schools from disciplining the students, and sought nominal dam-

ages. The case was dismissed by the U.S. district court on the grounds that the school authorities' action was constitutional and reasonable as an effort to protect school discipline.

The Supreme Court ruling in Tinker v. Des Moines, *delivered by former Justice Fortas on February 24, 1969, reversed the lower court decision, arguing that pupils are entitled to full protection by the First and Fourteenth Amendments in expressing their political views peacefully all the way from kindergarten through high school.*

By limiting the school's fiat when it collides with the First Amendment rights of students, the Supreme Court also expressed a philosophy of education that is crucial to the interests of librarians and other professional groups committed to free inquiry and expression. It showed a concern for the moral bases that validate authority—whose violation lies behind much student unrest—and an understanding of "relevance" that transcends the ken of most school administrators. And it argued that a school board suppressing controversy "must be able to show that its action was caused by something more than a mere desire to avoid the discomfort

57

*and unpleasantness that always accom-
pany an unpopular viewpoint." If these
principles are followed by our profession, they should usher in a new era of
freedom of selection for our libraries.*

FIRST AMENDMENT RIGHTS,
applied in light of the special characteristics of the school environment, are
available to teachers and students. It
can hardly be argued that either students or teachers shed their constitutional rights to freedom of speech or
expression at the schoolhouse gate.
This has been the unmistakable holding of this Court for almost 50 years.
In *Meyer* v. *Nebraska* (1923) and
Bartels v. *Iowa* (1923), this Court, in
opinions by Mr. Justice McReynolds,
held that the Due Process Clause of the
Fourteenth Amendment prevents states
from forbidding the teaching of a foreign language to young students.
Statutes to this effect, the Court held,
unconstitutionally interfere with the
liberty of the teacher, the student, and
the parent.

In *West Virginia* v. *Barnette* (1943),
this Court held that under the First
Amendment, the student in public
school may not be compelled to salute
the flag. Speaking through Mr. Justice
Jackson, the Court said:

The Fourteenth Amendment, as now
applied to the states, protects the citizen
against the state itself and all of its
creatures—boards of education not ex-
cepted. These have, of course, important,
delicate, and highly discretionary functions, but none that they may not perform
within the limits of the Bill of Rights.
That they are educating the young for
citizenship is reason for scrupulous protection of Constitutional freedoms of the
individual, if we are not to strangle the
free mind at its source and teach youth
to discount important principles of our
government as mere platitudes.

On the other hand, the Court has repeatedly emphasized the need for
affirming the comprehensive authority

of the states and of school authorities,
consistent with fundamental constitutional safeguards, to prescribe and control conduct in the schools. Our problem lies in the area where students in
the exercise of First Amendment rights
collide with the rules of the school authorities.

The problem presented by the present case does not relate to regulation
of the length of skirts or the type of
clothing, to hair style or deportment.
It does not concern aggressive, disruptive action or even group demonstrations. Our problem involves direct,
primary First Amendment rights akin
to "pure speech."

The school officials banned and
sought to punish petitioners for a
silent, passive expression of opinion,
unaccompanied by any disorder or disturbance on the part of petitioners.
There is here no evidence whatever of
petitioners' interference, actual or
nascent, with the school's work or of
collision with the rights of other students to be secure and to be let alone.
Accordingly, this case does not concern
speech or action that intrudes upon the
work of the school or the rights of
other students.

Only a few of the 18,000 students
in the school system wore the black
armbands. Only five students were suspended for wearing them. There is no
indication that the work of the school
or any class was disrupted. Outside
the classrooms, a few students made
hostile remarks to the children wearing
armbands, but there were no threats
or acts of violence on the school prem-
ses.

The District Court concluded that
the action of the school authorities was
reasonable because it was based upon
their fear of a disturbance from the
wearing of the armbands. But, in our
system, undifferentiated fear or appre-
hension of disturbance is not enough to
overcome the right to freedom of expression. Any departure from absolute
regimentation may cause trouble. Any
variation from the majority's opinion

may inspire fear. Any word spoken, in class, in the lunchroom, or on the campus, that deviates from the views of another person, may start an argument or cause a disturbance. But our Constitution says we must take this risk; and our history says that it is this sort of hazardous freedom—this kind of openness—that is the basis of our national strength and of the independence and vigor of Americans who grow up and live in this relatively permissive, often disputatious society. . . .

Our independent examination of the record fails to yield evidence that the school authorities had reason to anticipate that the wearing of the armbands would substantially interfere with the work of the school or impinge upon the rights of other students. Even an official memorandum prepared after the suspension that listed the reasons for the ban on wearing the armbands made no reference to the anticipation of such disruption.*

On the contrary, the action of the school authorities appears to have been based upon an urgent wish to avoid the controversy which might result from the expression, even by the silent symbol of armbands, of opposition to this nation's part in the conflagration in Vietnam. It is revealing, in this respect, that the meeting at which the school principals decided to issue the contested regulation was called in response to a student's statement to the journalism teacher in one of the schools that he wanted to write an article on Viet-

nam and have it published in the school paper. (The student was dissuaded.)

It is also relevant that the school authorities did not purport to prohibit the wearing of all symbols of political or controversial significance. . . . Clearly, the prohibition of expression of one particular opinion, at least without evidence that it is necessary to avoid material and substantial interference with school work or discipline, is not constitutionally permissible.

In our system, state-operated schools may not be enclaves of totalitarianism. School officials do not possess absolute authority over their students. Students in school as well as out of school are "persons" under our Constitution. They are possessed of fundamental rights which the state must respect, just as they themselves must respect their obligations to the state. In our system, students may not be regarded as closed-circuit recipients of only that which the state chooses to communicate. They may not be confined to the expression of those sentiments that are officially approved. In the absence of a specific showing of constitutionally valid reasons to regulate their speech, students are entitled to freedom of expression of their views. As Judge Gewin, speaking for the Fifth Circuit, said, school officials cannot suppress "expressions of feelings with which they do not wish to contend." (*Burnside* v. *Byars* 1966)

In *Meyer* v. *Nebraska*, Justice McReynolds expressed this nation's repudiation of the principle that a state might so conduct its schools as to "foster a homogeneous people." He said:

---

* . . . The testimony of school authorities at trial indicates that it was not fear of disruption that motivated the regulation prohibiting the armbands; the regulation was directed against "the principle of the demonstration" itself. School authorities simply felt that "the schools are no place for demonstrations," and if the students "didn't like the way our elected officials were handling things, it should be handled with the ballot box and not in the halls of our public schools."

In order to submerge the individual and develop ideal citizens, Sparta assembled the males at seven into barracks and intrusted their subsequent education and training to official guardians. Although such measures have been deliberately approved by men of great genius, their ideas touching the relation between individual and state were wholly different from those upon which our institutions rest; and it hardly will be affirmed that any legislature could impose such restrictions upon the people of a state without doing violence to both letter and spirit of the Constitution.

This principle has been repeated by this Court on numerous occasions during the intervening years. In *Keyishian* v. *Board of Regents* (1967), Justice Brennan, speaking for the Court, said:

'The vigilant protection of constitutional freedom is nowhere more vital than in the community of American schools.' (*Shelton* v. *Tucker,* 1960) The classroom is peculiarly the 'market-place of ideas.' The nation's future depends upon leaders trained through wide exposure to that robust exchange of ideas which discovers truth 'out of a multitude of tongues, [rather] than through any kind of authoritative selection.' . . .

The principle of these cases is not confined to the supervised and ordained discussion which takes place in the classroom. The principal use to which the schools are dedicated is to accommodate students during prescribed hours for the purpose of certain types of activities. Among those activities is personal intercommunication among the students.** This is not only an in-

evitable part of the process of attending school. It is also an important part of the educational process. A student's rights therefore, do not embrace merely the classroom hours. When he is in the cafeteria, or on the playing field, or on the campus during the authorized hours, he may express his opinions, even on controversial subjects like the conflict in Vietnam, if he does so "without materially and substantially interfering with appropriate discipline in the operation of the school" (*Burnside* v. *Byars*) and without colliding with the rights of others. . . .

Under our Constitution, free speech is not a right that is given only to be so circumscribed that it exists in principle but not in fact. Freedom of expression would not truly exist if the right could be exercised only in an area that a benevolent government has provided as a safe haven for crackpots. The Constitution says that Congress (and the states) may not abridge the right to free speech. This provision means what it says. We properly read it to permit reasonable regulation of speech-connected activities in carefully restricted circumstances. But we do not confine the permissible exercise of First Amendment rights to a telephone booth or the four corners of a pamphlet, or to supervise an ordained discussion in a school classroom.

**In *Hammond* v. *South Carolina State College* (1967), District Judge Hemphill had before him a case involving a meeting on campus of 300 students to express their views on school practices. He pointed out that a school is not like a hospital or a jail enclosure. It is a public place, and its dedication to specific uses does not imply that the constitutional rights of persons entitled to be there are to be gauged as if the premises were private property.

Censorship—Reevaluated

Dorothy Broderick

WHAT follows is what I like to think of as reflecting middle-aged maturity, although I recognize that for others it will be seen as postdoctoral senility. I like to think I would have eventually reevaluated my thoughts about censorship just as a matter of course. But I had a great deal of help and would like to acknowledge it.

You are all familiar with the domino theory. I never believed in it until it happened to me. My first mistake was to pay my ALA dues. This led to the arrival of *American Libraries*, which I insist upon calling *ALA Bulletin* despite my newfound mental flexibility. It is essential to keep in mind that we all carry within us the seeds of our own downfall. My weakness is that I am a compulsive reader and thus, month after month I continued to read the column on Intellectual Freedom, knowing full well it was driving me into the enemy camp, but unable to stop myself.

It took me months to figure out what bothered me. At first I thought it was the absence of phrases like "the selection process" and "weeding the collection." Only gradually did it dawn on me that anyone who can write about intellectual freedom as *ex cathedra dicta* cannot possibly be understanding the concept. Now, I fully recognize that

Judith Krug of the Intellectual Freedom Office could answer this charge with one of my favorite quotations, namely, "It is the misfortune of the purist to be considered arrogant when all he is doing is being right." That reply would get right to the heart of my objections. It is bordering on suicide to be a purist about so complex a question as censorship.

Besides, has something happened behind my back? Did librarians suddenly and magically become infallible? Has everyone learned never to make a mistake in adding a book or magazine to the collection? Has everyone found the time to ruthlessly weed out the hundreds and thousands of books that are no longer worthy of shelf space (if they ever were)? Is the complainant always and automatically wrong? Is there no occasion when we might be wrong? Somehow, to be self-righteous under the banner of intellectual freedom strikes me as the ultimate in absurdity.

Moreover, the dogma coming from the Office of Intellectual Freedom shows no signs of understanding either the history of the public library or recognition of concepts being developed in other fields concerning the question of freedom. Having decided once and for all to be in favor of intellectual freedom, a segment of our profession has then

61

closed its mind to all consideration of the opposing point of view. Again, this rigidity does not meet my definition of an intellectually free person.

In *On Becoming a Person*, Carl Rogers discusses why he chose not to become a minister. Rogers says:

My beliefs had already changed tremendously, and might continue to change. It seemed to me it would be a horrible thing to *have* to profess a set of beliefs, in order to remain in one's profession. I wanted to find a field in which I could be sure my freedom of thought would not be limited.[1]

That is how I thought of the library profession—a place where change and growth were possible. Now I discover that the only freedom being expounded is the freedom to believe in absolute freedom. Despite my reputation as some kind of weird radical, I would suggest to you that I have never accepted this premise. Everything I have written has been within the framework of the selection process and if, on occasion, I have seemed radical, it was in the cause of opening up that process—but not to do away with it.

This belief was reinforced during the process of writing my dissertation. Few people can probably claim that doing a dissertation changed their lives for the better, but mine did. And in the process, I came to feel strongly that if freedom meant the right to warp children's minds, to put our stamp of approval on bigotry, then I would do with a little less of it.

Before we return to the here and now, I want to take you on an historical excursion. The purpose of taking the historical route is to point out: 1) the public library was not founded as a bastion of intellectual freedom; 2) the early librarians understood and accepted this premise, and 3) librarians of our time have unilaterally broken the covenant that existed between the community and the library.

Libraries were founded originally to offer a growing literate populace *approved* alternatives to the wares of the newsstands. Dime novels, the girly magazines, and *The Police Gazette* had to be counteracted. While rarely mentioning libraries, Paul Boyer's *Purity in Print*[2] offers a fascinating account of the social forces that gave rise to Anthony Comstock and his compatriots and makes quite reasonable the need for anti-vice societies without making Comstock himself any more acceptable. The book ranks high on my reading list for the insights it offers into the relationship between social conditions and intellectual climate. And I strongly suspect that it is not accidental that the two major cities to give rise to Comstock and the Watch and Ward Society, New York and Boston, were also forerunners in the public library movement.

In 1895 the American Library Association conference concerned itself with the topic, "Improper Books: Methods Employed to Discover and Exclude Them."[3] Here are some of the choice quotes from that symposium.

From Theresa H. West, Librarian, Milwaukee Public Library:

The underlying principle of my own selection of books, for a library which is essentially for the people, is that books which speak truth concerning normal, wholesome conditions may be safely bought, however plain-spoken. While, on the other hand, books which treat of morbid, diseased conditions of the individual man, or of society at large, are intended for the student of special subjects. Such are bought only after due consideration of the just relation of the comparative rights of students and general readers.[4]

From the librarian of the San Francisco Public Library, George T. Clark:

What, then, shall be the standard for a public library maintained by revenues derived from taxation? To determine this, we must arrive at some definite idea as to the proper functions of public libraries. Why has the State enacted laws under which holders of property are compelled to pay taxes for the support of such institutions? It is expected that a public library will contribute to the general welfare of the people, and be an influence on the community. In fact, that it shall assist in the education of the people and the making of good citizens. Unless it does exercise these functions, what justice is there in making it a burden on the taxpayers? What right has it to exist?[5]

Since the beginning of libraries, there has always been the problem of how to respond to public pressure for a book the library would rather not buy, or having bought, would prefer to control its circulation. J. N. Larned of the Buffalo Public Library came up with this solution.

In the case of one recent book for which many applications were made in our library, I have been trying the experiment of sending a circular note to each applicant, briefly describing its character and saying that I am not willing the book should go into the hands of any reader without clear knowledge of what it is. The result has been to cancel a large part of the requests for the book, while those who read it take on themselves the whole responsibility in doing so. It seems to me that a general policy of dealing with such books may be framed on the principle indicated in this experiment.[6]

Before moving on to the next writer, I would like to suggest that we could have a nationwide contest sponsored by one of our periodicals to see who can write the best letter telling patrons that they are dirty old men without offending them. The prize would be an ex officio seat on the Intellectual Freedom Committee, which isn't any more ridiculous than Gaines serving on the Board of Trustees of the Freedom to Read Foundation.

The last of the contributors to the ALA conference was William H. Brett of the Cleveland Public Library. Brett makes a point I want to stress, so let me quote him at some length.

There are, as we all know, many books published every year on economics, politics, and other important subjects which, adjudged by opinions that are now accepted, are utterly worthless. But, at the same time, there is in those fields such a diversity, such a contrariety of opinions that we may well be very careful about excluding books because they differ from the opinions which are accepted now. We must remember that the cranky idea of today may possibly be the accepted belief tomorrow; so that there are none of these books that we, perhaps, should absolutely exclude.

It is only when we come to books which affect the question of morals, the question of conduct, that we feel that we have the right to draw the line of exclusion; that we will have therein the support of right-thinking people, no matter what their religious opinions may be, no matter what their belief or lack of belief. We are all practically united on what constitutes right living. Matthew Arnold says that conduct is three-fourths of life; yet, conduct is but the working out into life of what a man thinks, and what he believes, and this moulded largely by that he reads. Among the books which influence opinion and mould belief, are many which are classed as fiction, and it is largely in that class that the line of exclusion will be drawn. . . I believe that we have a perfect right to exclude from our shelves books which seem likely to prove harmful, no matter with what reputation as classics they come to us. I think we have a right to judge these books and exclude them, just exactly as we do books of the day.[7]

What Brett makes clear is that there is a difference between diversity and licentiousness, just as there is a difference between freedom and anarchy. But the major point is that the old timers were not frightened by the idea of making value judgments. They understood they had a charge from the community to act as professionals and make decisions.

In my opinion, the only thing that has changed from those days is the concept of "the good life." Despite the innumerable and seemingly insurmountable problems of our society, I am encouraged by the movement toward openness and the acceptance of cultural and racial diversity and a beginning awareness that all men are entitled to respect and dignity.

The role of libraries under these conditions is to support life-affirming materials. One Corrine Bacon, writing in a 1909 issue of *New York Libraries* on "What Makes a Book Immoral," put it this way:

What does it matter of what he writes so that his heart be true to the finer possibilities in human nature? The book which degrades our intellect, vulgarizes our emotions, kills our faith in our kind, is an immoral book; the book which stimulates thought, quickens our sense of humor, gives us a deeper insight into men and women and a finer sympathy for them, is a moral book, let its subject-matter have as wide a range as life itself.[8]

Were this a book instead of a talk, we could pursue this value judgment argument by further quotes from such *LJ* symposia as the one in 1908 entitled "What Shall Libraries Do About Bad Books?"[9] and its repeat in 1922 on the subject "Questionable Books in Public Libraries."[10]

Because time is short, we are going to jump to the early 1950s. For 100 years the public library religiously fulfilled its charge from the public that supported it. Then came the grand days of Senator Joe. Suddenly, it was not a question of whether men like Lawrence, Joyce, and Hemingway had a right to literary freedom; it was not even just a question of political diversity—this time it was libraries themselves under attack. And we fought back, much as the scribes in England fought against the importation of the printing press. It was our world that was being challenged. Make no mistake: we fought for self-preservation, not for the abstract concept of intellectual freedom.

We can learn a valuable lesson from

those days that has great application to our present situation in relationship to the turmoil within ALA. The *profession* took a stand against McCarthy's attacks. But, quietly, as Fiske and others have shown us, librarians were engaged in self-censorship that was often far more restrictive than the communities would have imposed. And there was that never-to-be-forgotten occasion when the big, brave librarians told Ed Murrow that it was all a lot of nonsense while refusing to have their faces photographed.

Even so, what the elder statesmen of ALA do not understand is that during those years of fighting McCarthy, they created an illusion that led many socially concerned young people—myself included—to think that being a librarian might be an honorable profession. Yet at rock-bottom, they resembled nothing quite so much as Brother Librarian in Miller's *A Canticle for Leibowitz*: "To Brother Librarian, whose task in life was the preservation of books, the principal reason for the existence of books was that they might be preserved perpetually. Usage was secondary, and to be avoided if it threatened longevity."[11] Miller might well have added, "or if it threatened the established social order."

The leadership had no intention of broadening the fight from the preservation of libraries to the idea that librarians—as librarians—might also feel compelled to fight for the preservation of the world in which we live. You may recall that as recently as the June 15, 1970 issue of *LJ* one Ervin Gaines took us to task for indulging in a faddist relationship with Vietnam and pollution. We were told to chant daily: "I believe that it is my duty as a public librarian to collection information to the maximum extent possible, to make it freely available to everyone, and to assist people to find and use that information to the best of my ability."[12] Eleven months later, May 15, 1971, Gaines, his *faddist* relationship with intellectual freedom relegated to the past explains to us that "everyone" only meant adults and not young people and that restricted shelves aren't such a bad idea after all.[13]

Buried as a news item in the same issue of *LJ* is the information that the San Jose Public Library had won a grand fight for intellectual freedom by keeping the racist *Epaminondas and His Auntie* on the open shelves. And here, after all these words, we come to the crux of the matter.

In the name of intellectual freedom we defend materials that perpetuate attitudes that hinder the growth of individuals who are intellectually free. No racist is intellectually free. Try as I may, I can see no issue of intellectual freedom involved in a request to remove *Epaminondas and His Auntie* from library shelves. Except for research libraries, the process known as weeding the collection should have eliminated the book years ago. But the library remains what it was when founded: a reflection of white ruling class values. As long as it is black people being offended we invoke intellectual freedom and tell blacks that bigots have rights, too.

In the case of the Minneapolis Public Library's fight over the alternate press periodicals, it was the establishment being attacked. That is not good. In the name of intellectual freedom we will let young minds be warped by racism, but let us keep youth from thinking that the American corporate structure needs revamping—or even elimination.

To quote my favorite public figure, let me make it perfectly clear: I do not believe in an abstract concept of intellectual freedom. If some men are more free than others, it is because they exist in environments that make such freedom possible. One does not have to accept Skinner's "technology of human behavior" theory to recognize the validity of his emphasis upon environment as a controlling feature of man's behavior. After all, that is precisely what goes on in a classroom if real learning takes place: the environment makes it possible for the person to change. That is what happens in therapy and sensitivity

training and that is what happens to us if we join a reasonably homogeneous group whether it be the Black Panthers, Gay Lib, NOW, or a political party.

We also know that when we find ourselves in an alien environment we have but two choices: change our attitudes or find a new environment.

What does all this have to do with libraries and self-censorship and the overwhelming problems we are faced with? For me, everything. Libraries are in themselves "an environment," but they are also a microcosm of the larger unit we call society.

The fight we are experiencing within the profession at the moment would seem to be built around two alternatives. The first is to go right on doing what we've been doing, namely, reflecting attitudes rather than affecting them. The second is to fight to make the library an instrument of social change. Should we opt for the latter, and frankly I cannot conceive of that happening, there are two steps necessary. First, we must have a public debate with our communities, asking that the traditional role of the library be redefined. We need a mandate from the public, for whatever our private convictions, we must keep in mind that we are talking about a public institution and if we don't like what the public wants, we can always find something else to work at.

Secondly, we have to recognize that such a fight cannot be carried out under the banner of intellectual freedom, unless that phrase is redefined to mean that we will do all in our power to offer individuals experiences through materials that will broaden, not limit, their possibilities for growth. That means making value judgments. That means we have to be brave enough to say that love is a better emotion than hate, that fear and distrust of others are destructive to the person holding such emotions.

Actually, there is only one question that need be asked about books in this relationship: how does this book reflect the sanctity of life? In these terms we can look at *Down These Mean Streets*, the book under discussion at the moment. The obscenity of the book is that our society has relegated segments of the population to lead the kind of life Piri Thomas describes. It is attacked, and censored, by those who, were they to admit its validity would then be forced to feel they should do something about the conditions the book describes. How much easier it is to label the book obscene than to face the fact that the real obscenities are racism and poverty.

It is right and proper that librarians fight for the right of youth to read *Down These Mean Streets* or *Soul on Ice* or *To Kill a Mockingbird*—they are all life affirming books. But we cannot say that "intellectual freedom" justifies pornography, nor should we confuse political and social diversity with pornography. Few librarians ever see any pornography; if more did, we might rephrase our intellectual freedom concerns more realistically and in the process make them more defensible.

For me, racist materials are simply another form of pornography. They are anti-human. And just as Laura Hobson in her *New York Times* article, "As I Listened to Archie Say Hebe,"[14] says it is cruel to subject children to the idea that bigotry is fun, so I object to the library stocking materials that say bigotry is just another point of view.

I fail to understand how the people who are concerned with social responsibilities can also be gung-ho for the current stance being offered by the Office of Intellectual Freedom. The whole concept of social responsibility implies value judgments—some things are right and some things are wrong and it is that simple. In modern jargon, that is known as an elitist point of view, and elitist is a very dirty word, indeed. But here I stand and until my next great change of life, here I remain.

REFERENCES

1. Rogers, Carl. *On Becoming a Person.* Boston: Houghton, 1970, p. 8.
2. Boyer, Paul. *Purity in Print.* New York: Scribners, 1968.
3. "Improper Books: Methods Employed to Discover and Exclude Them." Symposium. *Library Journal,* December, 1895, p. 32-36.
4. *Ibid,* p. 32.
5. *Ibid,* p. 33.
6. *Ibid,* p. 35.
7. *Ibid,* p. 36.
8. Bacon, Corrine. "What Makes a Book Immoral," *New York Libraries,* 1909.
9. "What Shall Libraries Do About Bad Books?" Symposium. *Library Journal,* September, 1908, p. 349-54.
10. "Questionable Books in Public Libraries." Symposium. *Library Journal,* October 15, 1922, p. 857-61. Continued in the November 1 issue.
11. Miller, Walter. *A Canticle for Leibowitz.* New York: Lippincott, 1969.
12. Gaines, Ervin. "Viewpoint." *Library Journal,* June 15, 1970, p. 2235.
13. Gaines, Ervin. "Viewpoint." *Library Journal,* May 15, 1971, p. 1687.
14. Hobson, Laura. "As I Listened to Archie Say Hebe." *New York Times,* September 12, 1971.

Acting for the Children?

James A. Harvey

IF ASKED three years ago to write an article about intellectual freedom problems and children's materials, I would have laughed and declined. After all, I am neither a children's librarian nor an expert on children's literature. I have only limited experience as a school librarian, and that in a junior high school. Add to those nonqualifications the fact that I have no children of my own, and I appear like a celibate priest pontificating about the sex problems of newlyweds. My only real (as versus acquired) knowledge about children is that I was a child not all that long ago, and, in many ways, still am. Incidental to that, I have the sometimes advantage of spending the past three years as Assistant Director of the ALA Office for Intellectual Freedom and as an editor of the *Newsletter on Intellectual Freedom*. While so ensconced, I watched, like Alice at the Mad Hatter's tea party, as children's literature rose from relative obscurity on the censorship spectrum to a position of national prominence, which would be laughable if its implications were not so serious for the future of intellectual freedom in libraries.

I refer, of course, to the "reevaluation syndrome," a craze sweeping children's librarianship with the rapidity and, hopefully, the same lack of lasting impact, as

the hula hoop swept the nation. "Reevaluation" is surely the most significant movement related to intellectual freedom and children's materials to occur in the past 20 years. To define it, I defer to two of its chief proponents, Sara Innes Fenwick ("Re-Evaluation 1971, 1972...," *The Calendar*, January-April, 1972) and Dorothy Broderick ("Censorship—Reevaluated," *SLJ*, November 1971, p. 30-32; *LJ*, November 15, 1971, p. 3816-18).

Ms. Fenwick says, "... reevaluation is the most crucial aspect of the total process of collection building in determining the quality level of a particular collection. This principle recognizes that any selector is likely to make errors in initial selection, but that there is little excuse for the retaining or replacing of materials that are less than acceptable in quality or usefulness." In some respects, then, reevaluation doesn't sound too far from traditional weeding. But, is that the true extent of it? It seems doubtful. Ms. Broderick (who seems to direct her remarks to children's and young adults' materials only, but who knows?) has extracted "value" from "reevaluation," equated it with Ms. Fenwick's "quality," and gone on to tell us that "... old timers were not frightened by the idea of making value judgments. They understood

THIS IS THE CHALLENGED STATEMENT

PROPOSED STATEMENT ABOUT REEVALUATION OF CHILDREN'S BOOKS

Librarians have a two-fold obligation in service to the child:

1. To build and maintain a collection of materials which provides information on the entire spectrum of human knowledge, experience, and opinion.
2. To actively introduce to the child those titles which will enable him to develop with a free spirit, an inquiring mind, and an ever-widening knowledge of the culture in which he lives.

Most books, whether intentionally or not, reflect the social climate and conscience of the era in which they were written, and their readers at the time of publication accept this reflection without noticing it. But social climate and conscience and man's state of knowledge are constantly changing. Therefore librarians must continuously reevaluate their old "standard" titles in the light of current progress.

In the process of reevaluation, it may be found that a highly respected title presents hitherto unnoticed misinformation or stereotypes in character, plot, dialog, and illustrations that are inaccurate in the light of current knowledge or beliefs and are demeaning to some segment of our society. When it is clear from the context in which these are presented that they reflect a past era, this title may still serve a useful role in a library collection. We cannot erase the past, and indeed it would be a disservice to the child to do so—to pretend that discrimination, prejudice, and misinformation never existed. But when it is not clear from the context that the book belongs to a past era, when it apparently fosters for the present day concepts which are now deemed to be false or degrading, then, despite the title's prestige, the librarian should question the validity of its continued inclusion in the library collection.

In making his decision, the librarian has a professional obligation to set aside personal likes and dislikes: to consider the "objectionable" material within the context of the book as a whole and then to consider the book as a whole with objectivity and respect for all opinions. Only *after* such consideration can he reach one of three conclusions:

1. That other qualities in the book are so fine they outweigh the new-found flaws and that therefore he will continue to promote it while at the same time alerting the reader to its faults.
2. That the book should remain in the collection to fill specific title requests but should no longer be actively promoted.
3. That in comparison with contemporary thought and social climate the title is so misleading, or superseded in coverage in literary quality, that it is no longer valid library material and should be permanently discarded.

they had a charge from the community to act as professionals and make decisions." She says, "The whole concept of social responsibility implies value judgments— some things are right and some things are wrong and it is that simple." In general, Ms. Fenwick best sums up reevaluation, saying, "Therefore we are involved, on a variety of scenes, in the development and refinement of criteria by which we can reevaluate the quality of the experiences, both manifest and implied, provided for children in our total literature with respect to the absorbing problems on our social scene today."

Obviously, neither Ms. Fenwick nor Ms. Broderick speaks of evaluating accuracy, up-to-dateness, style, theme, nor contents (traditional factors considered in weeding, according to Carter and Bank's *Building Library Collections*, Scarecrow, 1969) in a literal sense. Ms. Broderick speaks of reevaluation in terms of right and wrong, as if they were absolutes. Ms. Fenwick speaks of "quality of experiences." Both speak of discarding materials, not on the basis of traditional weeding considerations, but on the basis of highly subjective value judgments. That, then, seems to be the thrust of reevaluation. And, it becomes apparent that it is not synonymous with "collection building." It is more likely synonymous with censorship: the exclusion of library materials because of the *views* of the authors.

Having watched the evolution of the reevaluation syndrome these past few years, I accepted this assignment to write about intellectual freedom problems and children's literature this year, not in spite of my flimsy background in children's librarianship, but because of it. Enough has been said from the viewpoint of "experts" who would have us believe that children's materials, because of their special nature and because of the special nature of their intended audience, cannot be governed by the same principles of intellectual freedom which apply, in theory, to adult materials. My view of such experts parallels that of

Mary Kohler, who wrote in the March-April 1971 *Social Policy* that:

Children constitute one of the largest and most vulnerable minority groups. They have no voice in the political process. They participate directly in no lobbies on their own behalf. At a time when they are particularly weak and easily intimidated and manipulated, their rights are particularly vulnerable to infringement, perhaps at least as often by *those who declaim that they act in the children's regard.* (My emphasis.)

These contemporary efforts to rid libraries of objectionable children's materials, under the guise of reevaluation, are not much different in substance from traditional efforts. In some instances, the identity of the censors and the means they use have changed, but the motivation remains the same. The *superficial* motivation involved in such efforts has always been one of moral values, whether the subject matter was sex, politics, religion, race, or drugs. As Ms. Broderick so succinctly illustrates, rare is the censor who does not believe he is acting in a socially responsible manner, and "some things are right and some things are wrong and it is that simple" has been the credo of all censors since before the invention of the eraser.

The roots of contemporary and traditional censorship efforts, however, go deeper than the surface issues of moral values and value judgments. At the core of the problem in schools and libraries is a confused and potentially dangerous definition of education. Rather than viewing education as the development of the ability to think critically about social issues, some consider education to be the learning of a prescribed body of knowledge, and the learning of nothing which conflicts with that prescribed body of knowledge. This brand of education is a thinly disguised, refined form of propaganda. For some, the "body of knowledge" may be anything which supports the conclusion that The American Way (somewhere to the right of the Milky Way) is the only way. For others, and apparently Ms. Broderick is one, the body of knowledge may be anything that is "life-affirming." And for others, such as Ms. Fenwick, the body of knowledge may be anything that is not "less than acceptable in quality or usefulness" regarding "experiences, both manifest and implied, provided for children in our total literature with respect to the absorbing problems on our social scene today." The possibilities for the content of the prescribed body of knowledge seem as endless as the hangups of the individuals doing the prescribing . . . and proscribing. Invariably, in this view of education, censorship and propaganda are mutual essentials. That which is "right" becomes the subject of propaganda; that which is "wrong" becomes the subject of censorship. It is as simple as that, and to hell with critical thinking.

This is precisely the philosophy which, in 1950, prompted a taxpayers' suit in New York City against the Board of Education to suppress *Oliver Twist* (Holt, 1969) and *The Merchant of Venice* (Cambridge Univ. Pr., 1965) on the grounds that the works were "antiSemitic." In 1950 (and, I would suppose, in 1972) antiSemitism was wrong and tolerance was right and it was that simple—a moral question to which the answer was obvious. Dismissing the suit, however, New York Supreme Court Justice Anthony Giovanna saw another issue and said so: "Public interest in a free and democratic society does not warrant or encourage the suppression of any books at the whim of an unduly sensitive person or group of persons, merely because a character described in such book as belonging to a particular race or religion is portrayed in a derogatory or offensive manner."

The "moral value" philosophy is also the one which motivated two children's librarians to write in 1952 to the Newbery-Caldecott Committee chairman to assert that Mordvinoff's *Finders Keepers* (Harcourt) was not a fit recipient for the Caldecott Medal. Although the librar-

ians dealt peripherally with the book's illustrations, their main complaint was that they were "alarmed to find many points in the book itself which could be construed as subversive, in a most subtle way, of course." In 1952 (and perhaps in 1972) loyalty was right and subversion was wrong and it was that simple—another moral question to which the answer was obvious. But, the Caldecott Award was not revoked, nor did the United States' foreign policy topple because of *Finders Keepers'* subtle influence on the moral development of children who read it.

I cite these two incidents of 20 years ago only to illustrate that the "moral value" philosophy is not a new one and is indeed a traditional tool of the censor. It is the same theory which moved policemen to object to *Sylvester and the Magic Pebble* (S. & S., 1969) in 1970 (to portray policemen as pigs is "wrong") and Dr. David Davis to object to the same book in 1972 (*Sylvester* is an allegorical "trip" and "getting stoned" is "wrong"). More recently, the theory prompted children's librarians in Caldwell Parish, Louisiana, to paint tempera diapers on the naked hero of *In the Night Kitchen* (Harper, 1970) (nudity is "wrong").

Also, the theory is, in large part, responsible for the reevaluation syndrome. Because its promulgators are veteran children's librarians and experts on children's literature, I find this movement to be the most dangerous threat to intellectual freedom in libraries, at least so far as minors are concerned, since 1939 when the American Library Association adopted the first version of the *Library Bill of Rights*. It is dangerous because the reputations of its supporters give it a credence it would otherwise not have.

To my knowledge, the movement to reevaluate children's materials came to a climax in December 1971 when the Association of Children's Librarians of Northern California (ACL) suggested that its members re-read and reevaluate some of the older books in children's collections with an eye toward racist and sexist incidents and attitudes. The ACL project was not intended to stimulate a purging of children's collections, but rather to provoke debate and awareness of the content of children's literature (a good time filler, but whether or not it is a beneficial endeavor is highly questionable). The press, however, was not taken in by this seemingly reasonable rationale and picked up the story, noting censorship-like implications of the project.

After much talking and writing on the subject, the reevaluation situation culminated in June 1972 in the now infamous Statement on the Reevaluation of Children's Materials adopted by the Board of Directors of the ALA Children's Services Division (CSD). Among other things, the statement said ". . . when it is not clear from the context that the material belongs to a past era, when it apparently fosters for the present day concepts which are now deemed to be false or degrading, then, despite the title's prestige, the librarian should question the validity of its continued inclusion in the library collection." It said further, that, if "in comparison with contemporary thought and social climate the title is so misleading, or superseded in coverage and quality . . . it is no longer valid library material and should be permanently discarded." In other words, libraries should forego free access to all views—especially those out of step with the contemporary social climate—and collect only those not misleading (i.e., those within the "prescribed body of knowledge").

For some time, the ALA Intellectual Freedom Committee had been studying intellectual freedom problems involving reevaluation and racism and sexism in library materials. Understandably, the IFC was concerned when informed about the CSD statement *after* it had been released to the library press. The IFC advised the CSD Board of its concerns about apparent contradictions between the statement and the *Library Bill of Rights*, not to mention an array of ALA policies supporting and interpreting the basic document regarding intellectual freedom. The IFC and the CSD Board

agreed to meet together at Midwinter 1973 to discuss the conflicts. In the meantime, a press release was issued explaining that "The CSD Board is reviewing the Statement . . . and developing further clarification and explanation where it may be appropriate. It is therefore recommended that use and distribution of the original statement be delayed until the proposed revision is available."

Whatever the internal problems of communications between ALA's various units may be, the situation created by this *ex post facto* explanation can do nothing but confuse the matter further for working librarians confronted with pressure groups clamoring for the removal of *Little Black Sambo* (Lippincott, 1923) and other titles of the same ilk. The issue is certainly not resolved and probably will not be for some time. It is rooted deeply in the history of children's librarianship and even more deeply in society's view of children and education in general.

Ms. Broderick is most likely correct in thinking that "old timers" would have resolved the matter simply by making a "value judgment" and removing the objectionable material. Intellectual freedom has not always been viewed as one of the basics of librarianship as practiced in the United States. Yet, for the past 30 years in general, and for the past five years with specific application to children, intellectual freedom has been viewed by the profession—if we can accept ALA as the voice of the profession—as one of the library's inviolable tenets. This view sees the library as attempting to provide people with any information and knowledge which it is hoped will lead to critical thinking, wisdom, understanding, and informed actions.

Where the "some things are right and some things are wrong" school stumbles in pursuing this purpose is in the imposition of personal definitions of "information and knowledge" upon the library collections. They would do well to recall that, at one time, some librarians believed that wisdom could not be derived from any fiction; fiction was fodder for the idle mind. Ergo, fiction collecting was ignored. Further, we have just come through a decade when to be a political and social conservative was seemingly lacking in wisdom and understanding. As a result, many library collections contain little material to aid the conservative's intellectual pursuits. If the November election was any indication, we seem to be entering a period when to be a political and social liberal or radical will be viewed as unwise (i.e., outside the scope of "contemporary thought and social climate"). Will future collections reflect this shift? With apologies to Keats, wisdom, like beauty, is in the mind of the beholder, not just in the value judgments of librarians. This is a principle which, like it or not, applies to children as well as adults. Therefore, I can agree with Ms. Broderick's assertion that "When all is said and done, the major task of any library is to supply those books which the individual will find valuable and useful." What I cannot agree with is her assumption that some individual will not find valuable and useful those works she detests. Bigots pay taxes; bigots use libraries; bigots read. Can public-supported libraries deny them the materials *they* find valuable and useful any more than libraries can deny works requested by blacks, women, Native-Americans, Mexican-Americans, et al? Some librarians may say let them buy their books in bookstores, which is like saying let them eat cake. It also establishes a kind of separate-but-unequal philosophy of library service that is inimical to the rights of *all* library users. Lastly, it gives credence to the idea that the library is a tool of the educational propagandist who is really only the censor in disguise.

III
Images

Black Images
In Children's Literature:
Revised Editions Needed

Mavis Wormley Davis

IN our present nationwide involvement in the education of all the black children, the elementary-school librarian plays a unique and important role. It is widely acknowledged that the child's self-image is created in the early or formative years, and that it is partly through books that this image is formed.

The librarian is responsible for the selection of nontextbook materials and stories and therefore is in a position to contribute much to the successful development and growth of the ego of her young readers. For she is the one who must remove or exclude from her collection those books which may be damaging to the self-image of the black child as well as to that of the other children. It is she, also, who must seek and find those books which present positive images.

This is a two-fold task. First, there are many old and popular classics that offer a poor or caricatured racial image, which not only robs the black child of his confidence, but creates a negative attitude toward books and reading. Secondly, there is a dearth of children's books dealing with Afro-American life in America and also of books which present black people as an integral part of and as first settlers of our country, as indeed we were. In dealing with the classics, the librarian must rely upon the publisher as well as the author, for it is in the sensitive area of reevaluation or editing that the publisher must play a vital part. A case in point is the Doubleday edition of Kipling's *Just So Stories*, one of the favorite read-aloud books on the elementary level. Few people would deny that Kipling was a masterful storyteller, but one of his tales is racially offensive. "How the Leopard Got His Spots" is the story. It is an appealing tale of a leopard being given black spots by an Ethiopian. The animal, feeling proud of his spotted beauty, asks the African, "Why don't you go spotty, too?" The Ethiopian then replies, "Oh, plain black's best for a nigger." This line remains unchanged in even the 1966 Doubleday printing of the book. As early as 1957, however, Grosset & Dunlap, in its *Favorite Just So Stories*, amended it to read, "Oh, plain black's best. Now come along."

A few years ago, an organization well known for its intercultural activities issued a list of titles recommended for elementary-school-age children. Among them was Mabel Leigh Hunt's *Benjie's Hat*, included because it presented with warmth the life of a North Carolina Quaker boy and his hand-me-down hat. Early in the story, however, Benjie goes to visit his grandmother and there meets Eliphalet, nine-year-old son of Hamish and Dilcey, the free negroes (sic) who lived on grandmother's farm.

"Benjie and Eliphalet were great friends. Once in a while Grandmother would allow Benjie to go to the cabin when Hamish was playing. He would sit on the porch, a little fair-haired boy surrounded by the kindly, shining black faces of Hamish and Dilcey and Eliphalet."

One day while Hamish is seated in his doorway strumming his "beloved banjo," and his son, Eliphalet, is cutting a buck and wing in the dust, Benjie appears and scolds his friend's father: "Hamish, Grandmother says thee is not to play the banjo on her farm on First Day." Hamish sheepishly replies, "Reckon dis niggah done los' my min' disrememberin' dat Ol' Miss cain' have no music on Fus' Day." (p. 27)

Benjie is a charming Quaker boy, but Hamish, Dilcey, and Eliphalet are the worst kind of stereotypes, as portrayed by their speech, their behavior, and the illustrations. This book, published by Lippincott, is still in print but should be rewritten or withdrawn from distribution.

One of the most startlingly offensive children's classics is the ever-popular *Mary Poppins* by Pamela Travers. The edition I refer to is the Harcourt, Brace 1963 volume of *Mary Poppins and Mary Poppins Comes Back*, advertised as "the original Mary Poppins stories on which the Walt Disney motion picture is based." Every child is familiar with the delightful story of the magical English nana and her adventures with her charges, Jane and Michael. All is gaiety and outlandish fun until, in Chapter Six, on "Bad Tuesday," Mary Poppins finds a compass on the street and decides that she and the children will go round the world. First, they go to the North Pole, and then South, but apparently it's not the South Pole; it's Southern U.S.A. They encounter "a man and a woman, both quite black all over and with very few clothes on," and with beads "in their ears and one or two in their noses." "On the knee of the negro (sic) lady sat a tiny

black pickaninny with nothing on at all. It (sic) smiled at the children as its mother spoke: "Ah bin 'specting you a long time Mar' Poppins ... You bring dem chillun dere into ma li'l house for a slice of watermelon right now. My, but dem's very white babies. You wan' use a lil bit black boot polish on dem." As Mary Poppins leaves, the mother "laughed again as though the whole of life were one huge joke."

Cordial though she was, the black, scantily clad mother remains an objectionable stereotype, the perennially happy watermelon-fancier, bead-bedecked and uttering the deepest dialect. The "tiny black pickaninny" merely makes the stereotype more reprehensible. Disney eliminated this episode.

With Disney Productions' showing of Hugh Lofting's *Dr. Dolittle*, it is necessary to reevaluate this classic, too. Dr. Dolittle is an odd but kindly little man who loves animals and keeps a variety of pets. Polynesia, his parrot, teaches him animal language, which helps the doctor in his treatment of the animals when they are sick. When Chee-Chee, his monkey, brings news that the doctor is needed in Africa to stop the monkeys' sickness, the doctor and all his animals pack up and leave for the continent. It is here that they run into Prince Bumpo, the African prince who falls asleep reading fairy tales.

The illustration of Prince Bumpo is a grotesque caricature. He is drawn nude, with a large head and large feet and a nose that occupies half his face. However bruising to small black egos the illustration is, it is not as crushing as the prince's dialogue with Dr. Dolittle. He addresses the doctor imploringly:

"White Man (sic), I am an unhappy prince. Years ago I went in search of the Sleeping Beauty, whom I read of in a book. And having traveled through the world many days, I at last found her and kissed the lady very gently to awaken her—as the book said I should. 'Tis true indeed that she woke. But when she saw my face she cried out, 'Oh, he's black!' And she ran away and wouldn't marry me—but went to sleep again somewhere else. So I came back, full of sadness, to my father's kingdom. Now I hear that you are a wonderful magician and have many powerful potions ... If you will turn me white, so that I can go back to the Sleeping Beauty, I will give you half my kingdom and anything else besides you ask ... Nothing else will satisfy me. I must be a white prince."

Here again, the movie improves upon the book in deleting the offensive episode, but many a child will purchase or borrow the book, which at present still includes the prince's plea and the original illustrations. As a matter of fact, however, the entire book is unacceptable, for throughout Dr. Dolittle's attitude toward the Africans remains patronizing.

Years ago, Bannerman's *Little Black Sambo*, another classic which has been translated into many languages and read all over the world, was the focus of much controversy because of its caricatured and stereotyped illustrations. New editions were published with Sambo portrayed as a most attractive little black boy; nevertheless, some of the librarians were confounded when our superintendent of schools issued a directive to discard all copies of the book from our libraries. After all, they said, it is a delightful story, the children enjoy it and the earlier, offensive illustrations have been replaced. An incident just a couple of years ago with one of the fourth-grade classes in my school, however, proved the decision to be a wise one.

Mrs. Dungee's class had come for its regular library instruction period and the children had taken their seats, but a few of them were obviously restless at 9:35 in the morning. The source of the agitation proved to be Candace's new doll, which she proudly held up for all to see. There were some exclamations of admiration and some of disgust. Then Julie said matter-of-factly, "Candace's got a black doll."

"Aw, what you said, Awww, awww," protested Steve.

"What *did* she say, Steve, that's so terrible?" I asked.

"She said 'black.' My mother don't 'low me to say that word."

"Mine neither," blurted Eddie.

"That's a bad word," another black child said.

"I don't let *nobody* call *me* black," Steve spoke again.

All this happened in five or six minutes and I was annoyed and confused. My encyclopedia lesson had never begun and the class was out of hand because somebody had said "black." I remembered Mary O'Neill's "What is Black" in her lovely *Hailstones and Halibut Bones.* Somewhere in it there's a line that reads "Black is beauty in its deepest form ..." But the book was out, or misshelved, or perhaps in my desperation I just didn't see it.

I began telling the children about Africans I'd met, many of whom were handsome people and who proudly referred to themselves as "black Africans." I recalled the Senegalese model my husband and I had met in Dakar who was one of the darkest and one of the most beautiful women I'd ever seen, and who was leaving Dakar for Paris, where she had been offered a better-paying job to model.

The children listened in polite silence, no questions, no comments. There was only my voice pleading with 26 ten-year-olds (five of whom were black) not to believe that black is evil or black is ugly or that black is the worst thing in the world to be.

The class left and others came and somehow I muddled through the day, preoccupied and frustrated. After school, I consulted our new *Random House Dictionary of the English Language* for some occult clue to Steve's violent reaction to the word "black." I was struck, not by the innocuous definition of black, but by all the terms and definitions which followed:

blacken—to speak evil of; to defame

black eye—a mark of shame, dishonor, etc.

black face—an entertainer, especially one in a minstrel show, made up in the role of a Negro

black flag—a pirate flag

blackguard—a low, contemptible person, a scoundrel

black-hearted—disposed to doing or wishing evil; malevolent; malicious

blacklist—a list of persons under suspicion, disfavor, censure, etc.

blackmail—any payment extorted by intimidation, as by threats of injurious revelations or accusations

black mark—an indication of failure or censure

black market—a market in which there are violations of legal price controls, rationing, etc.

black sheep—a person who causes shame or embarrassment because of his deviation from the accepted standards of his group

The *New Century Dictionary of the English Language* had a few to add:

black book—a book containing the names of persons liable to censure or punishment, hence "to be in one's black book," to be in disfavor with one

black Friday—any of various Fridays on which disastrous events occurred, as in the U.S., September 24, 1869 and September 19, 1873, marked by financial panics

Black Hand—an anarchistic society in Spain; in the U.S., a secret society organized for the purposes of blackmail and deeds of violence

black hole—a military cell or lockup; a place of confinement for punishment.

Steve was not the only black child to react so vehemently to "black." Each year our sixth-graders are required to make a comprehensive report on a foreign country, including its geography, history, economy, education, religion, music, and art. In one of the classes, no one chose an African country, despite the fact that our collection on Africa is not only very extensive but up-to-date. The following Monday morning, when the class arrived, all the appropriate books on Africa were on display. We read from Courlander's. *The Cowtail Switch*, played Danny Kaye's recording of *The Tale of the Name of a Tree*, which was most enthusiastically received, and

ended with a brief discussion of African drums and art. I showed the class a reprint of a picture done by a famous African artist named Tall Papa Ibra, and one girl remarked that she thought the model in the painting was very pretty; whereupon dark-skinned Janice sucked her teeth and said, "How can she be pretty and black?"

The present attempts by some groups to make "black" a beautiful word will meet with some success, but it may take a generation or two to eradicate the negative connotations already indelibly impressed on our children.

As noted at the outset of this article, the librarian must select new literature designed to build a positive self-image for the black child. Such books should also engender in the white child a willingness to accept the black child as a valued American. Some 20 years ago, before most authors were sensitive to or aware of the self-image which a child develops from literature, the Beims were writing books in which they presented a positive portrayal of the black child. Their *Two Is a Team*, written for first- and second-graders, is a simple story of two little boys who play together, visit one another's homes, disagree and argue, but remain friends. There is no mention of race or color. Only the illustrations, simply and beautifully done by Ernest Crichlow (who happens to be a black artist) reveal that one of the boys is black.

More recently, Dorothy Sterling's *Mary Jane* portrays a southern girl and her integration into a previously all-white high school. The story realistically depicts the emotional climate of Mary Jane's household and her mother's anxiety and concern for her daughter's safety. Most of the white children are hostile, often threatening. One white classmate, however, shares Mary Jane's concern for an injured squirrel, and with the help of an understanding teacher and loving, courageous parents, Mary Jane succeeds in adjusting to her new school environment.

May Justus' *New Boy in School* and Janice Udry's *What Mary Jo Shared* are lesser books with a similar theme and well done, the latter on a primary level with significant illustrations in color.

Patricia Crosses Town, by Betty Baum, is a welcome contribution to the field of books about black children. Patricia Marley is the dark-skinned daughter of a janitor and a cleaning woman, both of whom are earnest, hard-working parents, struggling to rear their children in an atmosphere of love and self-respect, and determined not to go on relief. In juxtaposition to the Marley family is the Oliver family, who are light-skinned. Mr. Oliver is a school teacher and Mrs. Oliver is a social worker. Although the book deals frankly with the hostility between light-skinned and dark-skinned children, it does perpetuate the old stereotype of the domestic as dark and the professional Afro-American as light in color. Pat, however, manages to overcome her distrust of light-skinned Lucy Mae Oliver and of her new white classmate, Sarah Mellon, whose mother would not approve of her befriending the child of a black domestic. Pat muses at the end, concluding that "being black" hadn't stopped her from making friends; it hadn't kept her from learning.

The numerous biographies of outstanding black athletes, musicians, leaders, entertainers, scientists, etc., contribute a great deal to the building of good self-images for the black child. The one biography, however, which is most popular in our school with both white and nonwhite children, both boys and girls, is Ann Petry's story of the life of Harriet Tubman. The book is an old one, but the lucid, cogent presentation of the courageous slave woman evokes sympathy and immediate identification of the reader with the subject. The white child who is brought face to face with the extreme cruelties suffered by Harriet at the hands of her white masters and mistresses can find solace in the revelation of the underground railroad established by white abolitionists.

The black reader who laments Harriet's lack of beauty and education takes pride in her indomitable will and courage and mother wit. Perhaps more than any other biography, Mrs. Petry's *Harriet Tubman* describes in vivid word pictures the fortitude of an American who was both black and noble. These are the kinds of books which will be of inestimable value to all children, and their delineation of black characters will provide the black child with some means of identifying himself as part of the American scene.

Now that American writers and illustrators are conscious of the present need of young minds, we can expect children's books that will build the ego of the black child and help the white child to relate to others without racial prejudice. Publishers must be encouraged to seek and produce such books.

But, the editing of the classics to remove social stereotypes or to reduce ethnocentricity will prove to be a more difficult but necessary venture, precisely because of their agelong acceptance and popularity. The publishers will cry "censorship" and receive support from literary critics and libertarian organizations. And the black community, whether black nationalist or not, will be outraged at the suggestion that it continue to be maligned after all these years by the masterworks of the creative writers of the white society. All this can be avoided with good sense, good book selection, and judicious editing that leaves the literary values of the works intact.

REFERENCES

Bannerman, Helen. *Little Black Sambo.* Lippincott, 1946.

Baum, Betty. *Patricia Crosses Town.* Knopf, 1965.

Beim, Jerrold & Lorraine. *Two Is a Team.* Morrow, 1945.

Courlander, Harold. *The Cowtail Switch, and Other West African Stories.* Holt, 1947.

Hunt, Mabel Leigh. *Benjie's Hat.* Lippincott, 1938.

Justus, May. *New Boy in School.* Hastings, 1963.

Kipling, Rudyard. *Favorite Just So Stories.* Grosset, 1957.

————. *Just So Stories*. Doubleday, 1952.

Lofting, Hugh. *The Story of Dr. Dolittle*. Lippincott, 1948.

O'Neill, Mary. *Hailstones and Halibut Bones*. Doubleday, 1961.

Petry, Ann. *Harriet Tubman: Conductor on the Underground Railway*. Crowell, 1955.

Travers, Pamela. *Mary Poppins and Mary Poppins Comes Back*. Harcourt, 1963.

Udry, Janice May. *What Mary Jo Shared*. Albert Whitman, 1966.

Up-Tight Ain't Right

Dr. Kenneth Goodman

"I play it cool and dig all jive,
That's the reason I stay alive.
My motto, as I live and learn,
Is dig, and be dug in return."

Langston Hughes,
Montage of a Dream Deferred

·POETS can be expected to have an intuition about language and language difference because it's the medium in which they work, the clay that holds the shape of the ideas, emotions, and feelings that the artist is expressing. Langston Hughes expresses the essential truth that all language varieties have a particular suitability to maximize communication among the individuals who share a common interest, experience, culture, or way of life. Each dialect, a language variant developed in a community of language users, is the one best form of communication for dealing with the common experiences of its users. Hughes' poetry and prose reflect this understanding as do the works of other poets: Burns with his Scottish dialect and Paul Lawrence Dunbar, an earlier black poet whose critics never seemed to grasp the importance of the choice of dialect to the success of his poems.

Modern linguistic theory and research has only recently caught up with the linguistic intuition of the poet. A new, scientifically based view of language has emerged which must be understood and applied in creating and evaluating books for children so that they might utilize the full rich potential of language as children interact with literature.

This new full view of language has provided a number of key insights:

—Every language such as English, is in fact a family of related dialects. These vary to some extent from each other in every aspect: grammar, phonology, vocabulary, but they are not so different that speakers of one dialect can not understand speakers of another dialect. Differences are great enough to impede communication but not prevent it. When differences become great enough that dialects are not mutually understandable, then separate languages have evolved (as is the case between Spanish and Portuguese). No one dialect is the language from which all others have derived or wandered. Dialect differences emerge among people separated by time and space, age, or interest.

—Difference in language is not deficiency. Language cannot be divided into two forms: right and wrong. My dialect is not a funny way of speaking yours. All

81

dialects are fully formed. They are rule governed, systematic, and capable of expressing any experience common in the culture from which they stem. Furthermore they are flexible enough to deal with any new experience or view that the speakers of the dialect may encounter. One reason why linguistic change is so common and rapid is this ability of language to adapt to the needs of its users. Dialects may vary in the social prestige that they carry but this is a reflection of the social status of the people who use them. Low status people speak low status language because that is the status the general society assigns to all aspects of their culture.

—Children and youth play a particularly important role in linguistic change. Their experiences and the way they view them are likely to differ from their parents. Furthermore, use of the language of their parents seems to require an implicit acceptance of the life view of an older generation. Rejection of the values of the dominant groups in society leads to linguistic change. Sometimes this even means inversion of language with positive terms becoming negative and vice-versa. So about the best thing about a car some 16-year-olds can say is that it's "super-bad." All dissident groups (hippies are a recent example) develop language forms to replace those of the culture or system they reject.

—Thought, learning, literature are not the monopoly of those who speak high status language. Oral literature existed long before any written literature appeared. Furthermore, it flourishes most among low status groups who are less influenced by the mass culture of the larger society. The play party game, a folk song-dance combination, is found among poor black and Appalachian white children even when they are transplanted to Northern ghettos. Lorenz Graham found bible stories such as that of David and Goliath which were first, of course, a part of the oral tradition of the ancient Hebrews, transformed back into

the oral tradition as African converts translated them into an idiom which brought them into harmony with their own culture and experience:

The giant say, "Ho! Small boy done
    come to say how-do."
David say, "I come for fight!"
Giant say, "Do you mommy know
    you out?"
David say, "Now I kill you!"
Giant say, "Go from my face less I
    eat you!"

David stand,
He put rock in him sling,
He turn it all about and round and
    round,
The giant coming close,
The sling leggo,
Hmmmmmmmmm.......................bop!

The giant holler out,
He hold him head,
He turn,
He try to walk,
He fall,
He roll,
He twist about,
He die.

Then David's brothers come and say,
"You fool!
The war palaver be for men.
Go home!
Go home and mind the sheep!"

And David say, "Now I go."

Lorenz Graham,
(*David, He No Fear*, Crowell, 1971)

Science then, has brought us to the understanding the poets always had: all language has system, utility, and beauty.

A decade of highly productive research on children's language development has made clear that all children learn the language form first which is most useful in communication within their families and their immediate communities. This is true for all human societies. Even deaf children who are born to deaf parents will learn sign easily and well if that is the language of their homes. Though individuals will differ in their linguistic effectiveness, language development is not slower in one group than in another regardless of social, cultural, economic, or racial differences.

Receptive language, the ability to understand others, moves ahead of productive language in children's development of linguistic competence. They can understand more than they can express. This is true in first language acquisition but it is also true in learning second languages or second forms of the same language. Ironically this accounts for an advantage urban poor children have over their middle-class peers. Children who speak, as their mother tongue, a low status dialect of the ghetto will also acquire receptive control, the ability to hear and understand, the other dialects with which they come in contact. So they will be able, eventually, to understand the policeman, teacher, grocer, as well as those who speak their own dialect. This does not mean they will ever drop their own dialect for productive use or learn to use both productively but it is an advantage over the more privileged child growing up in a community where all the "worthwhile people" speak the way he does. Even if the suburban child sometimes hears low-status speakers he has no need to tune them in.

Modern linguistic science and the related interdisciplinary fields of sociolinguistics and psycholinguistics have also made possible a better understanding of the reading process and how it is acquired. Reading can be viewed as a receptive language process. The reader, a user of language, constructs a meaning from language which he hopes agrees substantially with that of the writer. Reading is not a matter of learning to match letters to sounds or name words. Rather the reader uses his language competence to get to the underlying language structures and the meaning. A key element in his success is that he must, as in listening, focus on meaning. He must ask himself as he proceeds whether he is getting sense from the print. As long as he does that he can use all of the linguistic competence that he has built in listening to succeed in reading since the underlying grammar of both written and oral language is the same. The more natural the language, that is the more like language as he knows it, the easier will be this task. The more relevant the content is to his experience and his conceptual background, the more he is likely to read and understand. For all readers the ability to get meaning from a particularly written text depends very much on the meaning which the particular reader brings to the task. This is true for adults reading a Russian novel or a recipe for baking a cake. It is even more true for children just acquiring reading competence. Less proficient readers need more relevant, natural materials. The lower the proficiency of the reader, the more important is the level of background knowledge he brings to the reading.

Motivation in learning to read is the same as it is in all language learning. There is a need to communicate, to understand and be understood, or as Hughes put it "to dig and be dug," which is a powerful force behind language learning. Reading materials which kids really need to understand are going to be most useful in helping them acquire literacy. Fiction is probably not a particularly good vehicle for beginning reading since its language has different grammatical constraints than conversational discourse and it is less universally familiar than other language forms.

Uptight, conservative notions of what is acceptable and suitable in children's books need to give way to freer criteria designed to achieve more acceptable, more natural, more varied, more realistic materials. Such books can be of tremendous help in making the acquisition of literacy a natural extension of the language learning that produces oral language competence. Authors and editors of children's books can base language decisions on a single pervasive principle: it must be real language as people really use it. It has taken black people more than a decade to fully realize that if black is beautiful so is the way black people talk. There is nothing demeaning about presenting the language of any group as they use it in coping with every day's experience and in communicating with each other. Purifying, standardizing, or homogenizing language not only misrepresents it and the people who use it, but is likely to result in a loss of some of the beauty and strength the more suitable language could express.

There has been, of course, a tendency in literature of earlier times to overdraw language just as there has been to overdraw characters: to create a kind of linguistic caricature like that of the minstrel show, of Amos and Andy or L'il Abner. Minority group members who have struggled for upward social mobility have worked hard to rid themselves of the stigmatizing lower class dialects and in the process have sometimes come to equate them with the stereotypes. They too must make peace with their cultural heritage so that they and other members of their groups may achieve the full ethnic self-respect so necessary in a pluralistic society.

There was a tendency in recent years for publishers to respond to indignant minority groups by replacing the caricatured dialect in their books with a fumigated form of English no one speaks. As a character in *Purlie* comments, "That ain't it either, Charley."

There is no need to create special phonic spellings for the sounds of varied dialects. English spelling is standard across dialects, which in reality is a major advantage. Pumpkin is the spelling regardless of how it's pronounced. There are at least four ways Americans say *almond*, some with an *L* sound and some without, but the spelling is shared by all. Artificial spellings in fact complicate the reading particularly for those unfamiliar with the dialect the writer is trying to represent.

It is not just the black child or the Chicano child or the Appalachian who needs books portraying real people tell-

int it like they do. All children need to encounter the richness in language, culture, and experience which is America. The illusion that many youngsters grow up with that everybody is like them except a few people who are either peculiar or quaint can only break down with exposure to reality.

Perhaps the best sign that Americans are becoming comfortable with their differences is the growing ability of groups to laugh at themselves and to enjoy the sorts of humor that linguistic diversity makes possible. This has finally found its way into books for children. An example is *The Dragon Takes a Wife* (Walter Dean Myers, Bobbs, 1972). Harry, a dragon, wants to beat the knight who always beats him, so he can win a wife. He seeks help from Mabel May Jones, a sweet and kind fairy. "I can dig where you're coming from," she sympathizes. She encants a spell to help him:

Fire, be hotter
And hotter than that
Turn Harry on
So he can burn that cat!

But this doesn't help. Harry keeps losing.

"Well, don't get uptight, honey: ain't nobody perfect!" she says. Finally, after several more failures, Mabel May thinks she knows what the problem is, "My magic thing ain't working because you got your mind set on losing. You got that losing stuff in your system and you can't move right." So Mabel changes herself into a dragon to show Harry how to move. He not only learns and wins, but falls in love with Mable May. Mabel May, who "never did dig fairying too much," marries Harry. Harry gets a good job in the post office and they live happily ever after.

Language is not a straightjacket for human expression. It is rather a tool as flexible as we choose to let it be, if we can take the advice Mabel May Jones gave to Harry the Dragon and "learn to move" with it.

Black English:
The Politics of Translation

June Jordan

WE ARE in a political situation in America where, on the one hand, there are the powerful who control and, on the other hand, there are the powerless who pay the consequences.

In America, we are knuckling under the rapid loss of freedom of speech, freedom of the press. Too many people in this country deliberately seek to enforce a homogenized, complacent, barbarous society where *standard* means *right*, where *right* means *White*. Therefore, *non*standard means *sub*standard, and means *wrong*, and means *dangerous*, and will be punished, even unto the death of the spirit.

We are talking about power: and poetry and books—history books, novels, what-have-you—none of these can win against the schools, the teachers, the media, the fearful parents, and the elite of this country, unless we understand the power of these politics.

In America, the politics of language has become obvious around the globe: it is American power that invented and imposed upon our minds the Vietnam vocabulary of "making peace by making war," of murdering people and calling that "pacification," of "advisory personnel," "protective reaction," and even the 1972 Twelve Days of Christmas "carpet bombing." There is an obscenely long list

of the lies and the euphemisms that have been printed and telecast in perfectly standard, grammatical, White English.

In America, the politics of language, the wilfull debasement of this human means to human communion has jeopardized the willingness of young people to believe *anything* they hear or read.

And what is anybody going to do about it? I suggest that, for one, we join forces to cherish and protect our various, multifoliate lives against pacification, homogenization, the silence of terror, and standards that despise and disregard the sanctity of each and every human life.

The Functions of Language

We can begin by looking at language. Because it brings us together, as folks, because it makes known the unknown strangers we otherwise remain to each other, because it is the naming of experience and, thereby, a possession of experience, and because names/language make possible a social statement of connection and lead these connections into social reality—for all these reasons, and more, language is a process of translation. Language is a process of translation whereby we learn and we tell who we are, and what we want, and what we need, believe, or why we tremble, or hide, or kill, or nurture and love. This is a political process, a process taking place on the basis of who has the power to use, abuse, accept or reject the words—the lingual messages—we must attempt to transmit to each other and/or against each other.

As a poet and writer, I deeply love and I deeply hate words. I love the infinite evidence and change and requirements and possibilities of language: every human use of words that is joyful, or honest, or new because experience is new, or old because each personal history testifies to inherited pleasures and/or inherited, collective memories of peril and pain.

But as a Black poet and writer, I hate words that cancel my name and my history and the freedom of my future. I hate the words that condemn and refuse the language of my people in America: I am talking about a language deriving from the Niger-Congo family of languages. I am talking about a language that joins with the Russian, Hungarian, and Arabic languages, among others, in eliminating the "present copula"—a verb interjected between subject and predicate. Or, to break that down a bit, I am talking about a language that will tell you simply, "They Mine." (And, incidentally, if I tell you, "they mine," you don't have no kind of trouble understanding exactly what I mean, do you?)

As a Black poet and writer, I am proud of our Black, verbally bonding system born of our struggle to avoid annihilation—as Afro-American self, community, and culture. I am proud of this language that our continuing battle just *to be* has brought into currency. And so I hate the arrogant, prevailing rejection of this, our Afro-American language. And so I work, as poet and writer, against the eradication of this system, this language, this carrier of Black-survivor consciousness.

The Politics of Black English

The subject of "Black English" cannot intelligently separate from the subject of language as translation and translation as a political process distinguishing between the powerless and the powerful in no uncertain terms. Here are a few facts to illustrate my meaning:

1) Apparently, "Black English" needs defense even though it is demonstrably a language: a perfectly adequate, verbal means of communication that can be understood by any but the most outrightly standard racist.

2) On the other hand, where is the defense, who among the standard, grammatical, White English mainstreamers feels the need, even, to defend his imposition of his language on me and my children?

3) "Thou know'st the mask of night is on my face.
Else would a maiden blush bepaint my cheek
For that which thou has heard me speak tonight.
Fain would I dwell on form, fain, fain deny
what I have spoke: but farewell compliment!
Dost thou love me? I know thou wilt say 'Ay.'
And I will take thy word; yet, if thou swear'st
Thou mayst prove false; at lovers' perjuries,
They say, Jove laughs."
(*Romeo and Juliet* Act II, Scene II)

Now that ain hardly no kind of standard English. But just about every kid forced into school has to grapple with that particular rap. Why? Because the powers that control the language that controls the process of translation have decided that *Romeo and Juliet* is necessary, nay, *indispensable*, to passage through compulsory, public school education.

4) "You be different from the dead. All them tombstones tearing up the ground, look like a little city, like a small Manhattan, not exactly. Here is not the same.

Here, you be bigger than the buildings, bigger than the little city. You be really different from the rest, the resting other ones.

Moved in his arms, she make him feel like smiling.

Him, his head an Afro-bush spread free beside the stones, headstones thinning in the heavy air. Him, a ready father, public lover, privately at last alone with her, with Angela, a half an hour walk from the hallway where they start out to hold themselves together in the noisy darkness, kissing, kissed him, kissed her, kissing.

Cemetery let them lie there belly close, their shoulders now undressed down to the color of the heat they feel, in lying close, their legs a strong disturbing of the dust. His own where, own place for loving made for making love, the cemetery where nobody guard the dead."

(*His Own Where*, first page)

Now that ain no standard English, either. Both excerpts come from love stories about White and Black teenagers, respectively. But the Elizabethan, nonstandard English of *Romeo and Juliet* has been adjudged as something students should take and absorb. By contrast, Black, nonstandard language has been adjudged as *sub*-standard and even injurious to young readers.

I submit that these judgements are strictly political and that they should be recognized as political and resisted, accordingly.

But language and the politics of translation affect more than the censorship of literature; we are talking about power, and about the perpetuation of power.

White Power

In the compulsory public school situation, demonstration of such power is a daily event: Black and White children enter the so-called educational system. Once inside, the White child is rewarded for his mastery of his standard, White English—the language he learned at his mother's White and standard knee. But the Black child is punished for his mastery of his nonstandard, Black English. Moreover, the White child receives formal instruction in his standard English, and endless opportunities for the exercise and creative display of his language. But where is the elementary school course in Afro-American language, and where are the opportunities for the *accredited* exercise, and creative exploration, of Black language?

The two languages are not interchangeable. They cannot, nor do they attempt to communicate equal or identical thoughts, or feelings. And, since the experience to be conveyed is quite different, Black from White, these lingual dissimilarities should not surprise or worry anyone.

However, they are both communication systems with regularities, exceptions, and values governing their word designs. Both are equally liable to poor, good, better, and creative use. In short, they are both accessible to critical criteria such as clarity, force, message, tone, and imagination. Besides this, standard English is comprehensible to Black children, even as Black English is comprehensible to White teachers—supposing that the teachers are willing to make half the effort they demand of Black students.

Then what is the difficulty? The problem is that we are saying language, but really dealing with power. The word "standard" is just not the same as the word "technical" or "rural" or "straight." *Standard* means the rule, the norm. Anyone deviating from the standard is therefore "wrong." As a result, literally millions of Black children are "wrong" from the moment they begin to absorb and imitate the language of their Black lives. Is that an acceptable idea?

As things stand, consequences of childhood fluency in Afro-American language are lamentably predictable; reading problems that worsen, course failure in diverse subjects dependent on reading skills, and a thoroughly wounded self-esteem. Afterwards, an abject school career is eclipsed by an abject life career. "Failing" English (Standard English) merely presages a "failure" of adult life. This, I submit, is a deliberate, political display of power to destroy the powerless.

Solutions

This punishment of Black children will continue until the legitimacy of Black language is fully acknowledged by all of us, Black and White. That will mean offering standard English as simply *The Second Language*. It will mean calling standard English studies "Second Language Studies" wherever that description accurately applies.

A sincere recognition of Black language as legitimate will mean formal instruction and encouragement in its use within the regular curriculum. It will mean the respectful approaching of Black children, *in the language of Black children*. It will mean an end to illegitimate, political use of language studies against Black life.

It is true that we need to acquire competence in the language of the powerful: Black children in America must acquire competence in standard English, if only for the sake of self-preservation. But I do not understand how anyone supposes that you will teach a child a new language by scorning and ridiculing and forcibly erasing his old, first language: all of his names for all the people and events of his black life prior to his entry into school.

I am one among a growing number of Black poets and writers dedicated to the preservation of Black language within our lives, and dedicated to the health of our children as they prepare themselves for life within this standard, White America which has despised even our speech and our prayers and our love.

As long as we shall survive Black, in this White America, we and our children require and deserve the power of Black language, Black history, Black literature, as well as the power of standard English, standard history, and standard, White literature.

To the extent that Black survival fails on these terms, it will be a political failure; it will be the result of our not recognizing and not revolting against the political uses of language to extinguish the people we want to be and the people we have been.

Politics is power. Language is political. And language, its reward, currency, punishment and/or eradication—is political in its meaning and in its consequence.

Recently, a White woman telephoned to ask me to appear on her television program; she felt free to tell me that if I sounded "Black" then she would not "hire" me; language is power. That woman is powerful if she feels free to reject and strangle whoever will not mimic her—in language, values, goals. In fact, I answered her in this way: "You are a typical racist." And that is the political truth of the matter, as I see it, as I hope you will begin to see it; for no one has the right to control and sentence to poverty anyone—because he or she is different and proud and honest in his or her difference and his or her pride.

There is a need to understand Black language, per se: A young friend of mine went through some scarifying times, leaving her homeless. During this period of intense, relentless dread and abuse, she wrote poems, trying to cope. Here are two lines from her poetry: "*What have life meanted to me*" and, "*You are forgotten you use to existed.*"

There is no adequate, standard English translation possible for either expression of her spirit because they are intrinsically Black language cries of extreme pain so telling that even the possibilities of meaning and existence have been formulated in a past tense that is emphatic, severe.

I deeply hope that more of us will want to learn and protect Black language. If we lose our fluency in our language, we may irreversibly forsake elements of the spirit that have provided for our survival.

Black language is not A Mistake, or A Verbal Deficiency. It is a system subsuming dialect/regional variations that leaves intact, nevertheless, a language that is invariable in fundamental respects. For example:

A) Black language practices minimal inflection of verb forms. (e.g.; *I go, we go, he go*; and *I be, you be, we be*, etc.) This is nonstandard and, also, an obviously more logical use of verbs. It is also evidence of a value system that considers the person/subject—the actor—more important than the act.

B) Consistency of syntax: for example, in Black English/Black language, the imperative case, the interrogative case, and the simple declarative case all occur within the same structural pattern. (e.g. *You going to the store.*) Depending on tone, that is a statement of mere fact, or a command, or a question.

C) Infrequent, irregular use of the possessive case. Therefore, in Black language, you say, "they house" at least as often as you might say, "their house."

D) Clear, logical use of multiple negatives within a single sentence, to express an unmistakably negative idea. e.g. *You ain gone bother me in no way at no time no more, you hear?*)

E) Other logical consistencies, such as: *ours, his, theirs,* and, therefore, *mines.*

Black language is a political fact suffering from political persecution. Black language and Black literature are political facts persecuted by the same powerful political people in this country who feel bold to say, in perfectly standard, grammatical, White English: ". . . let each of us ask not just what will government do for me but what I can do for myself."

(Of course that declaration is quite entirely at odds with another, perfectly standard, American concept: ". . . government of the people, by the people, and for the people.") As the President has since made plain, his standard English exhortation to self-help means the deadly reduction of government aid to every program against poverty, poor housing, inadequate education, and poor health.

This is a time when those of us who believe in people, first, must become political, in every way possible; we must devise and pursue every means possible for survival as the people we are, as the people we want to become. For Afro-Americans, this certainly means that we must succeed in the preservation of our language.

Let us cherish its long service to us, as a people.

Let us halt the mutilation of abilities to manage the world through language. Let us cease the destruction of one language for the sake of another. Let us present standard English as merely a second language, whenever that is the case. And let us undertake these goals with full awareness that the stakes are truly the political stakes of the power to kill or the power to survive.

And, as for the children: let us welcome and applaud and promote the words they bring into our reality; in the struggle to reach each other, there can be no right or wrong words for our longing and our needs; there can only be the names that we trust and we try.

RECOMMENDED BRIEF BACKGROUND READING

Goodman, Kenneth. "Up-Tight Ain't Right!" in *SLJ*, October 1972.

Labov, William. "Academic Ignorance and Black Intelligence" in *Atlantic Magazine*, 1972.

The 34th Man: How Well Is Jewish Minority Culture Represented in Children's Fiction?

Leona Daniels

THE TREMENDOUS outpouring of articles and books on Jewish literature has seen little reflection in the field of Jewish fiction for young people. This is curious in an age of ecumenism. Some sociologists say the Jewish community has become so enculturated that a specific fiction would only point up its few vestigial differences, in turn festering suspicion and fear, the seeds of anti-Semitism, at a time when understanding is necessary. Others, however, affirm the need for a literature to define the uniqueness of the subculture in a pluralistic society.

Authors themselves reflect this dichotomy, as some create the Jewish family in an atmosphere of ancient tradition, cultural awareness, and innate humor—as in the recent rabbi detective stories of Harry Kemelman and in Herbert Tarr's *Heaven Help Us*. Others offer little more than a story whose sterile characters happen to have Jewish names and celebrate the appropriate holidays. The popular juvenile *Carol's Side of the Street* is a typical example of such shallowness; few adult authors would develop such unsatisfying characters—though Stephen Longstreet's *Pedlock & Sons* does compete with its depiction of a non-ethnic Jewish family that is outside the living experience of most Jews of any generation or economic level. If the purpose of the ethnic fiction is to impart the feeling of a people, to create understanding and empathy, then a course in comparative religion would be more valuable than these pasteboard people in shadowed situations. It is perhaps this ambivalence that reflects the output and quality of children's fiction writing on the modern Jew in America.

In October 1967 a conference on children's books as a means of promoting international understanding was organized by the Danish Unesco School at Sophiehom, near Copenhagen. The participants formalized their agreement that good children's fiction—subject to the same standards as all literature —is essential to improving understanding among people and can be used with great educational effectiveness. They charged Unesco to encourage further study of the effect of children's fiction on attitudes.

These resolutions lend international prestige to the idea that fiction can be used to develop cultural awareness and sympathetic brotherhood. But its use depends on consistency and continuity, on seeing literature and exposure as inseparable twins, recognizing the interpretive depth and perspective that fiction gives the child as he identifies with characters and moves with them through plot and culture.

To apply this concept to the understanding of one minority, I undertook a study of the extent, range of theme, and quality of works treating the Jew in children's fiction. The Jewish population constitutes 3 percent of the total in America, and its contribution to American life is substantial enough to have created a definite focal point in our pluralistic society. What kind of statement does junior literature make?

I ruled out certain genres and periods —folklore, for example, despite Isaac B. Singer's recent excellent contribution with *Zlateh the Goat, When Schlemeil Went to Warsaw,* and *Mazel and Schlemazel.* Also excluded were biography, historical fiction, festivals, and early Jewish life in America in favor of stories on contemporary Jewish life in America. In these times of conflicting social patterns, "understanding" is a somewhat academic goal, disembodied from experience, while acceptance—the hope of a dynamic interchange *between* varying cultures— depends on identifying with today's ethnic groups.

Jewish youth may provide the hungriest readership today for a satisfying ego image, an objective exposure to their own life style; such fiction might play checkers with the generation gap, replacing some of the missing cultural heritage which the youth's parents could not pass down to him from the last generation of grandparents. And the non-Jewish reader, should be led to stories with which he can identify, yet that will take him into the modern Jewish home with its family patterns and values. Stories of people "born Jewish" are quite beside the point.

A modern ethnic portrait, in other words, would describe family relationships, community institutions and affiliations, social awareness, humor. It would describe characters who accept their ethnic identity, and share a sense of community with others of common origin across the world. And since "modern" Jewish life was shaped by the tragedy of the European upheaval of World War II, which unified world Jewry and brought Zionism to its goal of a national refuge, the terror of Nazism and the state of Israel are part of that portrait.

The search for titles in this literature area was difficult and disappointing. Extensive resources had to be searched. Bibliographies designed to promote understanding, such as those published by the American Jewish Committee's Institute on Human Relations, are more concerned with non-Jewish minorities than with Jews. It is true that there are more titles available in these areas, but it is also true that the bibliographies extant are far from definitive. The useful and very excellent *Red, White and Black: Minorities in America,* published by the Combined Paperback Exhibit, lists less than a dozen entries, out of nearly 600, that relate to the Jewish community. These are nonfiction and paperbacks, not the subject of this study but indicative of the disproportion evident in the catalogs available.

Nor do the standard bibliographic resources do much to promote Jewish fiction as a means of subcultural enlightenment in the U.S. Most resources can be counted on for only one or two titles—and these are generally the popular, familiar Taylors and Lewitons reflecting the community of a by-gone day, while it is a vastly different culture that has emerged since World War II and the birth of Israel. Jewish titles can be found under subject headings concerned with family and community life; girls' stories; growing up; or any number of allusive phrases. But no cross-referencing directly to Jewish content is found. In the standard Wilson selection tools, Jewish content is arranged under holiday stories; Nazi-Jewish stories; historical fiction; early settlement; and biography. Little or no effort is made to point to "Jewish life —Fiction." This seems to indicate a lack of awareness of the constant inclusion of Jewish influence in adult fiction, and even Jewish influence in daily living. Complete notation may be found in the Wilson *Fiction Catalog* for adult works. Why then, don't we find a similar tool for younger readers?

Picture books for the general trade are notably lacking in stories of Jewish children. Most are published by Jewish organizations, for a limited market, and are filled with unexplained religious and ceremonial allusions. Where regional stories about other groups often manage to slip in subtle definitions to clarify the concept without didacticism, countless Jewish books assume that the reader is familiar with the esoteric concepts and non-English vocabulary sprinkled throughout. For this reason alone, the books are of limited appeal and readership. Out of hundreds of titles, only a few had general appeal for the public school, non-Jewish child, rather than the religious schools that consume them. Among these were Mel Silverman's *Hymie's Fiddle* (World, 1960), reflecting lower East Side New York City in the days of the pushcarts; *The Mystery of the Missing Challah* by Freda Charles (Jonathan David, 1959) which, despite its parochialism, had whimsical drawings, religious explanations, and a quiet humor; and *Debbie in Dreamland* (National Woman's League of the United Synagogues of America), in which Debbie and her parakeet unfold the circumstances of ten holidays in a better-than-average text that compensates for the undistinguished format.

Publishers like Ktav or Behrman House have extensive lists. It's a pity their books don't appeal to the general market. What a shame that the better writers don't create titles for this market! Names as familiar as Leonard Kessler and Maurice Sendak are attached to books from these houses. They are early efforts, to be sure. Why can't people of this stature, with a feeling for children's needs, a knowledge of their own culture, and a talent for

writing and illustrating, put their creative efforts into this field of interest? Perhaps the general publishers should move in here, or perhaps Jewish publishers are overlooking a broader market. Even religious teachers complain of the lack of attractive material for the specialized library.

The one publisher notable for its attempt to bring Jewish heritage to the trade for young children is Crowell. Unfortunately the series it has developed concentrates not on fiction and cultural patterns, but on holiday material concerned with festivals and ritual. Authored by Molly Cone and Norma Simon, writers known for their talents in fiction, these books combine Biblical history with contemporary celebration. Some are beautifully illustrated by such creative artists as Ellen Rashkin in her stylized design-art concepts and by Symeon Shimin's sensitive charcoal sketches. Unfortunately there is an imbalance of presentation. Take the focus on foods. While it is true that in fiction foods do relate a definite cultural focus, it is crass to suggest that chicken soup gives meaning to a day set aside for dedication and peace, as the *Jewish Sabbath* does. The *Jewish Sabbath* and *Jewish New Year* imply Orthodox tradition with the latter illustrated in inappropriate cartoonstyle. They attempt to explain theological concepts not within the grasp of the primary audience for whom they were written. On the other hand, the *Hanukkah* and *Passover* stories are beautiful presentations of religious occurrences. What is still missing in all these retellings is the unfolding of Jewish culture patterns.

There is little parallelism between adult fiction treating the Jewish experience in America and fiction for younger people. Historically, we can begin this "modern" era with the waves of immigration caused by European pogroms which brought two million Jewish immigrants to America before 1922 (when Congress passed a law restricting immigration). Most of that great number settled in ghettoized communities in New York City, forced into insularity by the Depression and a flagrant anti-Jewish bias. Jews outside New York City, and those of older American origin, had an opportunity to develop economically and begin an acculturation which led to a polarization of the American Jewish community.

One author unique in his objective presentation of this experience is Charles Angoff, who in nearly a dozen titles takes the reader through three generations of a Jewish family saga, from the immigrant years to current times. He unfolds a history and culture that few comprehensive courses in the history of the modern Jew could equal.

Angoff's self-respect was evident in years when other Jewish writers expressed self-consciousness and discomfort in their role in an anti-Semitic world. Henry Roth's *Call It Sleep* has become another classic example of the story of self-accepting, nonassimilating Jews. His idiomatic portrait is a statement of unacculturated, ghettoized Jews whose lives are unaffected by the Gentile world beyond. Philip Roth, on the other hand, has come to be recognized as a cliché in his Jewish self-consciousness. The over-50 Jewish audience today can't even enjoy the movie version of *Goodbye Columbus*, lest someone identify them with the gross overabundance of the wedding scene. The polarization of values is forgotten as the audience overreacts to the one scene.

This same self-consciousness is exposed even in books for young people when authors tick off incidents without the atmosphere that make the characters authentic. While stories about the turn-of-the-century, such as those by Mina Lewiton and Sydney Taylor, and the Caldecott Award runner-up *Our Eddie* by Sulamith Ish-Kashor, have an ethnic charm, when history approaches the Thirties and the Depression, authors for young people make very few contributions.

Marilyn Sachs has written a light little trilogy of the Forties—*Amy Moves In, Laura's Luck,* and *Amy and Laura*—that adds so subtle a touch of Jewish life one recognizes it only through "Grandma's matzoh-brei." After establishing her characters as Jewish in the first book, she never hints at their identity again. Why the relationship in the first place without a cultural contribution throughout? But at least it offends no one. In so many stories the clichéd "gleaming white linen tablecloth, polished silver and best china set for the Passover table" makes one wonder how some of the characters, so economically deprived throughout the rest of the story, can own such lovely accoutrements to dress up the holidays. Certainly more positive statements might be made in the field of children's fiction about the educational, cultural, and economic contributions that were happening in the Jewish community of the Thirties and into the Forties. Juvenile authors might look to Gerald Green for clues to the perspective of this time.

The Nazi era offers both drama and thematic value, and just as the adult literary field used the trauma of the Holocaust, so material for young people is emerging. *Miriam* by Aimée Sommerfelt and the ever-favorite Ann Frank stories have wide readership. James Forman has written two excellent works on this era, *The Traitors* and *My Enemy, My Brother*. While Gerda Klein originally had an adult readership in mind when she wrote *All But My Life*, it was picked up by the high school level and now can't be put down by enthusiastic middle school girls.

After the Holocaust, when the world settled down to new social and political awareness, the partition of Israel offered wonderful new material for reading on all levels. Where Israel is the locale, the chauvinistic pioneer spirit lends itself to an awareness of social and political problems and a dedication to basic values. One wonders whether it is the lack of religiosity in

Israel that explains its lack of self-consciousness—a trait so apparent in American stories. The Israeli stories contain an interesting anti-Arab bias that says a great deal about Negro-white relationships in the United States. The implications of prejudice, taken out of the familiar and relocated across the sea in a strange, exotic culture, tend to refocus the problems to serve as an excellent reflective teaching tool. Adults relate to Israel through such works as Yael Dayan's *Envy the Frightened* and Yahuda Amichaie's *Not of This Time, Not of This Place*, while young people are as deeply stirred by the beautiful stories of Sally Watson and Thelma Nurenburg.

Nonfiction titles of Israel are also available at all age levels, from the Sasek's colorful favorite *This Is Israel*, to books designed to implement the social studies curriculum in schools. Biographies exist, of heroes such as General Yigael Yadin (*Desert Fighter* by Shane Miller, published by Hawthorn in 1967, and Israel Taslitts' *Soldier of Israel*, published by Sabra Books and distributed by Funk & Wagnall) and several on all age levels about David Ben Gurion and Theodore Herzl. Unfortunately, these have more political than social significance. Meyer Levin's *Story of Israel*, Harry Essrig and Abraham Segal's *Israel Today*, and Joan Comay's *Israel* are just a few of the many description and travel books that offer full range of information about this new nation. But none offer the perspective and balance of the fiction that children enjoy as recreational reading, never cognizant of the tremendous influence their pleasure reading can contribute to their social awareness and world-wide background.

As events move forward in time, the contemporary American scene is dealt with mostly in terms of prejudice —at least in the junior novel, some of which are excellent despite the stigma of the genre. Books treating non-problem themes of family life written in a humorous way are aimed mainly at the upper elementary child.

On the whole, the available books are excellent reading from a literary view. They offer a variety of patterns of Jewish life although the greater number of authors represent Conservative or Orthodox traditions. Certain ceremonials are distinctly non-Reform and do not represent the total Jewish community. If any stereotyping can be found in the characters, it can be defended by the recurrence of a type that is recognizable and identified with. Unfortunately, the mother in Elaine Konigsberg's *About the B'nai Bagels* uses certain ideolectic phrases that do not reflect the modern-day Jewish mother; this, then, is tantamount to stereotyping not frequently found. In stories concerned with neighborhood and school prejudice, the stereotyping is an intellectual one, using all the hackneyed arguments to label and then to explain the platitudes that have been found in discussions and literature on anti-Semitism ever since *Gentlemen's Agreement* made its shocking impact. But no untoward bias is evident in any of the characters or their life situations to add weight to a built-in prejudice held by any reader. While most authors of this group of books are Jewish, not all are. Most stories are satisfying and effective in mirroring an inherently Jewish community. Some, indeed, are too bland, and only an excuse to define holiday customs as if Jews were simply Americans who happen to celebrate different customs and rituals.

Only a few of the stories in print actually echo the nuances of the American Jewish family. These few, which include *Freckle-Face Frankel*, *A Promise Is a Promise*, and *Irving and Me*, do capture the subtleties of philosophy and humor and the commitment to community institutions that are indigenous to the Jewish family. Authors would do well to recreate this texture of kinship on all reading levels, rather than constantly emphasize Bar Mitzva,

Chanukah, and Passover, which are religious occurrences but have no daily influence in the lives of the people except as they occur in chronology for celebration.

Authors and publishers should be alerted to the limited output of contemporary Jewish fiction for young people. While the total number is adequate, they run the gamut from about the 4th grade reading level to fiction suitable for young adults. The themes are generally repititious, focusing on holidays for the younger readers and prejudice for the teens. The best stories in terms of literary excellence are those concerned with the European War and those that describe Israel. It is interesting to note the three titles of the Depression years are all new and reflect the New York City community.

Certain themes have never been attempted that are fertile for imaginative treatment—for instance, the terrible world of the Soviet Jew; the great population of the South African Jew; and the insecure world of the South American Jews who fled there from Europe in the Forties. Even in the U.S. there is that most interesting and little-known subculture within a subculture, the mystical, Kabbalistic Hassidic community of New York City and the colony in Rockland County. They are the subject of Chaim Potak's *Chosen* and brand new *Promise,* both suitable for young adults, but not written for them.

Hopefully, we should not only see more stories published, from tasteful picture books through young adult fiction, but also find better bibliographic techniques to identify this material. No previous study seems to be extant on this subject of Jewish fiction for young people except in a limited way, in Jewish periodicals. No one bibliography includes all the available titles or even a substantial portion of those appended below. Librarians might contribute to this lack in their dependence upon demand creating supply. It can be demonstrated that supply invites demand. Librarians must accept the challenge and create a reading interest by supplying the titles.

The bibliographic entries below are annotated wherever the books were available and evaluated. There may certainly be more titles not in catalogs and therefore not yet seen or known about. It was not unusual for me to find some titles mentioned in articles as relating to this field, and, after a reading, find the Jewish involvement so limited as to be irrelevant. One word does not become a theme. Even specific tools published by Jewish institutions, such as *A Book List For the Jewish Child,* published by the Jewish Book Council of America, and *A Guide to Jewish Juvenile Literature,* published by the Jewish Education Committee Press, reveal a very limited number of the total titles extant. If readers aware of other titles would send me an index card with entry and some annotation as to content, a definitive bibliography may be compiled.

Reading so consistently in one area of literature, one becomes saturated with the motif. Exposure concretizes attitudes, lights new dimensions, reinforces values. Obviously, Judaism is recognized as a religion; what becomes evident is that it is also a separate and distinct culture. The vigors and contributions achieved through the multifaceted cultures of America are what make our country the blend of goals and accomplishments that it is.

ABRAHAMS, Robert D. *Room For a Son.* Jewish Publication Society of America, 1951. (8+) o.p.
An unusually moving story of a displaced teenage boy who comes to America to become the foster son of a small-town Jewish shopkeeper. A mystical thread runs through the book, catching conscience and reality in a successful effort to help the boy adjust to American ways. It presents a Judaic theology and approach to life, a more profound depiction than the prevalent recounting of customs and traditions.

ARNOLD, Elliot. *A Kind of Secret Weapon*. Scribner's, 1969. (4-7)
Lars Anderson, a dedicated Danish newspaperman, and his 12-year-old son Peter are involved in the Danish guerrilla movement fighting Hitler's occupation, whose efforts involved the amazing rescue of Demmark's entire Jewish population of 8000. Among Anderson's activities in the Resistance is the publication of an underground newspaper, which eventually leads to his capture, torture, and death. Tracing Peter's involvement and maturation in this effort, it is a moving, unsentimental account of courage under stress.

BEIM, Lorraine. *Carol's Side of the Street*. Harcourt, 1951. (4-6)
A light story of the Meyers family's move to a new house where a family of kittens, remodeling, and an anti-Semitic neighbor create the action. Though references to Chanukah and Passover customs categorize this as an ethnic story, the flavor is bland, lacking a truly Jewish savour. A further misrepresentation of the word "Passover" makes this additional material, to be used only because of a lack of more colorful stories.

BERG, Leila. *A Box for Benny*. Bobbs-Merrill, 1961. (3-5) o.p.
A simple little story about a quite young boy who fantasizes a magical quality in a series of trades until he finally acquires the shoebox he needs for his nut games. Unique in being set in a poor Jewish neighborhood in Manchester, England, the story has Anglo-Judaic elements which reflect hues unlike those in an American story.

BIBER, Johoash. *Treasure of the Turkish Pasha*. Scribner's, 1968.
This story of Palestine during the British occupation describes how the guild of the guardsmen protected isolated villages from fearful ravages. A "dynamic view of the country and its people," says one reviewer.

BIDERMAN, Sol. *Bring Me to the Banqueting House*. Viking, 1969.
An eccentric boy living in a Jewish orphanage grows from the ages of six to 14 in a series of funny and colorful episodes. An adult book, this has been recommended for the older teen.

BISHOP, Claire Huchet. *Ten and Twenty*. Viking, 1954. (4-6)
This dramatic story of the frightening risks a nun took in hiding ten Jewish youngsters among 20 French children who were living in a convent during the Nazi occupation of France is based on a true incident.

COHEN, Florence Chanock. *Portrait of Deborah*. Messner, 1961. (6-8)
Perhaps as adult and mature as a young person's book can be, this well-written portrait of a young Jewish girl's senior year in high school is a sensitive balance of problems and solutions. Debbie reacts as any real girl would; her angers abated by social temptations, her disappointments softened by the complexities of school and family life. Anti-Semitism is realistically presented—with an honest lack of solution. The story ends with nothing really resolved beyond the hope that Debbie will win the musical scholarship which she learns requires such dedication. The theme of self-respect and integrity underscores the multiethnic characters who, though vaguely stereotyped, are drawn from consistently recurrent types in real society today.

COLMAN, Hila. *Mixed-Marriage Daughter*. Morrow, 1968.
Another attempt to depict anti-Semitism, this time with a new twist for the teenage reader. Sophie is the daughter of a mixed marriage, brought up without religious identity. Moving to her mother's home town, she is forced to see herself within the Jewish community where her family is settling into this pattern of living. Discrimination is explored as Sophie learns to accept her minority status.

CONE, Molly. *A Promise Is a Promise*. Houghton-Mifflin, 1964. (6-8)
Undertones of humor convey the relationships of a Jewish family in a non-Jewish neighborhood. Ruthie's desire for Bas Mitzva and her study for it permit the dialogue to discuss Jewish philosophic thought on a plane understandable by a little girl. A mildly smug tone, as if the author thinks being Jewish is being special, nevertheless reflects the family's wholesome self-acceptance. This light story offers an unusual depth and unique presentation of Jewish values and comparative

facets of a community. Typical of the humor and realism in this affiliated Conservative family are the comments about their rabbis . . . "the last one was too Orthodox; . . . this one is too Reform . . ." These are people we all know.

DAVID, Janina. *A Touch of Earth.* O'Rion, 1969.
Janina, saved from the Warsaw holocaust by a German-Catholic family, could only be protected by conversion from Judaism. This caused searing anxiety within a girl trained in two conflicting religions.

EMERY, Anne. *Dinny Gorden, Junior.* Macrae-Smith, 1964. (6-8)
The central issue of this story is anti-Semitism, though only two secondary characters are Jewish. The "in" crowd at a mid-Western suburban high school finds itself involved with the son and daughter of the first Jewish family to move into the community. One of the clique is dating the boy, Mike Goldman. The typical biases and usual bromides of the YA novel are probably suited to young teens who may never before have thought of this ever-present community problem. The revealing moment comes when Mike, and Debbie, his sister, articulate their side of the issue with understanding and tolerance . . . never acceptance, of course. It's too bad that the Jewish students are always portrayed as the intellectuals of the crowd.

FEDER-TAL, Karesh. *Stone of Peace.* Tr. from the Dutch by H. R. Kousbroek. Abelard-Schuman, 1961. (6-8) o.p.
A beautiful story of Arab-Israeli relationship with a universal plea for friendship and peace. David, a Moroccan Jew living in a southern kibbutz, becomes involved with an Arab boy in a plausible series of events. Their relationship draws in thieving Bedouins and a benevolent shiek. A reflection of attitudes, lore, and the essential differences in the characters of the Israelis and the Arabs add to the value of this well written, but not always well translated, book. Since there are no other stories that deal with this precise theme, it is unfortunate that this one is o.p.

FORMAN, James. *My Enemy, My Brother.* Meredith, 1969.
From the Warsaw Ghetto to a concentra-

tion camp, to a kibbutz, violence is evident in life as experienced by the teenage Daniel Baratz. A profound young adult novel, dealing with the issues of war and murder, Nazism and fraternity through the boy's doubts and questions.

————. *Traitors.* Farrar, 1968.
In Germany during the Nazi reign, a small band of "traitors" prevent the last-ditch Nazis from destroying Nuremberg. Noah, half-Jewish son of the local doctor, provides the source of conflict between two brothers whose patriotic loyalty is divided. Suspense and objective realism provide a moving experience.

HAMMRI, Laslo. *Flight to the Promised Land.* Tr. from the Swedish by Annabelle Macmillan. Harcourt, 1963. (6-8)
Early in the history of Israel, the community of dark-skinned, Biblical-type Jews of Yemen arrived in the land they believed was promised to them by the heritage of the Scriptures. They represented a mode of life incompatible with modern times, and still, nearly 20 years later, find the adjustment to sanitation, technology, and European habits an enigma and a fearsome thing. But some have learned Western ways quickly. Sholem Mizrachi, the young Yemenite hero thrust into 20th-Century Israel, learns the ways of kibbutz life, Arab aggression, and the thrills of modern miracles. This deeply stirring story gains in suspense as it moves to a military climax. A satisfying postscript adds veracity to an amazing and enlightening story of a culture within a culture.

HAUTZIG, Esther. *Endless Steppe: Growing up in Siberia.* Crowell, 1968.
A story of human triumph, this autobiography reveals the terrible years of deprivation as a "capitalist" family is torn from the beauty of its life and forced into labor in a Siberian gypsum mine.

HESKY, Olga. *Sequin Syndicate.* Dodd, 1969.
A mystery involving the Israeli secret service, a CIA agent, and a paunchy, incisive, folksy-type agent whose activities reveal relics of a 4000-year old culture.

HOBART, Lois. *Strangers Among Us.* Funk and Wagnall, 1957. (6-8)

An emotional but interesting Jewish family's move from New York City to a small New England town points up the contrast between two families. Alison becomes more involved than she intends as the interaction between the families develops social awareness and adjustment for all involved. Outdated concepts in medical research remove this book from the recommended list.

HOFF, Syd. *Irving and Me.* Harper, 1967. (6+)
Economic opportunity and healthier climate draw the Granicks from Brooklyn to a Florida community where Artie meets a new friend, Irving. Contrasts are drawn between Artie's family's way of life and the more Orthodox customs of Irving's family. The story line concerns Artie's conflict with himself and his friends, mirroring the rather typical insecurities of the nonathletic 13-year-old.

ISH-KISHOR, Judith. *Joel Is the Youngest.* Messner, 1954. (4-6) o.p.
Pedestrian descriptions and dialogue tell an unimaginative tale about Joel, the toughest in the family, who resents limited privileges because of his age. However, Grandpa Mendoza's rare and fascinating anecdotes tell about the roots of those segments of American Jewry who came from Spain, from Eastern Europe, and from Western European countries. This is a factual approach with no social overtones. Interesting references to Jews in American history occur in Grandpa's stories of such Jewish heroes as Luis de Torres, who gave us our English word for "turkey," and August Bondi, who was instrumental in the escape of John Brown.

KEIR, Leota Harris. *Freckle-Face Frankel.* Coward-McCann, 1959. (4-6) o.p.
A warm, funny, tender story of Debbie, the little tomboy who grows up overnight, a little unbelievably, but in a book that reflects Jewish family-community life with emphasis on social commitment rather than mere ritual. It is an unusually dimensional story, effective in depicting the upper middle-class Jewish family of contemporary America. Debbie is delightful; her family sensitive, cordial, typical, and multifaceted. The religious-secular conflict, however, is unrealistic.

KONIGSBERG, Elaine. *About the B'nai Bagels.* Atheneum, 1969. (4-8)
Mark's mother becomes the manager of his Little League team as her responsibility in her B'nai Brith chapter. Mark's big brother is drafted as the coach. This is one baseball story as concerned with family life, identification, trust, and loyalty as it is with the game itself. Mother Setzer is reminiscent of Tevye as she enjoys a running conversation with God. As a pattern of Jewish life, this is effective and humorous. From the point of view of realism, however, one might question the attitude of a 12-year-old boy whose play becomes a family matter.

KUPER, Jack. *Child of the Holocaust.* Doubleday, 1968 (8+)
The story of a young boy's desperate attempt to survive in Hitler's Poland after he is miraculously the only Jew not marched off from his village.

LEVIN, Yehuda Harry. *Miriam Comes Home: A Story of Our Israel Cousins.* L.C. Page, 1953. (6-8) o.p.
A poignant story of post-Nazi reconciliation, told against a background of kibbutz relationships and Israeli history and geography. The festival of Shevouth stands out as a seldom-told segment of an ancient tradition.

MUDRA, Marie. *Look Beyond Tomorrow.* Dutton, 1957. (8+) o.p.
A smoothly written junior novel about a Jewish boy's life in a city high school. The theme of acceptance is really one of self-acceptance as the key to friendship. Adjustment has many faces as Dave matures in his family relationships, his realization that problems are not exclusively his, and that what he considers a problem is often merely a fact of life. Jewish anti-Semitism is evident in Dave's attitude, as he misunderstands others' personal reactions to him, believing the cause to be his heritage rather than his habits. The religious content is well handled, informative yet casual. Misrepresentations, however, are found in a statement comparing Chanukah to Christmas; in a Freshie who works as a cantor in a temple; and in rather stereotyped allusions to 'swarthy skin,' a preference for cleanliness, and disdain for involvement in sweaty games.

OMER, Devorah. *Path Beneath the Sea.* Tr. from the Hebrew by Israel I. Taslitt. Sabra Books, dist. by Funk and Wagnalls, 1969. (5-9)
This novel is unusual on several counts. It is one of the earliest works of children's fiction to be imported from Israel. Because it is indigenous to that land, the story lacks the didacticism of "other-culture" fiction. Dealing with a young man's growing up, it actually has two distinct plots. The first tells how Taboul Cohen runs away from his roots and native Morocco, takes on a new name, and learns to understand himself in relation to others—a family story realistic in treatment and resolution. The second part, describing his involvement as a frogman in the Israeli-Arab Six Day War, offers the reader an exciting deep-sea story of our time. The format of the book is also notable; the eggshell-white of the paper and the type design seems startlingly different as the reader first observes the pages that were printed in Israel by Sabra Books.

NEVILLE, Emily Cheney. *Berries Goodman.* Harper, 1965. (6-8)
A story about boys, in which anti-Semitism is the main concern. The Goodman family is not Jewish but have lived in New York City amid many Jews. When they move to the suburbs, they find that Jews are heavily discriminated against. Berries, the protagonist, becomes confused and upset to realize the reaction works both ways—incrimination by the Gentile, suspicion from the Jew. No actual culture pattern emerges except through references made by the non-Jew; both subcultures reflect typical middle-class suburban values.

NURENBERG, Thelma. *My Cousin, the Arab.* Abelard-Schuman, 1965. (6-8)
The early stages of kibbutz life, when the pioneer spirit soared beyond the grim reality of scrubby land and rock-strewn hills, was also a time when chauvinistic fervor faded religion into an historic past. This complex story, with true-to-life characters, points up many of the conflicting elements of a new land where discrimination and antireligious cynicism exist as the result of a diverse, melting-pot society in which all have a common heritage but many attitudes and customs representing that heritage. The political problems of partition play an interesting game of see-saw in an Arab-Jewish love, while supporters of the British mandate reflect the impossibility of a British-Jewish relationship at a time when building the land had to be the main concern. An extremely helpful glossary completes a most rewarding reading experience both as recreational reading and as an excellent representation of Israel's early development.

RADIN, Gil. *False Start.* Harper, 1969.
Against the background of Jewish heritage in the days of the depression in New York, perceptive Rich Gould learns to cope with the weak and disappointing characters of the people around him. A realistic awareness tempered with compassion help him mature in judgment.

ROSE, Karen. *There Is a Season.* Follett, 1967. (8+)
An unusually sensitive and honest junior novel about the 15th summer of Katie, a wholesome, rather typical young Jewish girl. Crushes, kisses, and clashes help her discover the values necessary to her life. Her family, her religion, her community, her friendships, and most important of all, herself, in relation to those influences, take on a new perspective as she matures. Jamie, the Catholic boyfriend, serves as a pivot. The well-drawn characters of both Jamie and Katie offer revealing insight into human relationships and growth. If the solution appears pat to the mature reader, it will appeal to the younger because it is stunningly unexpected.

ROUNDS, Ruth. *It Happened to Hannah.* Dutton, 1954. (4-6) o.p.
An unlikely story of a Methodist girl who pretends she is Jewish in order to "belong" in her new school. Her experiences expose her, and the reader, to a panorama of Jewish heritage and, incidentally, some Catholic background as well. One might question such euphemisms as "a Star of David" to refer to a Jew. An unexplained anti-Semitic reaction which is never resolved, and an unnecessary return of a lottery prize, offer an unusual approach to an unsatisfactory story.

SACHS, Marilyn. *Peter and Veronica.* Doubleday, 1969.

A story of New York City during the late Thirties reveals rather typical conflicts over religious differences. A light touch avoids cliché.

SANDMEL, Frances Fox. *All on the Team*. Abingdon, 1959. (4-6)
A series of contrived situations to describe religious and social acceptance, using a small boy's interest in playing baseball as the plot. The book reads like a narrative travelogue of religious practices, but picks up toward the climax. As in *Freckle-Face Frankel,* the moral decision concerns a conflict between secular and High Holy Day activities. There is a blandness in the comparison between Jewish and Protestant religions, and an artificial attempt to point up similarities in the liturgy.

SANTALO, Lois. *Wind Dies at Sunrise*. Bobbs, 1965. (8+)
A novel of anti-Semitism and its effects on a Gentile girl who discovers her own ingenuousness as her best friend experiences discrimination. Del knows the life of a small mid-Western community where polite society, and the fact of no Jewish neighbors, mask the prejudiced attitudes she begins to realize exist. As she moves from junior college to a cosmopolitan campus, her Jewish friend, Jan, serves as a prism through which Del begins to realize the various hues of bias' in her environment. With Jan as the catalyst, Del sees herself and her world begin to change. The story is all too predictable in dialogue, description, and plot.

SATTLEY, Helen. *Shadow Across the Campus*. Dodd, 1957.
A junior novel about three coeds whose friendship is affected by racial prejudice as sorority rushing becomes an issue.

SIMON, Norah. *Ruthie*. Meredith, 1968. (6-8)
A sensitive study of a little girl of the Depression days in New York City, who stays with neighborhood friends during her mother's hospitalization and gains insight and understanding about herself and her heritage. This story lacks strong plot,

but substitutes a genuine religiosity and a focus on the language of the immigrant.

SOMMERFELT, Aimée. *Miriam*. Criterion, 1963. (6+)
Hanne and Miriam find themselves appreciating a true friendship until the Gestapo finally frightens Miriam Fraenkel's family and they attempt an escape to Sweden. They do not all succeed. Destruction, a horrible waste of life, deep sorrow, and racial prejudice tell a story of occupied Norway in 1941. This book is especially moving as Miriam experiences a realistic balance of tragedy and love.

WATSON, Sally. *Mukhtar's Children*. Holt, 1968.
Following the 1948 War of Liberation, an Arab leader faces conflict and rebellion as his village people begin to understand, and even envy, the enemy Israelis. Penetrating character studies and wry humor offer a depth of morality and cultures.

————. *Other Sandals*. Holt, 1966. (6+)
A study in human nature and psychological development set against a tricultural Israel; the agrarian kibbutz, the excitement of throbbing metropolitan Tel-Aviv, and an Arab village. This multidimensional story of two children who exchange environments depicts life and relationships built in the spirit of the pioneer. It is, on the one hand, the tale of an emotionally upset boy, tortured by his lameness, so it becomes a story of overcoming personal problems. It is also a story of prejudice that parallels the problems of our own country. Aside from being an excellent narrative, it portrays a realistic cultural picture.

————. *To Build a Land*. Holt, 1957.
Young European Jews pioneer in an Israeli children's kibbutz before the Arab-Israeli truce. There is fair handling of both sides of an issue that is exciting and moving. Many of the characters reappear in the sequel, *Other Sandals,* though the time is a generation later and the children in the later story are the offspring of marriages between the children who are introduced in this story.

WOUK, Herman. *City Boy; the Adventures of Herbie Bookbinder.* Doubleday, 1969 ed.

Written for adults in 1948, the story is appropriate for today's youth, presenting a realistic, yet hysterically funny, peek into summer camp through the experiences of an overweight and overprotected Herbie who schemes for social acceptance. A project to raise funds for the camp lead him to expose a plot to ruin his father's business.

The Plight of the Native American

Rey Mickinock

THERE ARE APPARENTLY three kinds of people in this hemisphere: those who believe Leif Erickson discovered America, those who think Cristoforo Colombo stumbled upon it, and those who know America was never really lost.

Obviously, most Americans of Scandinavian descent support the first view and those of Latin descent the second; the third is composed of those who wish their ancestors had told Leif, Cris, and a few dozen other explorers to "climb back into those disease-ridden, rat-infested tubs and go right back where you came from." Several million misconceptions of native Americans might have been avoided, not to mention the diseases the non-Indian brought with him. From Squanto's wiped-out Patuxets of New England, as reported in Willison's *Saints and Strangers* (Toronto, McLelland, 1945, o.p.), to the Ona, of whom three women remain, and the Yahgan, with only a handful left, both of Tierra del Fuego, as told in *National Geographic* (January 1971), many tribes were infected with measles, smallpox, and other diseases for which they had not previously needed immunity. From the Midwest to California, before and after the Civil War, the disease-spread continued. Quite a range for our conquering hero.

The misconceptions? These are spread by such children's "easy" books as Tillie S. Pine's *The Indians Knew* (McGraw, 1957), whose illustrator, Ezra Jack Keats, spoils a reasonably well done work by mixing hair styles of the Eastern tribes with the tipis of the West, the pottery of the Southwestern tribes with the travoix of the North. How is the Indian or non-Indian child to believe in the intelligence of the people with such drawings? Would you put a kilt on a Hollander? Or wooden shoes on a Scot? By the way, find a true Scot and ask him if he's "Scotch," then step back and listen, taking care there are no ladies present. Mr. Keats' "Willie" may be beautifully done but he seems to know as little as most whites about Indians. LeGrand Henderson is no better in his *Cats for Kansas* (Abington, 1948) illustrations when he shows a number of "braves" stretching a rope across the track to stop a train. His idea is most imaginative, but picturing four of the 15 men in the war bonnets of chiefs is unforgivable. No warrior who has counted as many coups as that would be involved in such labor. Nor does he identify any coup by nick, cut, or paint. Only such Chiefs as Red Cloud, or the Oglala Sioux, who had 80 coups in his lifetime, would be entitled to wear such a bonnet as Mr. Henderson puts on the four men.

Any Hollywood costume department would have known better. Four chiefs for 11 braves?

Perhaps, for understanding, it would be best to read such books as Mari Sandoz' *These Were the Sioux* (Hastings, 1961), reissued as a Dell paperback. *These Were the Sioux* ranges from the mother's gentle, foolproof method of teaching the 14 day-old not to cry, to the explanation of old He Dog who, at 92, told Miss Sandoz, "It is well to be good to women in the strength of our manhood because we must sit under their hands at both ends of our lives." Dr. Spock's readers could take lessons from Sioux children in the matter of crying, and of hunting begun at the age of four. Where the white man scoffed at the Indian woman's "drudgery" in carrying the bundles of dried meat and hides, managing the tipi, the children and the dogs in travel, and arrogantly reviled the "brave" who carried only his bow, arrows, and lance, any reasoning observer should know that man, in the days before the horse, had to walk ahead into the unknown, unencumbered and in command, if the group was to survive an ambush, or if he was to find a sudden opportunity for a kill of game that might provide many meals for his family, as he had been doing for thousands of years.

In marriage ceremonies, an "old one," usually female and related or borrowed from a family that had an "extra," was always expected to live in the couple's tipi, treated with respect as the bride's helper and teacher, who knew her place and was conveniently silent or absent when discretion required. The groom became a part of the bride's family, whatever the tribe. The practice still exists, though circumstances vary. Roger Talmadge, Chief Little Eagle, is a Sioux (he would prefer to be called the guttural, "Duh-koh-tah," their word for "allies"), is married to a Winnebago princess, and is Chief of the Winnebago tribe, at Wisconsin Dells. Fifteen tribes in three divisions make up the Dakota Nation.

Divorce was easy, but not taken lightly. If a woman wanted a divorce, she merely threw the man's possessions out of her lodge; if a man didn't want his woman anymore, he carved a giveaway stick and tossed it to whoever he thought might want her next, though the catcher had a choice until he or another decided to make it permanent. Divorce was fairly common, for nothing could make a Sioux, male or female, do anything he or she didn't want to do. Ann Landers may wish to make notes.

Biographic Lies, Authentic Fiction

In another of Miss Sandoz' books, *The Horsecatcher* (Westminster, 1957), readers can learn of the Cheyenne and also something of the neighboring tribes, acceping this as authentic fiction. It is somewhat different from Elizabeth Coatsworth's *The Last Fort* (Holt, 1952), in which she calls killing the enemy "counting coup," where in truth merely to *hit* the man with the hand, bow, or coup stick was the highest possible honor, while killing him usually counted as nothing unless he was touched first. In ABC-TV's *The Immortal* this January, Italian-American Sal Mineo, playing a pseudo-hip Navajo, spoke of counting coup on "the white guy," a practice unknown in that tribe, although he may have been joking about it, as something he had read. Any plains Indian could look at a man's headdress and tell all the brave deeds that man had done by the way of the feathers, or by the wolf tails, ermine, or weasel skins he wore according to the tenets of his tribal custom.

In John Bakeless' *Fighting Frontiersman* (Morrow, 1948, o.p.), Daniel Boone, when trailing Indians, is said "to know exactly what they were going to do next . . . would soon do thus-and-so . . . as invariably they did!" (p. 5); yet on page 164, Mr. Bakeless' Indians withhold the peace pipe from the whites at the "peace council" and easily trap Boone and nine others. Overlooking this internal inconsistency, one may note that, as an example of what is accepted as biographical "truth," at least as listed in Hannah Logasa's *Historical Non-Fiction* (McKinley, 1968, p. 158), this work may be interesting, it is still hardly factual. Mark Twain would have classed Bakeless with James Fenimore Cooper. It is incredible that such tales are accepted by young readers, degrading the race, not the man.

(And in the meanwhile, the fact is universally ignored that the Puritans— the *Puritans!*—first began the practice of scalping, in 1637, by offering rewards for scalps, with the ears attached, of their enemies, and that the English, by proclamation, reaffirmed it, in 1755!)

One may find more authenticity, again, in works of fiction. Evelyn Lampman's *Half-Breed* (Doubleday, 1967) is a story of the Crow Indians and the white mountain men who sometimes lived among them, married, and perhaps tiring of the settled life, left the tribe, not always taking their wives and children along. It is sincere, deep, with courage, truth, and shortcomings intermixed according to the people involved. Mrs. Lampman writes of the problems of "half-breeds," living with the non-Indian, the bigotry of all ignorant people, and the quiet intelligence of family love.

The prologue to the paperback edition of C. Fayne Porter's *The Battle of the 1000 Slain* (Scholastic, Starline School Book Service, 1969, abridged from the 1964 Chilton title *Our Indian Heritage: Profiles of 12 Great Leaders*); should be most enlightening to a reader unfamiliar with the contributions made to American culture by Indians—among these more than half the cash farm crops grown, all the medicinal herbs known to man, and many novelty items sometimes counted as staples. At the circus or ballpark, the vendor hawks his wares, "Popcorn, Peanuts, Crackerjacks, Chewing gum!"—all first used by the Indian. Only the wasted containers were invented by the white man. The starving Pilgrims kept starving in the midst of plenty, refusing to eat the clams the Wampanoags tried to persuade them to dig, in 1620. The cahuchi, the "weeping tree," furnished balls and other playthings for Indians centuries ago. Today it is cultivated by Firestone.

The Truth about Custer

In the matter of Custer, the gathering of misinformation about him, his motives, his orders, his behavior, and the result of the battle and related skirmishes have been done to death. When the lie is big enough and told often enough, it is believed. A careful analysis should reveal that Custer's men and all the Indians involved were victims of "progress," something not much contested until recently. No matter that the financial panic of 1873 delayed these events for three years by stopping the Northern Pacific railroad at Bismarck, named for that famous leader in an attempt to bring German money into its coffers; no matter that Custer's 1874 expedition to verify the Black Hills gold discoveries drove thousands of reservation Indians up into the Rosebud country and that even his great exaggerations brought no new investors for that railroad. No matter that this predecessor of the Burlington Northern brought about the political necessity of driving the western tribes from their homelands. No matter that Custer tried to attack a minimum of 4000 warriors, or that, if he had approached the three miles of tipis as he tried to, he would have had to face as many as 10,000 men, that there may have been 15,000 Sioux, Cheyenne, Arapaho, and others, led by dozens of "Generals," many of whom had already bloodied various army units. No matter that he lost only 225 men, which may have been only because that was all he had at that particular place. No matter that it was another unit of his Seventh Cavalry that mowed down the women, children, and old men at Wounded Knee in 1890. It only matters that the white man's greed for money and land caused the many deaths, and the ensuing loss of the homelands of the western Indians. Ecologists were a hundred years late.

Read Mari Sandoz' *The Battle of the Little Bighorn* (Lippincott, 1966), the nonfiction account not colored by any admiration for "Longhair"; or Ralph K. Andrist's *The Long Death* (Collier-Macmillan, 1969); which tells in detail of the short-haired, saberless Custer and some of his political problems as only an editor of American Heritage can; or Vine Deloria, Jr.'s *Custer Died for Your Sins* (Avon, pa. 1970), the new Indian best-seller; or the 93-page National Park Services' handbook on the Custer Battlefield National Monument ($1.25, U. S. Department of the Interior) with Robert Utley's text and Leonard Baskin's "very non-G.I." drawings, all of which prove whose "last stand" it really was.

Other books of verified accuracy and intelligent perspective would include—

Betty Baker's *Walk the World's Rim,* and *Killer-of-Death* (Harper, 1965, 1963)

Christie Harris' *Raven's Cry* and *Once Upon a Totem* (Atheneum, 1966, 1963)

Florence Means' *Our Cup is Broken,* (Houghton, 1969)

Mary Warren's *Walk in My Moccasins* (Westminster, 1966)

Mari Sandoz' *The Story Catcher* (Westminster, 1963)

Hal Borland's *When the Legends Die* (Lippincott, 1963)

Thomas Berger's *Little Big Man* (Dial, 1964), probably better known as a film

Dan Cushman's *Stay Away, Joe* (Stay Away Joe Publishers, 1968).

A good policy might be to check out the particular author first, then read the works in the area desired. Most public libraries can produce the greater share of these. In spite of many good books by some Eastern authors, generally avoid those who "live and love in New York" and claim to write about our "noble" American natives. It is a verifiable fact that there are fewer Indians east of the Mississippi river than Sitting Bull directed at the council preceding the Custer episode, which gets it down to less than 15,000. There are even fewer with

knowledge much better than the Hong Kong tribes, whose souvenirs are everywhere. New York Public can provide much authentic material, but the Indian mind is difficult to capture on paper, especially for one who may never have been beyond 125th Street.

In *Textbooks and the American Indian,* a 1970 publication of the American Indian Historical Society, 32 Indian scholars, students, and native historians effectively take apart over 300 books used as texts in public, private, and even Indian schools. Not one could be approved as a dependable source of knowledge about the history and culture of the Indian people in America. To repeat, *not one!* Yet, all these books are currently being used in our schools. A defective automobile is recalled. Ralph Nader, where are you?

On page two, *Textbooks and the American Indian* presents a copy of the "Memorial and Recommendations of the Grand Council Fire of American Indians," which tells yesterday as it is today, taking the white man to task for unfair books, unfair attitudes, such as "when the white man was victorious, it was a battle; when the Indian won, it was a massacre," and "If the Custer battle was a massacre, what was Wounded Knee?" The Memorial was given to the Mayor of Chicago in 1927 and printed in the Congressional Record on May 11, 1928. Forty-three years have had little real result.

It is said that the Indian doesn't talk much, that he has little to say to the white man. The Indian talks only when he wants to, sometimes says only what he thinks the white man wishes to hear, says Fayne Porter in the epilogue of *The Battle of the 1000 Slain.* Yet the day is even-changing, and today's Indian is also changing, but carefully selecting the ancient ways to cling to, and only some of the new, rather than making any blanket acceptance of the non-Indian way. In 1868, Chief Red Cloud told his people how to become wealthy like the white man: "You must begin anew and put away the wisdom of your fathers. You must lay up food and forget the hungry. When your house is built, your storeroom filled, then look around for a neighbor whom you can take advantage of, and seize all he has." (This is from Mr. Andrist's book, on page 134.) Yet the Indian cannot shed his religion or his heritage. The mixing of the ancient and the new is called "adjustment," and it can be an eerie experience for a tourist to attend a western movie in, say Battleford, Saskatchewan, and slowly come to realize that some "Indians" are being applauded and some cowboys or cavalrymen jeered at, that the silences and cheers are coming in places he is not used to, and that not all the warwhoops are on the screen, even if the movie isn't in "3-D" and "surround-sound." May Cherokee Burt Reynolds make as many movies as did Iron Eyes and Eddie Little Sky, for they were uncountable.

To quote from *Textbooks and the American Indian:* "Everyone has the right to his opinion. A person has also the right to be wrong. But a textbook has no right to be wrong, or to lie, evade the truth, falsify history, or insult and malign a whole race of people. That is what the textbooks do."

"There is a difference between a book for general readership, and one accepted for classroom use. In the first case, the individual has a choice, and this choice we must protect. The student has no choice. He is compelled to study from an approved book. In this case, we have a right to insist upon truth, accuracy, and objectivity."

Estelle Thomas in *Gift of Laughter* (Westminster, 1967) gives this line to one of her Navajos: "Washing*tone* [The government was always called that] is inclined to stare out over the Big Waters too much."

Whether it be a textbook in the field of government, history, geography, or whatever, a television program of any kind, a movie, western or otherwise, a radio or newspaper story, or even somebody's latest attempt at fiction, let us all "Pass . . . up . . . the forked tongue, please!"

Postscript

If anyone has to make a choice of what to read, and that person has a real desire to learn of Indian attitudes, the Indian sense of reality, let him begin with Vine Deloria, Jr.'s recommendations (all of these have been previously mentioned): Dan Cushman's *Stay Away, Joe,* Hal Borland's *When the Legends Die,* and Thomas Berger's *Little Big Man.*

And end with mine:

Ralph K. Andrist's *The Long Death,* Mari Sandoz' *These Were the Sioux* and *The Battle of the Little Bighorn,* Vine Deloria, Jr.'s *Custer . . .,* Estelle Thomas' *Gift of Laughter,* and Mary Warren's *Walk in My Moccasins. Custer Died for Your Sins* is the single choice for anyone who will read only one; although the Indian favorite is *Stay Away, Joe.*

And do you know what the Indian used to call America before the white man came? "Ours."

Me—Gway—Ch (Thank you.)

A Feminist Look at Children's Books

Feminists on Children's Media

IS THE PORTRAYAL of females in children's books sexist? That is, are girls and women assigned only traditional female roles and personalities? And when the female foot fails to fit that often too-tight shoe, is the girl or woman then seen as an unfortunate, troubled human being?

These questions were the basis of a group effort to scrutinize some of the more highly praised children's books. In our view, a non-sexist portrayal would offer the girl reader a positive image of woman's physical, emotional, and intellectual potential—one that would encourage her to reach her own full personhood, free of traditionally imposed limitations.

In selecting books to examine, we consulted a number of influential lists. These were the *Notable Books of 1969* (American Library Association), the Child Study Association's annual recommendations for that same year, and the Newbery Award winners.

It was a shock to discover almost immediately that relatively few of the books on these lists even feature female characters—let alone what we would consider *positive* female characters. Of all 49 Newbery Award

winners, books about boys outnumbered books about girls by about three to one. On that score, the years have brought little improvement. The ALA list for 1969 gave us a ratio of over two to one.

The Child Study Association list for the same year proved more difficult to analyze. It is very long, divided into innumerable categories, and many of the books can't yet be found in the libraries. However, we made a separate check of several categories. Under the heading of "Boys and Girls" we found a male to female ratio of two to one. Under "Growing Up" the ratio was over three to one. And "Sports," of course, like certain bars we could formerly name, was 100 percent male. The rest of the book list may not follow the pattern of this sampling, but suspicion runs high!

The thoughtful introduction to the Child Study Association list makes the following statement: The books a child reads "should not shield him from knowledge of destructive forces in the world, but rather help him to cope with them." We agree, for the most part. But why does the sentence read "shield *him*" and "help *him*"?

Sexism is such a destructive force in the world, that we feel the implicit sexism is this sentence should not be overlooked.

The introduction states also that a book's "possible emotional and intellectual impact on a young reader" must be considered. Right on! Not even a problem of gender there. The CSA continues: "from its inception, it has been aware of the mental health aspects of reading and asks that books for children present basically honest concepts of life, positive ethical values, and honest interpersonal relationships."

We ask no more than that. The CSA has clearly been struggling to encourage greater sensitivity toward racism in books for children. If only their future book selections could be made with an equally growing sensitivity to the impact of sexism! Many of the present selections fail to realize the promise of their own introduction. The list is guilty of sexism—if only through indifference.

Of course, a greater sensitivity to sexism would greatly curtail the current lists of recommended children's books—at least for the next few years. Yet, a scrupulous attitude on the part of prestigious organizations would surely serve powerfully in raising the general feminist consciousness of the children's book world, making forever obsolete Eve Merriam's recent and accurate comment that "sex prejudice is the only prejudice now considered socially acceptable." Habit dies hard.

We'd like to apologize for seeming to pick on CSA. It's just that such a praiseworthy introduction deserved attention in terms of its implications for the female image. Nor were we being picky in our examination of specific books: checking the prevalence of so virulent a disease as sexism requires the isolation of even potential carriers.

What would we like to see in children's books? What were our criteria? We wanted to see girl readers encouraged to develop physical confidence and strength without the need to fear any corresponding loss of "femininity." We would have liked to see the elimination of all those tiresome references to "tomboys." Why can't a girl who prefers baseball to ballet simply be a girl who prefers baseball to ballet?

Many women have to—or simply prefer to—earn a living. Can't we encourage girls to find satisfaction and fulfillment in work, and lay forever the suspicion that work outside the home for a *woman* is primarily proof of her inability to love a man, or to land a sufficiently lucrative one? Women do study seriously, work with enjoyment—or at least pride in their competence—get promoted, and (of course) fight sexism at work and in their families in order to progress. Let's show them as no less "feminine," despite the assertiveness and firm sense of self required in this untraditional role.

Margaret Mead has written that "man is unsexed by failure, woman by success." That's another brutal truth we'd like to see changed. And while we're about it, let's not overlook the fact that boys, too, are denigrated and cramped by sexism. Our current rigid role definitions require that a boy be all that a girl should not be: unafraid, competent at "male" jobs, strong. A weeping boy is a "sissy." Words like "sissy"—and "hero," too—should be dissected and exposed for the inhuman demands they make on growing boys. Children's books could help.

We object to a woman's being defined by the man she marries, or the children she bears, or the father she once obeyed. Let's see women who are people in their own right—

independent of such compensatory affiliations. And if a woman doesn't want children, or even a husband, must this be seen as peculiar? Why not encourage girls in a search for alternate life styles? Give a girl all the possible options you give a boy for her future life choices, all his freedom to inquire and explore and achieve. Her options don't have to be slanted toward certain currently socially imposed preferences.

There are books on superwomen. Okay. Superwomen do exist. But many more books are needed on women who simply function very well and freely wherever they choose—or are forced—to apply their abilities.

We are bitterly tired of seeing depictions of the woman as castrator. Even a well-known writer, whose portrayal of girls we frequently admire, slipped badly in some recent picture books. In one of these, the mother reproves her son for spilling the mud he is playing with—even though the scene is outdoors! In another, little sister (and we know where she learned *her* lesson) reproves brother for accidentally spilling paint off his easel. Little girls are as capable of making a casual mess and as freely lost in creative play as little boys. A picture book that does that beautifully is *Rain Rain Rivers* by Uri Shulevitz (Farrar, 1969) which we were delighted to find on both the ALA and CSA lists. (We were as pleased to find the two previously mentioned books ignored by both lists.)

And when, as must sometimes happen if books portray real life, there is an overcontrolling or too-bossy woman, she should not be made a fool or villain. A little understanding—of her problem, her frustration at not being allowed to play an equal role in her family or her world, and her consequent misuse of energy to project her ideas and ego through the lives of others—is long overdue.

How about books showing more di-

vorced and single-parent families? And, for heaven's sake, every divorced or widowed mother does not solve her problems through remarriage—or even wish to do so. (Few do, you know!) Maybe she can start on that career she never had—and discover a new concept of herself. The difficulties and the loneliness, are real, as are the child-care problems. But let the woman find a new self-reliance in fighting her own battles—and joy in winning at least some of them.

There is also the question of language. No more automatic use of "he" to mean "child," or "mankind" to mean "humankind." If at first the alternatives seem forced—and they will—they won't sound that way for long.

Despite our criticism of socially assigned roles, we don't mean to diminish or ignore the mother or housewife. She is often a strong, wonderfully rich human being. Her role can be vital, and sometimes she finds satisfaction in it. But let's not insist on that as *her* role. Men can also cope skillfully with household tasks—and not necessarily look for a woman or daughter to take them off the hook.

SEXIST BOOKS

The books we read—most from the lists mentioned earlier—fell, or were pushed by our merciless analysis, into several categories. One, plain and simple, was the Sexist Book, in which girls and women are exclusively assigned traditional female roles—although the material may, unhappily, be fairly true to life.

We were forcibly struck by the purposeful sexist propaganda between the covers of some of the recommended children's books.

Young women who have found it an uphill struggle to identify with the popular female image will recognize it as propaganda—and not simply as a natural reflection of life. Unfortunately the girl reader is not yet so experienced. Books that outline a traditional background role for women, praising their domestic accomplishments, their timidity of soul, their gentle appearance and manners, and—at the same time—fail to portray initiative, enterprise, physical prowess, and genuine intellect deliver a powerful message to children of both sexes. Such books are a social poison.

Take, for a horrible example, the attitude exemplified in the following line: "Accept the fact that this is a man's world and learn how to play the game gracefully." Those words fell from the lips of a *sympathetic* male character in Irene Hunt's 1967 Newbery winner *Up a Road Slowly* (Follett, 1966). Or take this juicy bit from the 1957 winner *Miracles on Maple Hill* by Virginia Sorenson (Harcourt, 1956).

> For the millionth time she was glad she wasn't a boy. It was all right for girls to be scared or silly or even ask dumb questions. Everybody just laughed and thought it was funny. But if anybody caught Joe asking a dumb question or even thought he was the littlest bit scared, he went red and purple and white. Daddy was even something like that, old as he was.

Does that passage describe real life? Indeed it does! But a good book for children should comment and leave the child feeling something is wrong here. This one does not. In fact, we voted it our supreme example of the most thoroughly relentless type of sexism found in children's literature. The girl, Marly, never overcomes her hero worship of brother Joe or her comparative inferiority. And it certainly would have been relevant to explore the toll that maintaining hero status takes on Joe's character.

Such perfect examples, of course, are not the rule. But there was a surplus of books whose thesis might seem less obvious, but whose refrain was predictably the same. A little girl in the 1955 Newbery winner *The Wheel on the School* (Harper, 1954) asks her boy playmate: "Can I go, too?" And the response is "No! Girls are no good at jumping. It's a boy's game." Meindert DeJong leaves it at that—and another eager little girl reader is squelched.

Those fictional girls who join the prestigious ranks of male adventurers often do so at the expense of other members of their sex. And small wonder, the tomboy-turned-token-female is simply the other side of the coin. The message is clear: if a girl wishes to join the boys in their pranks and hell-raising, or to use her imagination and personality in leading them, she renounces all claim to supposedly feminine characteristics—tears and fears and pink hair ribbons. The line between traditionally assigned sex roles is drawn sharp and clear. The girl who crosses that line is forced to desert her sex rather than allowed to act as a spokeswoman for a broader definition.

Take *Lulu's Back in Town* (Funk & Wagnall, 1968). The proof provided by author Laura Dean to show Lulu's final acceptance by the boys is the clubhouse sign: "FOR BOYS ONLY. No Girls Allowed. (Except Lulu.)" This is seen by the author, who unfortunately happens to be a woman, as a satisfactory ending. But our committee was not so pleased. (Except to find that neither ALA nor CSA had listed it.)

COP-OUTS

The Cop-Out Book is often the most insidious. At its worst, it promises much and delivers nothing. But the better ones are the most infuriating, for often they are only a step away from being the exact kind of literature we'd like to see for girls *and* boys *about* girls. The actual cop-out may be only a crucial line, a paragraph, the last chapter. But somewhere a sexist compromise is made, somewhere the book adjusts to the stereotyped role of woman, often for the sake of social pressure and conformity. The compromise brings with it a change, and this change is not only disturbing, but often distorts the logical development of the character herself. Suddenly her development is redirected—or, rather, stunted.

The many Cop-Out Books we found are probably a fair reflection of the social uncertainties and inner conflicts of writers, publishers, and reviewers in our sexist society.

Caddie Woodlawn by Carol R. Brink (Macmillan, 1935) is a Newbery winner. Not a recent one, but still extremely popular. Caddie is a young pioneer girl, allowed to run free with her brothers. She is happy and strong in her so-called tomboy role. Though her mother pressures her to become more of a "lady," the reader feels serenely certain that Caddie will remain her own person. Alas, as the book draws to a close, Caddie's father pleads: "It's a strange thing, but somehow we expect more of girls than of boys. It is the sisters and wives and mothers, you know, Caddie, who keep the world sweet and beautiful. . . ." Thus subdued, she joins the insipidly depicted girls at the weaving loom. True, the boys do ask her to teach them how to weave. Apparently they may choose to join women at their work, but no longer may Caddie choose to run free in the woods. And we are left feeling cheated. Why should it be the *right* choice for her obediently to join the "sweet and beautiful" women of the world on their pedestals? Why shouldn't she continue to struggle for a life in which she might fulfill some inner potential?

The linking of a girl's growing up to the abandoning of her "tomboy" ways is a depressingly frequent theme in these books. As a stage in growing up, tomboy behavior appears to be acceptable. But the girl must in the end conform to more socially approved behavior. In a widely used bibliography compiled by Clara Kirchner in 1966 entitled *Behavior Patterns in Children's Books* there is an entire section called "From Tomboy to Young Woman." Here are two random descriptions:

A Girl Can Dream by Betty Cavanna (Westminster, 1948): Loretta Larkin, tops in athletics but poor in social graces and jealous of a classmate who shines socially, finds out that being "just a girl" can be fun.

Billie by Esphyr Slobodkina (Lothrop, 1959): Billie, who wore faded jeans and played boys' games because she didn't like being a girl, came to think differently after she took ballet lessons to limber up a sprained ankle.

These books fit into the following categories: Womanliness, Growing Up, and Popularity.

Young readers of such grievous cop-outs are forced to believe that the spunk, individuality, and physical capability so refreshingly portrayed in tomboy heroines must be surrendered when girls grow up—in order to fit the passive, supposedly more mature image of a young woman. But where is that earlier energy to be spent? Is depression in the adult woman perhaps linked to the painful suppression of so many sparks of life?

In a way we could call the Cop-Out Book the "co-op" book, for it permits the tomboy reader to believe she can pass comfortably over into that other world at a safely future date. Real life is rarely like that.

A new book recommended on both the ALA and the CSA lists is Constance Green's *A Girl Called Al* (Viking, 1969). The main character comes across as a nonconformist who truly enjoys her individuality, and throughout most of the book she eschews traditional female worries—how she looks, hooking boyfriends, etc. Wonderful. But the ending is a neat little all-American package. Al gets thin, gets pretty, and now she will be popular. All these sudden switches hit the reader in the last few pages. Her pigtails make room for a feminine hairdo. Her closest friend explains: "Her mother took her to the place she gets her hair done and had the man wash and set Al's hair, and now she wears it long with a ribbon around it. It is very becoming, my mother says. She is right. But I miss Al's pigtails. I wanted her to wear it this way but now that she does I'm kind of sorry. She looks older and different, is all I know."

Again, we are led to believe that another character in our long line of individual heroines will conform to the role society has rigidly defined for her. We find it hard to buy the sudden change in Al. And we also miss the pigtails.

Sometimes it is the focus of a book that makes it a cop-out. When we read the 1959 Newbery winner, Elizabeth Speare's *The Witch of Blackbird Pond* (Houghton Mifflin, 1958), we praised Kit's independent spirit, her rejection of bigoted values, and her truly striking courage at a time when women were burned for witchcraft. From a feminist standpoint, the book is marred only by the plot's revolving around the standard question: "Whom shall Kit marry?" In too many books we find the male character worrying about *what* shall he be—while the female character worries about *who* shall he be.

Only a few hairs are out of place in *Next Door to Xanadu* by Doris Orgel (Harper, 1969), also listed by ALA

and CSA. The main character faces the too-often very real hatred of preteen boys toward girls. She meets it with strength, earning respect. The only boy-crazy girl in the book is deemphasized. But one scene allows our society's pervasive sexism to come shining through.

At a going-away party for one of the girls, a woman parades as a fortune-teller. "She took out a bowl, put it on the table, filled it with all sorts of strange little things. Then she said 'Who among you dares to delve into the secrets the future holds in store?'" Here were the fortunes of the girls: The girl who pulled out two safety pins would be "the mother of a fine pair of twins." Chalk meant another would be a teacher. The one who picked a little sack of soil would be "a farmer's wife." One pulled a penny: she would be very rich. One picked a little plastic boy doll and she would meet a "fine young man." "Great happiness" was in store for the one who got a bluebird's feather. When one of the girls pulled out a jack, the fortune teller chanted: "Butcher, baker, candlestick-maker; tailor, sailor, teacher, preacher; doctor, lawyer, carpenter, smith—she would have kept it up, but Helen guessed it. Betsy would marry a jack-of-all-trades."

Not *be* a jack-of-all-trades, but *marry* one. Not *be* a farmer, but be a farmer's wife. The only vocation predicted was that of teacher. Unfortunately, fortune-tellers will be like that, until we have feminist fortune-tellers. That would certainly bring brighter futures.

At the risk of carping, we felt that such a fine book as *A Wrinkle in Time* by Madeline L'Engle (Farrar, 1962), the 1963 Newbery winner, had a hint of acceptance of woman's second-class status. This is almost the only science fiction book in which a girl is the main character. We even find a mother who is a scientist, perhaps one of the only scientist moms in juvenile fiction. But why did father have to be a super scientist, topping mom by a degree or two?

POSITIVE IMAGES

Happily, if not of course, there are some books for children which show female characters in flexible, diverse roles. They allow for character development beyond the stereotype, and do not disappoint us in the end.

At first we tried calling these "Non-Sexist." But we found many books were not precisely either Sextist or Cop-Out, though somehow they did not quite fit our exacting feminist standards, usually because they did not deal with the questions they posed in a sufficiently clear, real, and affirmative way. The rare book that did succeed, even in this, is our Positive-Image Book.

Certainly, these categories overlap a bit. *A Wrinkle in Time* really belongs among the Positive-Image Books. We just couldn't resist putting down papa's degrees. Unfair, we admit, because of the especially fine, honest relationship between Calvin (the boy who is a friend, as opposed to Boy Friend) and the girl protagonist. They respect each other's heads, and his ego does not stand in the way of her saving the day with an act of courage that rescues her little brother from it. We also applauded the image of the mother as a brilliant scientist who instills pride in her children.

Another Newbery we salute is the 1961 winner, *Island of the Blue Dolphins* by Scott O'Dell (Houghton Mifflin, 1960), one of the rare books showing a girl with strong physical skills. She kills wild dogs, constructs weapons, kills a giant tentacled sea fish, and hauls a six-man canoe by herself. The Indian girl protagonist, Karana, spends 18 years alone on a bleak and lonely island. And there we are indeed tempted to ask why such a marvelous heroine can only be encountered alone on an island—and never in the midst of society?

While on the subject of positive images, there is a new book we hope will appear on the 1970 recommended lists. *Rufus Gideon Grant* by Leigh Dean (Scribners, 1970) is about a boy, but we were taken by the following reference to a woman: "There inside this magazine was this lady, climbing giant trees and playing with wild chimpanzees. . . . " And Rufus asks: "Can a boy be a zoologist?"

If we had time we would also like to discuss such essentially positive-image books as *Strawberry Girl* by Lois Lenski (Lippincott, 1945), *From the Mixed-Up Files of Mrs. Basil E. Frankweiler* by E. L. Konigsburg (Atheneum, 1967), Vera and Bill Cleaver's *Where the Lilies Bloom* (Lippincott, 1969), and *Pippi Longstocking* by Astrid Lindgren (reissued in paper by Viking, 1969). Padding our Positive-Image list a bit we might add commendable classics like Lewis Carroll's *Alice in Wonderland* (first published in 1865), *Anne of Green Gables* by Lucy M. Montgomery (Grosset & Dunlap, 1908), and *Rebecca of Sunnybrook Farm* by Kate Douglas Wiggin (Macmillan, 1903). Of course there are some positive books that escaped our notice, just as some of the negative ones may have slipped by, but we wanted to cover a fourth and extra category that seems to overlap all the others.

ESPECIALLY FOR GIRLS

This category appears on a number of publishers' lists and on lists of recommended books. It's called "especially for girls." The reason advanced by librarians and publishers for having such a category at all is that while girls are perfectly happy to read "boys' " books, no self-respecting boy will read books about girls.

In our male-dominated society, unfortunately, this is probably true. But listing a separate group of books for girls provides boys with a list of books *not* to read, further polarizing the sexes.

There seems only one possible justification for a separate category of books for girls: to spot and recommend those books which, according to our highest, most stringent feminist standards are not sexist. Pursuing this logic, when children's literature no longer supports sexism, there will no longer be any reason to list books "especially for girls."

The current lists of girls' books promoted by publishers, show a preponderance of stories about love, dating, and romance. And there are the companion books about young girls with problems like shyness, overweight, glasses, acne, and so on, that are supposed to interfere with romance. Certainly, problems facing young girls should be dealt with in the books they read, but we resent the implication forced on young girls that romance is the only fulfilling future for them. Boys, too, are involved in romance, but their books are about other things.

The lists for girls also include career books about nurses, secretaries, ballet dancers, stewardesses. Why not more female doctors? Bosses? Pilots? Aquanauts? Present books simply reinforce the sex roles imposed by society—and even then virtually all the careers end in a cop-out. When the girl marries she gives up the career. But *must* marriage and career be mutually exclusive? These books are justified by their publishers in terms of the market—they are meant to sell rather than to edify. We happen to believe that career books that edify will also sell, and far more lastingly, as women gain struggle for their freedom.

But what about those lists of currently recommended books that *are* intended to edify? In 1969, for example, the Child Study Association listed eight books "Especially for Girls." Of all of these, we were disheartened to find that only one was free—or almost free—of sexism. Two more were Cop-Out books. The rest were middling to very bad.

Let's start with the best. *The Motoring Millers* by Alberta Wilson Constant (Crowell, 1969) not only shows delightful girls and women behaving responsibly and delightfully—and doing many things the men do, but the question of sex roles is specifically aired. In the story, the winner of an auto race turns out to be a young girl. When the wife of a college president says to her: "I want you to know that I am highly in favor of your driving in this race. Women should advance their cause in every field," the winner replies, "I didn't think about that. I just love to drive. Taught myself on our one-cylinder Trumbull when I was ten." We welcome both reactions.

Two more books on this list, *A Girl Called Al* and *Next Door to Xanadu*, have already been described above as Cop-Outs, though we did consider them both *almost* commendable. To those three acceptable books, we would also add *Julie's Decision* by Rose A. Levant (Washburn, 1969) except that we were disturbed by what seemed a paternalistic white attitude especially inappropriate in a book about a black girl.

But, after these titles, the CSA girls' list deteriorates into sexism. It is shocking to find "recommended for girls" a book like *The Two Sisters* by Honor Arundel (Meredith, 1969), which not only reinforces the stereotype of girls as romantic, clothes-crazy, and spendthrift, but whose moral says that, when all is said and done, love is a woman's proper vocation and her future ought to be subordinated to her husband's. The young heroine in *The Two Sisters* has just told her father that she may abandon her university scholarship to follow her husband who has gone off to find a better job in another city. Her father says gently: "Geoff's quite right to be ambitious and you're right not to stand in his way. A man who doesn't get a chance to fulfill his ambition makes a terrible husband." It doesn't occur to either that a woman who sacrifices her potential can also end up making a terrible wife.

John Rowe Townsend's *Hell's Edge* (Lothrop, 1969) is just as bad. The motherless teenage heroine cooks all the meals and does the housework for her teacher-father, whose domestic ineptitude is paraded as one of his endearing qualities. A pair of sisters in the book are set up with mutually exclusive stereotyped female traits—and then shot down for them. One is described as a "half-wit" for being concerned with looks and clothes; the other sister, a bookworm, is denigrated for not caring about her looks or clothes. Damned if you do and damned if you don't.

In another CSA recommendation, the boys in the family are considered more important than the girls, even though the book is supposedly for girls. (Well, it happens in real life too!) The name of that prize is *One to Grow On* by Jean Little (Little, Brown, 1969).

In *A Crown for a Queen* by Ursula Moray Williams (Meredith, 1969), the plot revolves around—get ready—a *beauty* contest with the boys as judges! The most memorable (and most offensive) line occurs when the heroine, Jenny, finally gets the beauty crown. As we might predict, she "never felt happier in her life." This is scarcely the positive female image we'd be looking for, even if we could all be beauty queens.

As our consciousness of "woman's place" changes, our recommendations of books for girls must change. As must books themselves. Eventually, we will have no more need for any list recommended "Especially for Girls."

Girls Grow Up to Be Mommies: A Study of Sexism in Children's Literature

John Stewig and Margaret Higgs

SPECIALISTS in children's literature have in recent years been euphoric over the advances made in books for children. While there are always a few unexpected clinkers to stumble over, the general quality is high. Books are available on a variety of topics undreamed of five years ago. Technological advances in printing have made it possible, quickly and cheaply, to produce visually sophisticated books, which delight both the artist who designed them and the child who reads or looks at them. It is probably safe to say that more children are in contact with better books than ever before.

Yet, suddenly, with an abrasive intensity which staggers us, we are made aware that much of this literature is considered dross. Those of us involved—from editors who choose the manuscripts to librarians who buy the books—are indicted for a sin of commission on the children to whom we are responsible. The charge? Sexism—the portrayal of women in undesirable and demeaning roles. Spokeswomen for liberation groups tell us emphatically that children are exposed to books which help mold their ideas of women's roles, albeit unconsciously, so that little girls grow up with a view of themselves as second-class citizens, destined only for motherhood.

Those who rail against such literature

are aware of the figures which indicate that 42.6 percent of the women in this country are employed outside the home, with almost 40 percent of these working in professional level jobs. Are childrens' books reflective of this situation, or do they in fact present distorted views of women's roles, so that boys and girls perceive girls' ultimate destiny as motherhood?

Opinions and Research

Recent years have seen numerous articles on the topic of sexism in children's literature, but these require careful reading. Often details concerning samples used, methods of investigation, as well as inclusiveness and accuracy of reporting leave something to be desired. Many publications from various groups, as well as newspaper, popular magazine, and professional journal articles are long on rhetoric and exhortation, citing "outrageous" examples, culled selectively from sources which may or may not be identified. Noticeably lacking in a number of these is information on the number of books investigated, the actual number of women portrayed, and percentages and types of role presentations involved. The researcher interested in an unbiased understanding of the actual conditions prevailing in children's books must pick his or her way carefully through the brambled underbrush of opinion to reach the firm ground of fact.

Of course, popular journalism often minimizes or ignores specific details and factual data. "What Are Little Girls Made Of" (*Parents Magazine*, February 1972) examines 15 major reading series, but neglects to mention the names of the series. Such articles, because of their lack of substantive data, remain rhetorical. Unfortunately, even articles in the more scholarly journals sometimes lack concrete and up-to-date information. "The Role of Male and Female in Children's Books" by Mary Key (*Wilson Library Bulletin*, October 1971) refers to a 1962 study and recommends a book based on a 1946 study. The first can only be considered dated, and the second is purely of historical interest. (Key does report substantive data on four elementary reading series, and she also indicts three trade books by name.)

"Sex Roles in Early Reading Books" by Ramona Frasher and Annabelle Walker (*The Reading Teacher*, May 1972) is an admirable examination of some 700 stories from reading textbooks. The authors list the series included. But, even here, the critical reader will note that one series is over ten-years-old.

Despite the foregoing, there are numerous published studies which are of considerable value. For comprehensive coverage, readers are referred to *Women Studies Abstracts* (Quarterly, P.O. Box 1, Rush, N.Y. 14543), an extremely valuable quarterly abstracting periodical articles related to many facets of the study of women. Among some articles of special note are those by Aileen Pace Nilson and Lenore J. Weitzman. In "Women in Children's Literature" (*College English*, May 1971), Nilson's careful research is evident in her reporting on a sample of 80 books—the Caldecott winners and runners-up. Her results are reported in objective terms, and the conclusions drawn are firmly grounded in evidence. Undoubtedly, the strongest part of her article is the thoughtful analyses of the reasons behind sex stereotyping which she found in books.

"Sex Role Socialization in Picture Books for Preschool Children," *American Journal of Sociology* (May 1972), is a model article, worthy of emulation by other writers. Weitzman, et al report on an examination of all of the Caldecott books, and a selected sample of other titles. The authors meticulously investigated portrayal of character, titles, location (indoor or outdoor) of main character, rescue function, and roles of children. The writing is concise, and ratios of men to women clarify the points made. An extensive bibliography is included.

Picture Book Survey

In an effort to clarify what the actual facts are in relation to women's roles, the authors of this article decided to conduct a simple survey of one specific type of children's literature—picture books. Our results are reported in the hope that they will shed some light on an issue primarily noted for the heat it generates. We limited our study both because of the quantity of children's books in print and the important influence of early learning on the child.

From the first birth cry until they enter kindergarten, children are engaged in a prodigious task: developing up to 50 percent of their intelligence. Psychologists agree that more intellectual development takes place in these early years than in any others. The amount of learning which takes place is only matched by the variety of this learning.

In addition to developing basic intelligence, the child is also busy assimilating fundamental role concepts. It has been clearly established by researchers that basic sex role identification begins in the earliest months of life, and is essentially completed by the time a child is five-years-old.

One of the elements in children's environments which encourage learning are the books which mothers—and later, teachers—share with them. Long before

TABLE ONE
The Homemaking Role of Women

Role	Number of Instances
Cooking	26
Watching over a child	26
Shopping	19
Standing, sitting in a crowd	18
Being upset with a child	13
Knitting	8
Eating	8
Sleeping	7
Planting or gardening	7
Riding	6
Reading	6
Washing clothes	5
Dancing	5
Visiting	5
Cleaning house	4
Feeding animals	4
Crying	4
Washing dishes	4
Having tea or coffee	3
Partying	3
Sewing, Helping child with task, Pushing baby carriage, Admiring child's work, Walking dog, Singing and Talking on telephone	2 each

they can cope with decoding the printed word, most children are exposed to picture books. From the artist's point of view they are a visual delight. How do these same books measure up when one considers what their content conveys about women's roles?

Our analysis included 154 picture books, representing the work of 78 authors, randomly selected from a collection of 957 picture books available in a university education department library (a complete list of books used in the study is available from the authors upon request).

The selection was made at random by having a clerical assistant in the library, not otherwise connected with the project, remove from the shelves the desired number of books. The books—both those in the total collection and those used in the survey—were judged representative of those typically available to children in school and public libraries. The total collection was judged representative because books in it were chosen by a professional librarian on the basis of recommendations included in such widely used bibliographic tools as *Children's Catalog* (H. W. Wilson), *Bulletin of the Center for Children's Books* (University of Chicago), The *Booklist* (ALA), the *School Library Journal Book Review*, and *The Kirkus Reviews*. The books in the study were judged representative because of the random means of selection, the spread of 68 years in publication date (1903 to 1971), the distribution of authors alphabetically, and the presence of award and nonaward winning books on this list. Of the 154 titles, 63 were published between 1963 and 1972 (41 percent of total sample of books), 64 were published between 1953 and 1962 (41 percent), 14 were published between 1943 and 1952, (nine percent), nine were published between 1933 and 1942 (five percent), and four were published before 1942 (two percent).

We used the definition of picture books discussed by Charlotte S. Hick and Doris Young Kuhn in *Children's Literature in the Elementary School* (Holt, 1968): the pictures are designed to be an integral part of the text. The fusion of both pictures and text is essential for the unity of presentation.

In our analysis, all representations of women were noted and categorized. A simple tabulation of total number of women in these stories was made. In addition, roles were indicated on Table One, which itemizes the many different types of homemaking-related roles in which women were shown. Table Two itemizes the different roles women are shown in, which are unrelated to the homemaking function.

Results

The unfortunate conclusion reached as a result of our research is that women do indeed play a subordinate, home-related role. In fact, in 13 of the books surveyed, no women were included *at all,* though these books did include men. In $17\frac{1}{2}$ percent of the books, only animals were present and four percent (primarily alphabet and number books) had no people at all. Thus, 65 percent included women in some role.

Of the books which did portray women, 83 percent of them showed

TABLE TWO
Professional Roles of Women

Role	Number of Instances
Teacher	10
Maid	5
Nun	4
Nurse, Flower vendor, Store clerk	2 each
Post Office worker, Stewardess, Cafeteria worker, Factory worker, Librarian, Street car conductor, Cook, Gypsy, and Fat Lady in a circus	1 each

women in the first category—homemaking roles, only 17 percent showed them in more professional roles (Table Two).

What do the women in these books do while they are at home? While it may be argued that cooking and knitting tasks can be creative, the conclusion reached from studying Table One is that women's homemaking roles in picture book literature are not essentially intellectual or creative. While reading is included, it is not prominent. Artistic expression (painting, playing musical instruments, creative writing) is minimal or nonexistent.

The analysis of the 17 percent of women's roles unrelated to the home revealed some interesting stereotypes. By far the most prevalent occupation for women outside the home was that of teacher (30 percent of the women portrayed). This perpetuates a stereotyped view of the profession dominated by women which educators have been trying to eradicate for some time. The next most prevalent (15 percent) was that of maid, simply an extension of a homemaking function into another setting for pay. Twelve percent of the women were nuns, certainly a subservient role. While the rest of the women's roles include some

which are interesting, in general they are at best semi-professional or untrained roles. As a group they are characterized as tasks requiring little or no formal education and providing few opportunities for expression of creativity. Noticeably absent, at least in the books surveyed, are women portrayed in such professional roles as doctors, lawyers, concert musicians, scientists, and many others. A contrastive summary of the two types of roles is included in Table Three.

Male Roles in Books

Three of the books surveyed did not include men, as compared to 13 omitting women. Apparently, it is easier for some authors to write a story without women than to write one without men.

Professional roles of men are analyzed in Table Four. In addition to the roles summarized on this table, there were single instances of 15 other occupations, ranging from waiter to photographer, from mountain climber to astronaut, and from optician to hobo. Only *one* man played the role of teacher.

A cursory examination of the first four tables shows that men are portrayed more frequently, and in a wider array of

TABLE THREE
Summary

Category	Percent
1. Books including no people or animals	4%
2. Books including animals, no people	17½%
3. Books including men, no women	13%
Total =	34½%
Of the remaining 65½% which did include women:	
4. Books including women in homemaking-related roles	84%
5. Books including women in professional roles	17%

TABLE FOUR
Professional Roles of Men

Role	Number of Instances
Fisherman, sailor, or other roles related to water	32
Farmer or rancher	23
Shopkeeper	21
Policeman	19
Guard or soldier	16
Horseman	13
Musician, Constrcution worker	12 each
Carpenter, Businessman, and Cowboy	9 each
Street vendor or Indian	8 each
Chef	6
King, Mailman, Janitor, Circus employee, and Gardener	5 each
Football player, Baseball player Thief, Hunter, Tailor, Fireman	4 each
Mover, Milkman, Shepherd, Logger Railroad man, Chauffer, Clock-maker, and Zookeeper	3 each
Principal, Preacher, Doctor, Matador, Gypsy, Baker, Mayor, and Barber	2 each

TABLE FIVE
Recreational Activities of Men

Activity	Number of Instances
Eating	19
Driving (other than as chauffeur)	16
Sleeping	13
Reading	10
Painting	8
Cooking	6
Flying	5
Dressing	4
Kiteflying, Skiing, Swimming	3 each
Talking on phone, Playing, Dancing	2 each

professional roles than are women. Of course, the accuracy of this portrayal of men could be questioned. While it is undoubtedly true that men's options are wider than those of women, the representativeness of these is uncertain. The two most frequent portrayals of men were in occupational roles related to water and to farming. These are hardly representative.

An analysis of the activities of men was also made, in an attempt to see what diversity was depicted from professional roles. This analysis is included in Table Five.

In addition to the roles summarized on this table, there were single instances of such other activities as mowing a lawn, crying, shaving, singing, and surfboarding. The nonprofessional activities in which men are depicted are not as wide-ranging as are the professional roles shown, but the variety does exceed that for women. Many of the activities in which men are shown are active ones, in contrast to the more sedentary activities depicted for women. Again, the accuracy of the portrayals of men is questionable when one notes their lack of participation with domestic duties, with the exception of cooking. The books seldom show men involved in the household tasks that many of them perform today, as a result of having a working wife.

Conclusion

Our analysis of 154 picture books reported substantiates indeed the too frequently vague and unscientific claims of sexual discrimination in books. In this particular group of picture books, women were portrayed in one of two ways:

—Primarily as a housewife and mother, and within this general category, as doing essentially dull and uninteresting tasks, or

—as semi-professionals engaged in occupations typically considered appropriate for females.

The inescapable conclusion to be drawn from this set of books is that women are *not* depicted in the rich variety of professional roles in which they are engaged today.

A wider presentation of women's roles in picture books would undoubtedly result in young children, particularly girls, having a more realistic picture of career opportunities now open to women. This seems especially crucial in picture books which are used at a time when children are extremely impressionable and learning much in the way of both facts and attitudes. Attitudes would be more positive if the facts presented through picture books were more reflective of the nature of our society today.

IV
Themes and Genres

No Bargains for Frances: Children's Trade Books and Consumer Education

Katherine M. Heylman

IN AN EXAMINATION of children's trade books for both their explicit and implicit approaches to consumer education, first prize goes to Russell and Lillian Hoban's *A Bargain for Frances.* In this recent (1970) addition to our favorite badger series, Frances' "friend" Thelma cons her into buying an ugly plastic tea set with red flowers, when she had her heart set on a real china set with pictures in blue of "trees and birds and a Chinese house and a fence and a boat and people walking on a bridge." Thelma tells her that that kind breaks, is very expensive, and besides, the stores no longer sell them. She kindly sells Frances her own ugly set for $2.17, all the money Frances has in the world. Agreeing to a policy of "no backsies," Frances pays her money and trots home with her acquisition, only to discover that the set she wanted is readily available at $2.07. Using the same psychological trickery that was used on her, Frances eventually gets the tea set with the blue pictures, plus a dime left over. Along the way, the first or second grade reader for whom the book is designed receives several valuable lessons in consumerism. An analysis of Thelma's sales pitch shows that Frances was taken in by: 1) the immediate availability of the ugly tea set; 2) the misrepre-

sentation of the saleslady (Thelma) about the availability of the competing product; and 3) the desire for a bargain without bothering to find out first if it indeed is a bargain.

Frances and Thelma agree to give up trying to trick each other because it's a big nuisance having to watch each other so closely when they play together. "Do you want to be careful or do you want to be friends?" asks Frances, and the implication is clear that the buyer-seller relationship automatically precludes friendship.

Unfortunately, the realism exhibited in this seemingly simple and charming little "I-Can-Read" story is notably absent in all but a few of the factual books relating to consumer education written for young and not-so-young children.

The Child As Consumer

Since consumerism as a movement has been largely left to the adult world, juvenile material on the subject is pretty scanty. But if writers, publishers, and educators have until now largely ignored the child as consumer, advertisers have not. Almost from infancy, today's child is bombarded with exhortations to: "Buy, buy, buy! Consume, consume,

125

consume! Discard, discard, discard! And buy, buy, buy again!"

Though it may be years before he will know what the word "consumer" means, he still knows that he *must* have the particular brand of cereal that he sees on the supermarket shelf because it's going to make him strong and healthy and loveable. In many households he (or she) also knows how to cajole, wear down, or bulldoze his parents into getting some of the marvelous cars, planes, dolls, or what-have-you that perform so realistically on TV and so disappointingly in actual life.

Certainly the modern child is as ripe for consumer education as his parents are. Fortunately, it seems that in more and more places he will be receiving it at a younger and younger age. The President's Committee on Consumer Interest, under the direction of Mrs. Virginia Knauer, has published *Suggested Guidelines for Consumer Education, Kindergarten Through Twelfth Grade,* plus a "Consumer Education Bibliography," an annotated list, comprehensive rather than selective, of over 2000 books, pamphlets, films, filmstrips, etc., including a number of juvenile titles. The bibliography, prepared by the Yonkers Public Library, is presently in the process of revision, and the new edition, according to a letter from Mrs. Knauer, will contain "an expanded section on materials for children's resources."

Librarians and Consumer Education

The *Guidelines* discuss the need for consumer education, methods of implementation, program, roles, and instructional resources. Four possible methods of implementation are suggested and it's refreshing to note that in the systems approach, the school librarian is included in the planning sessions.

Community involvement in a consumer education program is emphasized throughout the *Guidelines*. The school or public librarian can be very effective in finding out about and informing teachers and administrators of local agencies which might be helpful. Any consumer or environmental agency cannot only provide information and assistance itself, but can often lead to other concerned and helpful resource people. In Cleveland, two Nader groups, the Ohio Public Interest Action Group (OPIAG), and the Auto Safety Research Center at Case Western Reserve University, proved extremely helpful to this writer. Similar organizations in other places will be equally glad to be of service. Unfortunately, newspapers often softpedal activities of consumer groups, so the librarian who wishes to act as a clearinghouse for community resources must watch the newspapers carefully. It also pays to talk to a lot of people.

Even if your particular school does not now have a consumer education program, it's quite likely that they may have one in the near future, or that individual teachers will be working it into related units. As the scouts say; "Be prepared."

Finding material is not going to be easy. Standard sources of free material can all be used, of course, though such material is almost all sponsored and should be presented accordingly. "The use of biased, narrow-interest or self-serving materials does have a place in the Consumer Education classroom, but only when used with a full understanding of the purpose of the producer," says the *Guidelines*.

A particular paucity exists in material for inner-city schools. The *Guidelines* warn that "many of the instructional materials and aids required to insure relevance and authenticity in an inner-city school or class with special needs which arise out of ethnic or racial living patterns will have to be created . . ."It will be interesting to see when, how, and by whom. In the meantime, an examination of what we presently have reveals that there is precious little in children's trade books that can be recommended without qualification in a consumer education program.

Trade Books

A variety of material lends itself to use in a consumer education program, much of it free or inexpensive, such as ads from current newspapers and magazines, junk mail, articles in newspapers and both adult and juvenile magazines. Not so inexpensive is audiovisual material, but the criteria established for books will naturally apply to a/v material as well, though one suspects the latter will present more problems with vested interests than will the book field, with its long history of responsible editorship.

Of course, almost all of the books in the 600's and half of the 300's can be used in a consumer education program, since the more one knows about how things work and how material is moved and what institutions control it, the more likely one is to be a clever consumer. But to narrow the subject to reasonable proportions, this article will consider only those juvenile trade books, from preschool to early high school, which deal with things, agencies, or ideas that affect the individual's actual buying of goods or services, indicating the type of books that can be used for consumer education and the problems one encounters with them.

Books that will assist the child in becoming a responsible consumer should help him to develop one or more of the following abilities: 1) the ability to make logical and reasoned choices based on his own priorities; 2) the ability to know what information is relevant in making these choices and to be able to find it out; and 3) the ability to recognize emotions and emotional appeals. In addition, they should give the child a sense of active involvement in the process of buying and using products and services so that as an adult he will recognize his own political and economic power as a consumer, and not view himself simply as a helpless recipient of whatever product happens to be available.

This is a tall order. Books cannot possibly fulfill these goals for an individual. He needs, first of all, a good general education. One obviously cannot become a "good" consumer if one is a functional illiterate or if the simplest mathematics remain a mystery. But the converse is not necessarily true. One *can* be a brilliant mathematician and a bad shopper. We are concerned here with finding books that will help the child apply the skills he has to the business of being a consumer.

Store-Buying

A report on *Children as Consumers* by James McNeal indicates that training children early in the consumer role is uniquely American, uniquely modern, and that their first independent buying experiences are almost always in the grocery store or supermarket. Two books for primary children that appear frequently on recommended lists are Jeanne Bendick's *The First Book of Supermarkets* and J. M. Goodspeed's *Let's Go To The Supermarket*. It's interesting to examine the assumptions in these books. In the simpler Goodspeed book, the child is given the impression that everyone is there just to "help feed you." The slightly more sophisticated Bendick book, while giving much of the same factual behind-the scenes reportage, also alerts the young shopper to the fact that the "owners want to sell as many things as possible, so they try to design the supermarket to make a person buy even more than he went in for!" She describes an experimental design where, to make the buyer add more things to his cart than he really wants, "one row leads you into another, and you can't skip any." The necessity for making choices is also explicitly stated in the Bendick book, where she tells the young shoppers to get all the necessities first, such as green and yellow vegetables, milk, etc., and *then* such extras as candy and gum. (One suspects that the impact of such exhortations is relatively slight).

I Know a Grocer by Lorraine Henriod shows the owner of a small inner-city cooperative grocery store explaining its workings to two children. Though pleasant, it's clear that he's there to make money. He even tries a humorous softsell on the children to unload one of his mistakes, a nice carrot-pineapple cake mix. (Consumer lesson: watch out for "bargains.")

Another attractive title is *The Great American Shopping Cart: How America Gets Its Food Today* by Ada and Frank Graham. Based on the *Report to the President of the National Commission on Food and Marketing,* it is suitable for use anywhere from upper elementary through high school, and is intended to help the reader become a "wise shopper." But, despite the inclusion of a picture of an Ekco Food Cost Saver to help figure out prices per ounce, and an illustration of a steam iron purportedly worth $22.50 in trading stamps that sells for $14.95, one gets the distinct impression that the authors were pulling their punches. A fascinating chapter on the pecking order in the milling and baking industry nowhere mentions the consumer, though certainly he must be at one end or the other —determining what the final product will be and insisting through both economic and political means that it be of high quality and fair prices, or taking whatever limited varieties of bread the industry decides to give him after fighting it out among themselves. They also foster the "built-in maid" concept of convenience foods, without suggesting that the young reader compare nutritional values of, say, potato chips and fresh potatoes. All told, though, the book is extremely provocative. The authors give arguments on both sides of such questions as "Why not have consumer grades on more foods?," or "Is advertising good or bad?," and they do give the reader some very specific, practical ideas about what he can do to become a good shopper.

Though William Sebrell's *Food and Nutrition* was not specifically written for young people, it's frequently found in children's libraries. Reading this often fascinating study of everything about food from soup to nuts, including its history, present status, and possible future developments, lulls the reader into the comfortable assumption that the average American supermarket contains the best possible array of foods for good nutrition. When it comes to health foods, which he allows are "not harmful," just expensive, the author totally loses his objectivity. Tiger's milk, for example, "smells like floor wax, but tastes like soap." He ridicules health food "faddists" who will eat "only vegetables grown 'organically,' that is, fertilized in the old-fashioned way by manure or garbage." His five references to pesticides mention only their marvelous benefits, none of their possible dangers. Such writing does little for the cause of intelligent consumerism.

As a group, supermarkets understandably account for more child buying hours than any other kind of store, but McNeals's study shows that as a child moves into upper elementary school he is involved more and more in decision-making as far as other purchases are concerned. After supermarkets, a child's next most common experience is with department stores. *Children's Catalog* recommends *This Is a Department Store* (Romano and Georgiady) for third through fifth grades, though many much younger children could read it. Here again, the young reader is informed both directly and subtly that the store exists just to help him, that advertising merely lets people know what there is to sell and what it is like, that the display department spends a lot of time fixing things up just because they want everything to look nice. There is absolutely nothing about advertising *persuading* people to buy, nor about salespeople working because they get paid for selling. Certainly it is nice to instill in a child the idea that the world is a great big friendly place. After all, most people *are* friendly, and especially so to children. But in a book of information about a store, what is so shocking about the idea of profit that the authors leave it out entirely?

Craft and Hobby Books

Needs generated by particular hobbies create consumer demands and it's interesting to examine a few books on various subjects to see what kinds of marketing advice, if any, they provide the young reader.

David Stiles' very popular *Fun Projects for Dad and the Kids* gives such excellent consumer information as the dimensions of a 2 × 4 (1⅝" x 3⅝") and an Army surplus store or Section 14 of the *New York Times* as supply sources. Most cookbooks for children have very little to say about the actual purchasing of food, but in *Kids Cooking: a First Cookbook for Children*, authors Aileen Paul and Arthur Haskins seem to realize that a child old enough to use the book would be old enough to be getting some of the material him- (or her-) self, so they include such useful shopping hints as the best buy in ground meat or the importance of reading labels. Among other useful buying hints, *Pets for Pennies* by Joy Spoczynska, tells the reader not to buy paint with lead in it for animal cages, warns against buying a bird with puffed-up feathers, and informs the readers of several free or inexpensive services that are available to him as a pet owner.

More hobby and craft books could do this sort of thing. Perhaps all of us should become more aware of what a child needs to know to be an intelligent buyer in any particular field. For one thing, he often needs to know what *kind* of a store to look in for a particular item. It may be obvious to us that if you need a ⅝" socket wrench and your father doesn't have one, you go to a hardware store to buy it. It may not be to a ten-year-old-girl trying to work her way through a mechanical project. The child buyer also needs to know what constitutes quality and how he can distinguish between shoddy and good merchandise. The more specific clues an author can give him, the better. While it is very difficult to be specific about prices in a trade book, some idea of relative values can be given. In a particular art project, for instance, could either art tissue or crêpe paper be used? If so, which would give more satisfaction for the money? In a woodworking project, can scrap material be used? If so, this would be sound both from a consumer and an environmental point of view, both of which may be at odds with the profit motive. (But, old-fashioned thrift is becoming more and more new-fashioned, and planned obsolescence may soon itself be obsolete.)

Money, Credit, and Stocks

No area of consumerism is more emotionally charged than money. Children are aware of the enormous power of the stuff at a very early age, particularly as it applies to purchasing.

The consumer certainly needs to know *What Can Money Do?*, the title of one of the Community Helper series by Jene Barr. This simple little book is generally clear and fairly interesting, dealing with making a budget, including establishing priorities. The emphasis is on spending and spending well, rather than on saving.

Two primary titles which give behind-the-scenes information about banking are *Let's Go To a Bank* by Laura Sootin, and *At The Bank* by Elinor Rees. Both manage to give the impression that the bank charges interest on loans just so that it can pay its customers interest on their deposits. Otherwise, they are factual, useful and unexciting.

An older title, Louis Wilcox's *What Is Money?* deals with, among other things, investing and saving. Muriel Stanek's *How People Earn and Use Money,* designed for grades two to five, uses and clarifies such terms as consumer, credit, interest and budgeting. A book for older children is Kathlyn Gay's *Money Isn't Everything: The Story of Economics at Work.* On one hand the book seems geared to increasing the GNP: "Want spurs us on." But then we're told, "the more we prevent wants or learn to use leftovers, the less we have to worry about running out of materials to produce goods we need and want."

Elmer Kane's *How Money and Credit Help Us,* one of the textbooky-looking Basic Concepts Series, designed for grades four to seven could, according to the *SLJ* reviewer (February 1967, p. 80; *LJ*, February 15, 1967, p. 894), be better used as supplementary material in junior high. The author has done a commendable job in clarifying difficult concepts, notably the idea of money "dying" when a loan is repaid. From a consumer education point-of-view, he might have been more helpful if he had emphasized the necessity for finding out the actual terms of and interest on a loan before signing any papers.

The inner workings of the stock exchange, mysterious to many adults, are explored and explained in *The Bulls and Bears* by Adrian Paradis. The reader follows a little man, the inventor of "Instant Cleaner," through the stock exchange as he interests people in manufacturing and marketing his product. A good school project suggests picking out a whole portfolio and following it through a period of ups and downs. Two other books on the stock exchange are, in approximate order of difficulty, Dorothy Sterling's *Wall Street,* and James Playsted Wood's *What's the Market? The Story of The Stock Exchange.*

Floherty's *Money-Go-Round,* basically an excellent tale of the history and theory of money (and as such outside the scope of this article), includes a warning, backed up by several sad stories, against loan sharks who operate both within and without the law and says that if a person is refused credit by a bank the bank is in effect saying that borrowing any more money will probably increase his financial woes rather than solve them.

Books on personal budgeting are, of course, consumer education in its purest form. Unfortunately, nothing terribly valuable has come down the turnpike recently. Mary Beery's *Young Teens and Money* has some pertinent information on banking, tipping, and charging, but the discussion format is so confusing that the reader can't tell whether the

advice is that of the author or one of his contemporaries. For example, when discussing saving money, one paragraph suggests that you can save on long distance calls home by reversing the charges and letting your parents pay!

Of all the books examined for their usefulness in consumer education, there is only one that is really basic to the subject. Though a little too difficult for most elementary school students, Marc Rosenblum's *Economics of the Consumer* makes excellent source material. The series is well-named, the book well-written, concise, clear, and simple. The final chapter, entitled "The Intelligent Consumer," recommends that one avoid going into debt unless absolutely necessary, that one find out true interest, and that one ask whether one really needs what one is buying, or whether one is buying on impulse or due to clever advertising. Shopping ideas for consumers include such items as making lists, comparing prices in ounces, and knowing where the nearest state and federal regulatory agencies are located. Rosenblum tells it like it is, but does not scare the reader or unduly discourage him. Rather, he emphasizes the consumer role and encourages the reader to become active in it. Books like this on a slightly younger level would fill a real need.

Making Choices and Advertising

To choose between two things seems like a fairly simple process until one starts thinking about it. A favorite example of medieval scholastic philosophers was the ass who, precisely midway between two bales of hay and lacking free will, starved to death. Knowing what influences our choice of one brand of cereal (hay?) over another, or our decision to spend our money on pop rather than chewing gum, can help us make more intelligent choices and end up with what we want rather than with what someone else tells us we ought to want.

An excellent book on the subject of making choices is John Maher and S.

Stowell Symmes' *Learning About Why We Must Choose*. The authors, in commendably simple and pleasant style, go into the business of economic scarcity, wants, needs, and an analysis of our own motives. This book can readily be used in upper elementary school and is suitable for junior high, and even basic courses in senior high.

A very simple title on choosing is *What Can I Buy?* by Mickey Klar Marks. Uncle John gives a little boy a quarter and tells him not to spend it all in one place. Another Watts title, *Spending Money*, discusses decisions made on the basis of having, needing, wanting. Dull, but inclusive.

Drs. Luther Terry and Daniel Horn explore in depth the reasons behind choices, psychological and otherwise, in *To Smoke or Not to Smoke*. While basically a book on health, it provides a beautiful illustration of the individual's free choice in the matter being obscured and manipulated by commercial interests "who were afraid that a decrease in cigarette sales would threaten their own pocketbooks." Tobacco interests themselves have committed two million dollars a year for five years for studies by independent studies on the effects of smoking on health. "However," the authors point out, "the amount of money the industry spends on the program is less than one percent of what it spends on advertising."

It's one thing to say that advertising is self-serving, often misleading, and in its very nature manipulative. But how do we counteract its effects? Just knowing how it works is a start. G. Allen Foster's *Advertising: Ancient Market-place to Television* is a difficult but fascinating history of advertising, with a particularly frightening section on modern techniques, particularly subliminal projection—(pictures or messages are flashed on the screen so quickly that the eye cannot read them or even be aware that they are there). Nevertheless, the poor brain gets the point, and properly "washed," it takes its owner out to the theater lobby to buy popcorn or coke or whatever it was subliminally told to do.

The First Book of Advertising by Richard O. Pompian is far simpler and an absolute mine of facts about the industry and the people in it. Some common criticisms given and rebutted, *e.g.*, "advertising tends to brainwash people" are refuted by the statement that in spite of a huge sales campaign the Edsel bombed. The author (one wonders what he does for a living) admits that the problems are "very complicated."

Perhaps the best answer to advertising is training in logic. Irving Adler's *Logic For Beginners* is pretty difficult, abstract, and based heavily on mathematics. Wellsuited for high school, a good choice for junior high, but much too much for elementary school. Alvin Schwartz' *What Do You Think? An Introduction to Public Opinion: How It Forms, Functions, and Affects Our Lives*, is still difficult but a little more down-to-earth. Probably the best book for all three levels is Hyman Ruchlis' *Clear Thinking* with exceptionally clear writing and good examples. Even though only a few uppergraders could benefit directly from it, it's excellent for teacher reference. Opinion-molding devices such as "plain folks," "scapegoat," "wife-beating," and "band-wagon" are discussed and illustrated. Children are almost always able and more than willing to bring in their own examples of these devices.

Exposure to the ideas in the foregoing books will hopefully lead the young person to question the logic, meaning, and impact of a statement like the oft-repeated, "Everyone is talking about doing something about pollution. [So-and-so] is doing it."

Who Says You Can't?

It's one thing to know you're being had, it's another to do something about it. Intelligent buying, proper use of credit, and resistance to the blandishments of advertising all add up to making a good individual consumer. But, in order to have the safest toys and automobiles, the most nutritious food, and the fairest prices, it is often necessary to work as a group. The government, of course, is the most able to take group action, and books on government agencies can provide good material for consumer education units. The implications in some of the books, however, bear watching. Most books that mention the Food and Drug Administration, for example, indicate that no drug is ever released unless it is absolutely safe to use as directed. A lively account of the FDA from its inception is Josephine Hemphill's *Fruitcake and Arsenic,* which does not gloss over some manufacturer's past attempts to circumvent both the law and common decency, but does give an unreal feeling of assurance that nothing like that could happen *now.* Ironically, the book must have been going through press just as the FDA's Dr. Frances Kelsey was single-handedly resisting enormous pressures to release thalidomide. Her successful efforts are well-described in Samuel and Beryl Epstein's *Who Says You Can't?,* a collection of biographies of individuals —including Ralph Nader—who proved that it's still possible for the individual citizen to take effective action.

Mary Sagarin's *Washington Alphabet* deals with the seven independent agencies which regulate our country's business. Created by the president, they are accountable to no one and are, she cautiously states, "often considered" tools of industry. Rebecca Schull in *Government at Work,* adds that Congress is considered their watchdog, but "the watchdog can be muzzled." Except for the Epsteins' book, which can be appreciated by some sixth-graders, the books about government agencies and citizen recourse are all young adult.

It's difficult to know how far books for young readers should go when dealing with the depressing details of governmental pressure and corruption. While they obviously should not dwell on the subject, neither should they—by actual statement or implication—foster the notion that big brother is taking total care of us, that the ordinary citizen need never lift a finger to protect his own interests.

Fiction

So far, no bargains for young children have appeared in nonfiction books concerning consumerism. The world of fiction and folktale, however, proves far more realistic, with many fewer concessions to nice-Nellyism. Trickster and the so-called "numbskull" tales are fun, good exercises in logic, and (perhaps dubiously) increase the listener's sense of self worth by contrast (*I* would never be *that* stupid!). A child who has caught on to the flummery in Marcia Brown's *Stone Soup* is less likely to be duped in later life by promises of "something for nothing" which turn out to cost him all kinds of money.

Money, gold pieces, treasures are common motifs in nursery rhymes and fairy tales, and stories for children of elementary school age are frequently concerned with the getting and spending of money.

In *Evan's Corner* by Elizabeth Hill, a small ghetto dweller desperately wants a place he can call his own. Two rooms plus eight people—one corner each. Evan's mother lets him choose his own corner, and the slight but heartwarming book deals with his decisions and efforts at fixing it up, only to discover that consumerism is *not* an end in itself.

Picture books abound in consumer details, *e.g.,* the store in Sendak's *In the Night Kitchen,* and what can possibly get down to more basic definitions of producing and consuming than Leo Lionni's *Frederick,* where the seemingly nonproductive mouse has been busily storing up words and colors and poetry for the long winter days ahead?

While scarcely great literature, Hazel Wilson's *Jerry's Charge Account* humorously illustrates the perils and advantages of going into debt, especially with someone else's money.

It would be informative to hear a psychologist's explanation of young children's interest in shoes, for there must be dozens of books on the subject, from Ellis Credle's *Down, Down the Mountain,* to Masoko's *A Pair of Red Clogs,* to Evelyn Ness' *Josefina February* who is willing to give up her little burro for a pair of new shoes for her grandfather.

For older children, the forays of the Melendy family in *The Saturdays,* the careful spending of the children in *Where the Lilies Bloom,* the doling out of money in Elaine Konigsburg's *From the Mixed-Up Files of Mrs. Basil E. Frankweiler,* represent a very few of the titles that can build up much more realistic attitudes toward money, choices, and spending than do most of the currently available nonfiction titles.

Certainly the most gratingly realistic book, and one that is obviously not for the nursery rhyme set, is Eve Merriam's *Inner City Mother Goose:*

To market,
Supermarket,
To buy a full quart;

Home again,
Open it;
Measure is short.

Or:

Taffy is a storeman,
Taffy is a thief;
Taffy overcharges
For a tough piece of beef.

And so on. Grim. But too often true. Which brings us to the final question.

How Much Realism?

How much does a child need to know to grow into a responsible adult consumer? He needs, first of all, to establish a sense of his own identity and then to learn and articulate something about his own emotions. As he gets older, he needs specific information about the products he himself might buy and what criteria are used to judge them. He needs to know what institutions in our society exist for his protection as a consumer and how they operate. He needs to see himself as an important link in the economic process, with potential power to change things for the better.

But, just as it is impossible to teach democracy in an autocratic situation, so is it impossible to teach children healthy respect for themselves and for others as producers and consumers when you allow them to be exploited and manipulated. In the aforementioned McNeal study, the author tells of consumer training, under the guise of arithmetic skills, in which an organization named Educational Foundations, Inc., distributed a "model store" to thousands of elementary schools. The schools got it for nothing. Manufacturers paid $10,000 each to have their brands exclusively used. In Nona Walker's *Medicine Makers* the information was obtaned right from the horse's mouth by asking the drug manufacturers themselves. The facts may be accurate, but the reasoning can be astonishingly fallacious. E.g., in discussing the "conmensurately reasonable" prices of today's medicines, the author compares penicillin at $20 a dose in 1943, to "two cents as it left the manufacturer" sometime after 1951. It fails to state that penicillin was still very much in the experimental stage in 1943 and almost unobtainable by the public.

An example of the attempted encroachment of business into education is given in Sidney Margolius' *The Innocent Consumer Vs. The Exploiters.* Some business associations, he says, "exaggerate to the point of wildness, as did the Advertising Federation of America in attacking a consumer-education program in a Yonkers, New York, high school as creating doubt and suspicions in [our children's] minds as to the integrity and dependability of the country's business firms and their advertising practices!" Mr. Margolius goes on to say that many individual businessmen and Better Business Bureaus are thoroughly delighted with the programs.

By what stretch of the imagination does teaching a young person to read contracts, shop around for real values, and analyze advertisements always create doubt and breed suspicions? If the contracts are valid and fair, the bargains real, and the advertisements true.

Certainly books that point out to children the pitfalls in his role as consumer are not going to be half as disturbing to him as those that inform him that all is well and everyone that is trying to sell something is thinking only of his welfare, only to discover later on in life that not half of what he's learned in books has anything at all to do with the real world he encounters every day.

Picture Books

Brown, Marcia. *Stone Soup.* Scribners, 1947.

Hoban, Russell. *A Bargain for Frances.* Harper, 1970.

Lionni, Leo. *Frederick.* Pantheon, 1967.

Matsuno, Masako. *A Pair of Red Clogs.* World, 1960.

Ness, Evaline. *Josefina February.* Scribners, 1963.

Sendak, Maurice. *In the Night Kitchen.* Harper, 1970.

Juvenile Fiction

Cleaver, Vera and Bill. *Where The Lilies Bloom.* Lippincott, 1969.

Credle, Ellis. *Down, Down the Mountain.* Nelson, 1961.

Enright, Elizabeth. *The Saturdays.* Holt, 1941.

Hill, Elizabeth Starr. *Evan's Corner.* Holt, 1967.

Konigsburg, Elaine. *The Mixed-up Files of Mrs. Basil E. Frankweiler.* Atheneum, 1967.

Wilson, Hazel. *Jerry's Charge Account.* Little, 1960.

Nonfiction: Primary & Intermediate

Barr, Jene. *What Can Money Do?* (Community Helpers series), Albert Whitman, 1967.

Bendick, Jeanne. *The First Book of Supermarkets.* Watts, 1954.

Georgiady, Nicholas P. & Louis G. Romano. *This Is a Department Store.* Follett, 1962.

Goodspeed, J. M. *Let's Go to a Supermarket.* Putnam, 1958.

Henried, Lorraine. *I Know a Grocer.* Putnam, 1970.

Marx, Mickey Klar. *What Can I Buy?* Dial, 1962.

Rees, Elinor. *At the Bank.* Melmont, 1959.

Rossomando, *Spending Money.* Watts, 1967.

Sootin, Laura. *Let's Go to a Bank.* Putnam, 1957.

Stanek. *How People Earn and Use Money.* Benefic, 1968.

Wilcox, Louise K. & Gordon E. Burch. *What Is Money?* Steck-Vaughn, 1959.

Nonfiction: Intermediate & Junior High

Floherty, John J. *Money-Go-Round.* Lippincott, 1964.

Foster, G. Allen. *Advertising: Ancient Market Place to Television.* Criterion, 1967.

Graham, Frank & Ada Graham. *The Great American Shopping Cart: How America Gets Its Food Today.* S. & S., 1969.

Kane, Elmer R. *How Money and Credit Help Us.* (Basic Concepts series), Benefic, 1967.

Maher, John E. & S. Stowell Symmes. *Learning About Why We Must Choose.* Watts, 1970.

Paradis, Adrian A. *The Bulls and the Bears: How the Stock Exchange Works.* Hawthorn, 1967.

Paul, Aileen & Arthur Hawkins. *Kids Cooking: a First Cookbook for Children.* Doubleday, 1970.

Pompian, Richard O. *Advertising* (A first book of). Watts, 1970.

Marc Rosenblum. *Economics of the Consumer.* Lerner, 1970.

Schull, Rebecca. *Government at Work.* (Bold Face Books), Sterling, 1962.

Spoczynska, Joy. *Pets for Pennies.* Hawthorn, 1965.

Sterling, Dorothy. *Wall Street.* Doubleday, 1955.

Stiles, David. *Fun Projects for Dad and the Kids.* Arco, 1963.

Terry, Luther L., M.D. & Daniel Horn. *To Smoke or Not to Smoke.* Lothrop, 1969.

Wade, William W. *From Barter to Banking: The Story of Money.* Crowell Collier, 1967.

Nonfiction: Young Adult

Adler, Irving. *Logic for Beginners.* Day, 1964.

Beery, Mary. *Young Teens and Money: Earning, Saving and Spending.* McGraw (Not yet published.)

Epstein, Samuel & Beryl. *Who Say's You Can't?* Coward, 1969.

Hemphill, Josephine. *Fruitcake and Arsenic.* Little, 1962.

Ruchlis, Hyman. *Clear Thinking.* Harper, 1962.

Sagarin, Mary. *Washington Alphabet: Seven Agencies That Regulate Business.* Lothrop, 1968.

Schwartz, Alvin. *What Do You Think? An Introduction to Public Opinion: How It Forms, Functions, and Affects Our Lives.* Dutton, 1966.

Sebrell, William H. *Food and Nutrition.* (Life Science Library), Time Life, 1967.

Wood, James Playstead. *What's the Market? The Story of the Stock Exchange.* Dutton, 1966.

Walker, Nona. *Medicine Makers.* Hastings, 1966.

Adult

Margolius, Sidney. *The Innocent Consumer Vs. the Exploiters.* Trident, 1967.

McNeal, James V. *Children as Consumers,* Marketing Study, Series #9, Bureau of Business Research, U. of Texas, Austin, 1964 ($1.00).

President's Committee on Consumer Education. "Suggested Guidelines for Consumer Education: Kindergarten through Twelfth Grade." U.S. Government Printing Office, 1970 ($.65).

President's Committee on Consumer Interest (Yonkers Public Library) "Consumer Education Bibliography," U.S. Government Printing Office, 1969 ($.65).

Unclassified

Merriam, Eve. *The Inner-City Mother Goose.* S. & S., 1969.

Africana: Folklore Collections for Children

Gertrude B. Herman

. . . Afric's Sunny Fountains

From Greenland's icy mountains,
From India's coral strand,
Where Afric's sunny fountains
Roll down their golden sand;
From many an ancient river,
From many a palmy plain,
They call us to deliver
Their land from error's chain.

What though the spicy breezes
Blow soft o'er Ceylon's isle;
Though every prospect pleases
And only man is vile:
In vain, with lavish kindness,
The gifts of God are strown;
The heathen in his blindness
Bows down to wood and stone . . .
            (Reginald Heber, 1783-1826)[1]

HEAD ringing to the marching rhythm of the lusty old hymn, the child that I once was clutched her pennies in hand and dropped them, one by one, into the Sunday School missionary box, noting with satisfaction the kneeling white-robed heathen lad atop it, who nodded his black papier-maché head gratefully as each coin clunked in to start on its appointed way to deliver his land from error's chain. The rich imagery of the hymn's words merged in my mind with Dr. Dolittle's African garden where thick-lipped, stupid Prince Bumpo lay dreaming of a white princess. Through the jungle echoed the cries of Tarzan; and all the while someone later personified by Deborah Kerr, with stiff British upper-lipmanship, was hacking her way through the bush to King Solomon's Mines.

My vision was not unique. Of such lush materials the fantasy world has been woven which many American children have carried around in their heads as their image of Africa. Even as adults we have our illusions. We, who tolerate the daily body count from Vietnam and who have been able to accommodate to

memory the murder of Europe's Jews, were almost disappointed when the predicted blood-bath by "savages" failed to materialize in Biafra at the conclusion of the Nigerian war. And when the heathen's wood and stone were assembled in the Metropolitan Art Museum a few seasons back, we were astonished by the compelling power of the spiritual force and beauty revealed.

The decade of the 60's forced us to listen to many hitherto unheard voices, among them those of the African peoples. As new-old nations emerged from the collapse of colonialism, we discovered that our old images needed revision. A burst of publishing in the juvenile field occurred and continues to flourish. Works of fiction and nonfiction have proliferated, among them a considerable number of collections of African folklore, as well as picture books in which the traditional tale has provided a vehicle for the illustrator's talents. Children's librarians have welcomed the new stories, not only as a means of correcting old errors, but also of bringing to both black and white children some of the rich heritage hitherto denied the black American.

136

But enthusiasm has sometimes outrun critical acuity, and we have tended not to apply rigorous enough standards to our evaluation of African folklore collections for children.

Few American librarians in services to youth are trained as folklorists or anthropologists; some have travelled more or less extensively in Africa; the number who can read or understand an African language is probably infinitesimal. Nevertheless, it is possible to inform ourselves by reading, viewing, and listening. It seems worthwhile, therefore, to define once more some general criteria for the evaluation of folklore for children; to identify some of the particular characteristics of African folklore; and to present a selected bibliography of recommended books.

Basically, the questions one should ask about any book which purports to be folklore are: 1) what is the authority of the book? where do the stories come from? who collected them, from whom, and under what conditions? and 2) how honestly and artistically does the literary form preserve the cultural and stylistic integrity of the original? In the case of folklore intended for children, one should also inquire: 3) how appealing will the material be to children, whether for reading or listening, and at what ages? and how does the format of the book support or enrich the content?

When one examines the question of sources and authority, one finds that many of the African collections for children are not primary material, i.e. collected in the field by the compiler. In many cases they are adaptations from literary sources, most often from the works of 19th and early 20th Century missionaries, colonial officers, and scholars.[2] Unfortunately, acknowledgement is not always made to these sources, for many of them have passed into the public domain, presenting the same opportunities for exploitation as do Grimm, Perrault, Asbjornsen and Moe, etc.

A second kind of collection is that gathered by the compiler himself, sometimes combining field work with literary sources or the work of a collaborator, in which case he usually makes a point of identifying his sources specifically and accurately.

A third kind of collection is that in which authority is very nebulous, often printed only on the book jacket, and couched in such vague phrases as "told among the Bantu people," or "the author has travelled in Africa, where he heard these stories told by village storytellers." In what language, one wonders, and in what villages? Literary sources are implied but not specified in such equally cloudy authority as "research in the libraries of Nairobi (or Accra, or wherever)."

A fourth recent and important kind of collection is that containing stories set down by native Africans. Source identification is equally important for such works, and is often supplied in introductory materials or notes.

The authority of the work having been determined, one turns to consideration of how to evaluate the written form of an oral art. Field collectors emphasize the role of the audience and the stylistic devices employed by the narrator in the transmission of oral literature.[3] In the culture from which the literature arises, the audience brings to the performance a whole complex of assumptions, past experiences, etc. The story is not new to this audience; it is interested in the plot, but more profoundly in the skill which the narrator brings to his particular rendering of it. The accomplished performer draws his audience into the experience through words, but also through music, dance, body gesture, tonal variations, etc. The audience participates by singing, clapping, dancing, hissing, taking sides in the outcomes of the story, etc. A range of multimedia devices might capture some of the essence of what appeals to the eye and ear, but the social matrix which nourishes the art will continue to elude the alien observer. As the score of a Mozart concerto symbolizes, or stands for, the living music, so the printed form of an oral narrative is but the record of a living, changing, aural event. How effectively can the adaptor translate such an experience to the printed page?

Harold Scheub, of the University of Wisconsin, who in 1967-68 was a member of the audience of over 4000 performances created by some 2000 Xhosa and Zulu artists in South Africa, has said:

> The basic problem for the translator rests with those elements of the performance which most clearly identify it as an oral work—the non-verbal elements of production. . . . New tensions must be introduced into the recast work. . . . The rhythmic sounds of the language have indeed been replaced by a language which is no longer itself an oral language, but this does not mean that it is not a poetic language. . . . [The translator] must be something of an artist himself, for the only way an oral narrative-performance can survive the translation into the written word is as a new work of art.[4]

A third critical question is: how appealing will the material be to American children, whether for reading or listening, and how does the format of the book support or enrich the content? Dundes warns against ethnocentricity, "the retouching of oral tales . . . in the children's literature field where reconstructed, reconstituted stories written in accordance with written not oral conventions are palmed off as genuine folktales."[5] The elimination of unfamiliar elements and reliance upon western literary devices are common faults. The stories must retain faithfulness to the oral style and the cultural content of their African prototypes, but a faithfulness which is lively enough and dramatic enough to draw children into an unfamiliar world.

Format, including print and illustrations, ought to be attractive to children. It should reinforce the ethnic origins of the content, including distinctions in artistic motifs, colors, landscape, costume, and artifacts of the particular culture from which the stories come.

What are some of the stylistic features and story elements one might expect in

African folklore? Many of the stories are analogues to familiar European stories, but they are analogues with a difference, testifying to their unique origins, each culture using familiar motifs to fabricate its own unique works of art. All African stories are not alike. Just as there are important cultural differences between Navajo and Iroquois American Indian stories, so are there important differences among the stories and artistic conventions of various African peoples. It is important not to repeat the errors made in treating all American Indian groups as undifferentiated.

As an example one might consider the Trickster stories which are to be found all over Africa. Among the Ibo the Trickster is Tortoise; among the Ashanti, Spider; among the Bantu peoples, Hare; and among the Bushmen, Mantis. The central theme of all Trickster stories is the triumph of brain over brawn. But each Trickster is distinctively Ibo or Ashanti or whatever, and the stories reflect societal differences.

> . . . All these tricksters, however, are adaptable. They are able to turn any situation, old or new, to their advantage. The tortoise, we are told, now aspires to white collar status in Southern Nigeria and attends adult education classes, while the spider, Ananse, referees football matches among the Ashanti in Ghana. (From "Tricksters and How They Differ")[6]

Some common stylistic elements of African folktales are: formulaic openings and closings; repeated songs and chants; direct conversation rather than narrative; ideophones (words used to represent sounds, as "he knocked on the door—ngo! ngo! ngo!");[7] the use of repetition as adverb ("he walked a long way, a long way, a long way"); and proverbs added at the end of stories. Some story motifs are: talking animals; supernatural creatures differing from the European stock, e.g. few fairies, instead one-legged monsters, and ogres (the Hausa "Dodo," the Zulu "Zim"); magical oxen as symbols of beauty and/or power; the metamorphosis of human spirits into animals, particularly birds; heroines frequently protagonists. (Incidentally, the Dodo and the Zim are both cannibalistic, which somehow worries us more than the flesh-eating propensities of trolls or Jack's giants. Visions of missionaries in pots still haunting us?)

Implicit in all African stories are the values of the people telling them. In those parts of Africa where Islam is dominant, Muslim elements will be pervasive. The extended family and the obligations of kinship are reflected consistently all over Africa. Stories from Africa south of the Sahara reflect the force of custom, the importance of the welfare of the group, and the respect accorded to the ways of the elders.

The late A. G. Jordan, a black South African in exile and a scholar of African oral tradition, once said: "Traditional literature is the artistic property of the community." Respect is due. The emphasis in human relations books has often been, "We are really all alike." Actually, of course, we are not all alike. To understand and to value difference rather than to deny it, is a more difficult, but more human concept. All people are limited by the "error's chain" of their own cultural conventions, not only superficially but on unconscious and linguistic levels. The probability is that one should refrain from attempting to interpret another culture unless one is seriously committed to acquiring particular and deepening knowledge of that culture. African life and oral literature are rich and interesting enough to inspire that kind of commitment, so that we may select wisely and interpret adequately to children.

For advice and counsel, the author wishes to thank Professors Harold Scheub, A. Neil Skinner, and the late A. G. Jordan, all of the Department of African Languages and Literature, University of Wisconsin-Madison.

REFERENCES

1. *Oxford Dictionary of Quotations*, 2d ed., Oxford Univ. Pr., 1955, p. 240.

2. Dorson, Richard M., *The British Folklorists: A History*, Univ. of Chicago, 1968, p. 349-71.
   Finnegan, Ruth, *Oral Literature in Africa*, Oxford Univ. Pr., 1970, p. 26-47.

3. Finnegan, *op. cit.*, p. 1-25; Scheub, Harold, "Translation of African Oral Narrative-performances to the Written Work," *Yearbook of Comparative and General Literature*, 20, 1971, p. 28-36.

4. Scheub, *op. cit.*, p. 36.

5. Dundes, Alan, "Folklore as a Mirror of Culture," *Elementary English*, (April, 1969), p. 472.

6. Finnegan, p. 345.

7. Scheub, p. 31.

AARDEMA, Verna. *More Tales from the Story Hat.* illus. by Elton Fox. Putnams-McCann. 1966. Gr 3-5.

_____. *Tales for the Third Ear.* illus. by Ib Ohlsson. Dutton. 1969. Gr 3-5.

_____. *Tales from the Story Hat.* illus. by Elton Fox. Coward. 1960. Gr 3-5.
Literary sources acknowledged in notes. Attractive formats and fairly easy reading.

ARKHURST, Joyce Cooper. *Adventures of Spider: West African Folk Tales.* illus. by Jerry Pinkney. Little. 1964. Gr 3-5.
Trickster stories from Ghana and Liberia, collected by author. Handsomely illustrated.

ARNOTT, Kathleen. *African Myths and Legends.* illus. by Joan Kiddell-Monroe. Walck. 1962. Gr 4-6.
Mainly from early literary sources. Some include repeated chants.

BERGER, Terry. *Black Fairy Tales.* illus. by David Omar White. Atheneum. 1969. Gr 4 up.
Maidens, ogres, magic oxen, talking birds. Stories adapted from Bourhill and Drake (1908).

BERTOL, Roland. *Sundiata: the Epic of the Lion King.* illus. by Gregorio Prestopino. Crowell. 1970. Gr 4 up.
An epic of Mali, from Arabic, French, and oral sources.

BRYAN, Ashley. *The Ox of the Wonderful Horns: and Other African Folktales.* illus. by author. Atheneum. 1971. Gr 4 up.
Striking woodcuts based on African motifs. Stories from early collections, cited.

BURTON, W.F.P. *The Magic Drum: Tales from Central Africa.* illus. by Ralph Thompson. Criterion. 1961. Gr 4 up.
Tales from the Congo, re-told by a present day missionary.

COURLANDER, Harold. *The King's Drum: and Other African Stories.* illus. by Enrico Arno. Harcourt. 1962. Gr 4-6.

————— and Ezekiel A. Eshugbayi. *Olode the Hunter: and Other Tales from Nigeria.* illus. by Enrico Arno. Harcourt. 1968. Gr 4-6.

————— and Wolf Leslau. *The Fire on the Mountain: and Other Ethiopian Stories.* illus. by Robert W. Kane. Holt. 1950. Gr 4-6.

————— and Albert Kofi Prempeh. *The Hat-Shaking Dance: and Other Tales from the Gold Coast.* illus. by Enrico Arno. Harcourt. 1957. Gr 4-6.
Basic collections; excellent notes for each story with literary and/or oral sources identified. Collaborators from African countries; suitable art motifs.

DAYRELL, Elphinstone. *Why the Sun and the Moon Live in the Sky: An African Folktale.* illus. by Blair Lent. Houghton. 1968. Gr K-3.
A Nigerian creation myth as a handsome picture book. From collection published in 1910.

DORLIAE, Peter G. *Animals Mourn for Da Leopard: and Other West African Tales.* illus. by S. Irein Wangboje. Bobbs. 1970. Gr 4-6.
Retold by a Liberian paramount chief, and illustrated with woodcuts by a Nigerian artist. African humor.

FOURNIER, Catharine, adapt. *The Coconut Thieves.* illus. by Janina Domanska. Scribner. 1964. Gr K-3.
Picture book adaptation of a Trickster story.

FUJA, Abayomi, comp. *Fourteen Hundred Cowries: and Other African Tales.* illus. by Ademola Olugebefola. Lothrop. 1971. Gr 4 up.

Traditional Yoruban folktales collected by a Nigerian and illustrated by a West Indian. Shrewd commentary on the ways of man and beast.

GLEASON, Judith, retel. *Orisha: the Gods of Yorubaland.* illus. by Aduni Olorisa. Atheneum. 1971. Gr 6 up.
Selection of myths and legends about pantheon of Yoruba gods. Fascinating, but obscure. Source for interpretive story-telling. Author an Africanist.

GUIRMA, Frederic. *Princess of the Full Moon.* illus. by author. Macmillan. 1970. Gr K-3.
Picture book of maiden who is rescued by a magic flute. Author an Upper Voltan.

—————. *Tales of Mogho: African Stories from Upper Volta.* illus. by author. Macmillan. 1971. Gr 4-6.
Recalled by the author out of the oral tradition of his own people (the Mossi). Magical, imbued with values of traditional society.

HALEY, Gail E. *A Story, A Story.* illus. by author. Atheneum. 1970. Gr K-3.
An Ananse (Spider) story first recorded by Rattray (1930).

HASKETT, Edythe Rance, coll. & ed. *Grains of Pepper.* illus. by author. John Day. 1967. Gr 3-5.
Liberian folktales. No individual notes. Author spent two years as teacher in Liberia.

—————. *Some Gold, a Little Ivory: Country Tales from Ghana and the Ivory Coast.* illus. by author. John Day. 1971. Gr 3-5.
Shape-changing, witchery, and help from talking beasts, in stories collected by the author.

HEADY, Eleanor B. *Jambo, Sunqura: Tales from East Africa.* illus. by Robert Frankenberg. Norton. 1965. Gr 4-6.

—————. *When the Stones Were Soft: East African Fireside Tales.* illus. by Tom Feelings. F. & W. 1968. Gr 4-6.
Competently re-told stories from literary and oral sources.

HELFMAN, Elizabeth S., retel. *The Bushmen and Their Stories.* illus. by Richard Cuffari. Seabury. 1971. Gr 4-6.

Mantis is the Trickster in stories from the Kalahari, collected early in the century by W. H. I. Bleek, a German scholar.

HOLDING, James. *The King's Contest: and Other North African Tales.* illus. by Charles Keeping. Abelard. 1964. Gr 4-6.
Arabic sources determine the flavor of these tales.

HOLLADAY, Virginia. *Bantu Tales.* ed. by Louise Crane. illus. by Rocco Negri. Viking. 1970. Gr 4-7.
Tshikashi Tshikulu (the little woman of the forest who can be friend or foe), and animals who "catch friendship with the moon." Collected in 1930 in the Belgian Congo.

JABLOW, Alta, tr. & adapt. *Gassire's Lute: A West African Epic.* illus. by Leo and Diane Dillon. Dutton. 1971. Gr 4 up.
Striking graphics complement re-telling of epic poem set down in 1909 by Leo Frobenius.

KAULA, Edna Mason. *African Village Folktales.* illus. by author. World. 1968. Gr 3-6.
"Twenty stories, learned by listening in the villages of West, Central, East, and Southern Africa."

KIRN, Ann. *Beeswax Catches a Thief: from a Congo Folktale.* illus. by author. Norton. 1969. Gr K-3.
No source given for this prototype of "Bre'r Rabbit and the Tar Baby," well-known throughout Africa. Excellent illustrations.

————. *Tale of a Crocodile: from a Congo Folktale.* illus. by author. Norton. 1968. Gr K-3.
A pourquoi story. Moral: if you want something, do it yourself. No source.

NUNN, Jessie Alford. *African Folk Tales.* illus. by Ernest Crichlow. F. & W. 1969. Gr 4-6.
Kenyan "legends of long ago that hold both the sweetness of honey and the sting of the bee." African internal evidence, but no sources cited.

OKEKE, Uche. *Tales of Land of Death: Igbo Folk Tales.* illus. by author. Doubleday. 1971. Gr 5 up.

Significant stories, but so skeletal in written form as to need interpretation. Poetry.

ROCHE, A. K. *The Clever Turtle.* Adapted from an African folktale and illus. by author. Prentice-Hall. 1969. Gr K-3.
Turtle is the trickster in a variant of "Bre'r Rabbit and the Briar Patch." Oral elements of dialogue and repetition. Identified as from Angola, but no source cited. Strong woodcuts.

ROCKWELL, Anne. *When the Drum Sang: an African Folktale.* illus. by author. Parents' Magazine Pr. 1970. Gr K-3.
Handsome picture-book of well-known South African story. No sources, and fundamental song is omitted.

SCHATZ, Letta, retel. *The Extraordinary Tug of War.* illus. by John Burningham. Follett. 1968. Gr K-3.
Picture-book of well-known Hausa tale, recorded by Rattray (1913). Illustrations more distinguished than re-telling. No source cited.

————. *Never-Empty.* illus. by Sylvie Selig. Follett. 1969.
Wordy re-telling of Nigerian Trickster tale.

SEED, Jenny. *Kulumi the Brave: a Zulu Tale.* illus. by Trevor Stubley. World. 1970. Gr 3-5.
Freely adapted elements of Zulu legends and stories. Use of Zulu words and illustrations authentic. No sources cited.

STURTON, Hugh. *Zomo the Rabbit.* illus. by Peter Warner. Atheneum. 1966. Gr 3-6.
Hausa stories of Hare as Trickster, retold from Johnston. Oral style well simulated.

TRACEY, Hugh. *The Lion on the Path: and Other African Stories.* illus. by Eric Byrd and music transcribed by Andrew Tracey. Praeger. 1968. Gr 3 up.
A unique collection, retaining much of oral style including ideophones, repetition, songs, and idioms. Includes musical notations.

WALKER, Barbara. *The Dancing Palm Tree: and Other Nigerian Folktales.* illus. by Helen Siegl. Parents' Magazine Pr. 1968. Gr 4-6.
Yoruban tales told by Nigerian student to the author. Handsome woodcuts, glossary, and notes.

The Little House Syndrome vs. Mike Mulligan and Mary Anne

Katherine M. Heylman

THIRTY-ODD years ago, Virginia Burton wrote two books, beloved of children ever since, which represent opposite approaches to the problems of environmental change. In *The Little House,* when the encroachments of the city become intolerable, the title character is simply moved out to what is still country, where "Once again she could watch the sun and moon and stars. Once again she could watch Spring and Summer and Fall and Winter come and go."

But in *Mike Mulligan and His Steam Shovel,* the problem of technological unemployment is solved by a neat adaptation to changed circumstances. The steam shovel, Mary Anne, ends up in a lovely symbiotic realtionship with the town hall, rather than in the city dump where her rusting bulk would have been a blot on the landscape.

Legend has it that the solution to Mike Mulligan's dilemma was suggested to the author by a small boy of her acquaintance. One wonders if this same small boy, still on the fair side of forty, is presently involved in some form of environmental control, possibly thinking up schemes to recycle solid waste (we used to call it junk) into the economy by methods more

practical, but certainly less picturesque, than having an old steam shovel heating up the town hall.

The Little House represents an escape syndrome that is no longer realistic in 1970, if indeed it was in 1942. On the other hand, *Mike Mulligan and His Steam Shovel* represents an ecological answer to planned obsolescence that Miss Burton's consultant instinctively hit upon as a more valid solution than escape. It is to be hoped that his generation, now young-middle-aged, will come up with some similarly imaginative solutions to the problems of crowding and waste and pollution that plague our planet. In any case, there is no dearth of writing about the subject for what may be the last audience of children who will have a chance to do anything about it.

The truism that children's literature is a sensitive mirror reflecting contemporary concerns and values is certainly borne out by the number of juvenile books that have appeared recently about our environmental crisis. What follows is an attempt to define the area of environmental control, to establish some special criteria for juvenile books in this area, and to present a selection of books, new and old, fiction and nonfiction, which deal with it in one way

142

or another and are suitable for inclusion in an elementary school library. A large number of these will also be appropriate for a junior high school library, but the junior high library would no doubt want to add a few more advanced titles, as well as drop the picture books and some fiction.

Toward a Definition

The phrase "environmental control" could be interpreted so narrowly as to include little else besides devices to control pollution, or so broadly as to include every animal book in the library. The books under discussion here will deal with ecology, conservation, and air and water pollution. Not included are books on the chemistry of air and water, on identification of plants and animals, and on propaganda and government, though some or all of these would find their way into any extensive study of environmental control. Also outside the scope of this article are audiovisual materials, not because they are unimportant but precisely because they are so very important and can have so strong an impact that they should be discussed at greater length than is here possible.

In addition to meeting ordinary standards of literary quality, accuracy, pleasing format and so on, books in the environmental field have some special stumbling blocks. In any book, of course, the ideas conveyed should be suitable for the age of the intended reader. But strong feeling, whether it be about religion or race relations or pollution, often engenders an uncontrollable urge to proselytize the young. A pictorial polemic for five-year olds will either be unduly disturbing or, a more likely result, go right over their heads.

A case in point is *The Last Free Bird*, by A. Harris Stone. Beautiful wash drawings show the progressive destruction of the birds' nesting area until it has become a concrete jungle, and only one bird is left to tell the tale. A sad and beautiful little book, that could provide a basis for discussion from the second grade up, but misses the mark for younger children, who have very little control over their own lives, let alone birds.

Perhaps, for very young children, about the most suitable books in the area of environmental control are those which instill an appreciation of nature and of nature's own controls. Refraining from littering is about the one positive thing they can do to improve their environment, and so far no one seems to have written about the life cycle of the litterbug.

In general, juvenile books in the area of environmental control should in one way or another instill certain broad concepts, or perhaps "approaches" would be the better word. One is ecologic, the idea that for every gain something is lost and must ultimately be returned. The idea of man as ultimate consumer without giving anything back represents the frontier rather than the ecologic approach.

Where appropriate, books should indicate what the reader can do as an individual and what he can do as a member of a group. Whether it be picking up his own trash, or planting trees, or feeding birds, or making the most self-sacrificing decisions, such as forgoing automobile transportation when not absolutely essential, the reader should feel that in some manner he is involved in the problem and can contribute to its solution. For a writer to cry doom to an audience still politically helpless is not only sadistic but pointless.

Picture Books

For the youngest readers (or listeners), there are countless books calculated to increase appreciation of nature and animals. *Ask Mr. Bear, Millions of Cats* (Malthusianism carried to its ultimate conclusion), *Timothy Turtle, Rain Drop Splash, The Happy Owls* (especially effective as a movie), *A*

Tree is Nice, and *The Biggest Bear* all carry immediate and lasting impact.

Two recent picture books which depict animals in the grim reality of their surroundings are *Nobody's Cat* (Miles), the story of a stray cat living by his wits in the city, and *The Barn* (Schoenhert), where an owl and a skunk battle for survival. These represent a new breed of picture book and are certainly not for very young children, but their appeal, though limited, is real and quite different from that of *The Last Free Bird,* which is remote and unreal to most children.

More traditional in style but up-to-the-minute in theme are *Chicken Ten Thousand* (Jackson), *Farewell to Shady Glade* (Peet), *Just Right* (Moore), *Swamp Spring* (Carrick), and *The Old Bullfrog* (Freschet/ Duvoisin). Of these the most successful is *The Old Bullfrog.* A heron stalks a dozing frog. The frog leaps away at the last second. He is a wise old frog. That is why he has lived so long here at the pond. The stylized pictures of pond life are superb, and the simple tension-release story line constitutes true drama. Despite the fact that our particular frog gets away, the basic facts of pond life are clear, since obviously not all of the frogs are old and wise, and the heron does not look as though he is starving to death.

Swamp Spring, dedicated to "the conservationists who hold back the day when swamps exist only in brooks," evokes the feeling of a swamp with stunning pictures and muted prose. In the Peet book, a group of animals, evicted from their home by a bulldozer, hop a train and try to find another field. But the train stops only in smoky stations and near polluted streams. A rock slide saves them, and they hop off the train out in the open country, safe at last (for a while, anyway). The humor in the drawings does not blend with the bleak tale, and the story does not *quite* come off. *Just Right* is about an old farmer who wants to sell his

farm, but not to one man who wants to dry up the farm or to another man who wants to cut the lumber. The house is finally sold to his own son, who plans to come back from the city and stay down at the farm, raising his little boy the way he himself was raised. As a blatant plea for conversation, this is all right, but as a story it lacks zip.

Chicken Ten Thousand (Jackson) is a back (way back!)-to-nature story full of feeling and slightly sophisticated humor. The title character escapes from an egg factory, meets up with a rooster, and starts laying real eggs that turn into real chickens that scratch in real dirt. The message here hits adults with greater impact, since their lives are usually more circumscribed and synthetic than that of children. This is not to say that there is no message in it for children, though it is one that may suddenly hit them ten years from now.

Fiction

Recent fiction also has its share of environmental concerns. When he discovers that a legal quirk still makes him owner of the land he had supposedly sold, Fletcher Larkin's grandfather in *Henry 3* wants to evict all of the ex-urbanites from the land and turn it over to potatoes. And in *Tucker's Countryside,* Tucker Mouse and Harry Cat visit the country only to find that Chester's meadow home is about to be bull-dozed for apartments. Their human friends picket unsuccessfully, and the end seems near. But Tucker edits an old sign to make the powers-that-be think the Meadow has historical significance. When he finishes his chewing and chopping, he asks, "How's that for a 'benign deception'! " And Harry answers, "Very good. As a forgery it isn't bad either." Right or wrong, the deception saves the Meadow for its many inhabitants.

When it comes to action, no one can beat the kids in Felice Holman's *The*

Blackmail Machine. In order to save a swamp, they refuse to come down from their flying tree house until the Mayor and their parents promise to do what they can to halt the depredations of progress. Here is a book, clever and light and frothy on the surface, that can lead to some solid discussion and soul-searching concerning ends and means and man's role upon the earth and like that.

Ester Wier's *Action at Paradise Marsh* also involves an attempt to save land, this time a swamp. The young hero sacrifices his favorite trout to convince the legislature to leave things as they are. This makes for a duller book that either of the foregoing, but it *is* a more socially acceptable solution, though hard on the trout.

In the future we can evidently expect more fiction titles concerning pollution and conservation. A publisher's announcement just received tells of a science fiction story about poisoning the sea with "DDT and other chlorinated hydrocarbons." Good or bad, this is a story that wouldn't have been published five years ago, even assuming it might have been written.

City stories about children who act positively to influence their environment are *Miguel's Mountain* (Binzen), *The Big Pile of Dirt* (Clymer), and *A Small Lot* (Keith). In each of these stories, quite small children have figured out ways to persuade authority to leave them some contact with nature.

Survival stories, from *Robinson Crusoe* to *The Cay* (Taylor), and including along the way *My Side of the Mountain* (George), *Island of the Blue Dolphins* (O'Dell), *Zeb* (Anderson), and *The Summer I was Lost* (Viereck), all are powerful reminders of our dependence on nature, even when their main theme may be something more subtle. In each of these titles, the environment is really one of main characters, and the plot revolves around some conflict and resolution involving it.

The imaginative librarian will undoubtedly think of many more fiction titles that can be used in relation to environmental studies. Stories of the Westward movement, the Gold Rush, the lumber camps, can all be used as springboards for discussion of what effect man's activities had on the neighborhood. It would be easy to overdo this type of thing, though, and end up turning poor Babe the Blue Ox into a villain.

Ecology

Ecology, a term that until recently was no more familiar than the vice-president's name, has now become a household word. Though often used in a narrow, biological sense, it can include the study of human communities, a sign that we are beginning to see ourselves as part of the natural process, albeit one of its most disruptive forces. Thus studies of the city, such as the Radlauers' *What Is a Community?* for younger children, and Schwartz's *Old Cities and New Towns* for upper grades and junior high, belong in a bibliography of books on environmental control at least as much as Rachel Carson's *The Sea Around Us* or Farb's *The Land and Wildlife of North America.* Books about the inner city, including *It's Wings That Make Birds Fly* (Wiener), or *The Way It Is* (Holland, ed.), or *J. T.* (Wagner), or *Miguel's Mountain* (Binzen, mentioned earlier) should certainly stimulate discussion, be the discussants familiar or unfamiliar with the specific environment. Since most children's trade books depict white middle-class environments, one doesn't need a special list.

An adult book that kindergarten children may seize upon for the photographs and that can be used for reference in the middle grades is Peter Farb's *Ecology.* Books for very young readers in this field are scarce indeed, though the concept of the balance of nature can certainly be understood to some extent during the early school years. Material from some of the more difficult books can be used by the teacher either to read aloud or to adapt in some way to the needs of her class. An exception to this is *Patterns of Nature,* by Jeffrey Baker, a photographic essay which would no doubt be more effective with adult assistance. Some third-graders could read *A Tree Called Moses,* by Laura Nelson Baker, but it would be an even better choice as a read-aloud. One giant sequoia is followed from the time, around 2500 B. C., when the acorn was carried to the earth by a red squirrel. A deer nibbles at the seedling, Indians come and go, the white man comes and stays. John Muir visits the tree. A dramatic fire almost detsroys it. The reader will find himself totally involved in the life of the tree and the surrounding plants and animals. The author manages to write all this without a hint of anthropomorphism.

Phyllis Busch's *Once There Was a Tree,* similar in concept to the above title, and more suited to independent reading, was written with the specific purpose of encouraging "the very young child to experience his environment esthetically as well as intellectually." For older readers, the Milnes' *Because of a Tree* consists of brief studies of individual trees, such as the apple, the date palm, the aspen. "Each tree [draws] together a little community of creatures [who] come because the tree is there."

The Tale of Whitefoot (Brandhorst), for upper elementary students, is a fascinating study of the recycling of elements, through decay and growth, in the person of a whitefoot mouse on the Kansas prairie.

Millicent Selsam always seems to know what to put in and what to leave out, getting information across without burying the reader under it. Her *Birth of a Forest,* telling the story of the growth of a forest from its beginning

in a pond long years ago, will interest readers in fourth through sixth grades.

Young people who think that swamps are good only for mosquitoes, might think differently after reading Delia Goetz' *Swamps,* or *The First Book of Swamps and Marshes* by Frances Smith. The first title can be read by a third-grader, but the pictures, green and black drawings by Louis Darling, make it valuable even through the sixth grade. One would have to look far to find a more expressive depiction of the speckled limpkin (p.20). The Smith book, with an index and indifferently-reproduced photographs, contains more information about specific swamps, and can even be used in junior high.

By thinking small, sometimes larger concepts fall into place. Two books on symbiosis, Dorothy Shuttlesworth's *Natural Partnerships* and Earle's *Strange Companions in Nature* illustrate the interdependence of life in an immediate and intriguing way.

For general reference in the field and as individual reading, the set *Community of Living Things* covers the waterfront (it also covers Parks and Gardens, Forest and Woodland, Field and Meadow, and the Desert). Done in cooperation with the National Audubon Society, its pedigree is impeccable, but its format leaves something to be desired. The 1967 edition, little changed in text from 1960, is in double columns with photographs that were probably gorgeous in color but translated into black-and-white seem rather dull and textbookish.

Three books on ecology for older readers are Elizabeth Billington's *Understanding Ecology,* the Darlings' *A Place in the Sun,* and S. Carl Hirsch's *The Living Community: A Venture into Ecology.* The first uses the most direct approach, with diagrams and a glossary and a list of practical projects. The book by the Darlings tends to be a little chatty, but it does throw down the gauntlet to the reader as far as doing something about the dreadful conditions we have allowed to occur. Perhaps the best of these three (and they all have their uses) is the Hirsch. It is also the earliest, having been something of a trailblazer in 1966. It is not a book to be used for reference, though if you want to find out how the Australians coped with rabbits by spreading a virus disease among them, you'll be able to. Rather, it is a book to be savored, with its careful building of concepts, its quotations from Darwin and Genesis and Donne, its attractive format and illustrations, and its low-keyed wit. This author, too, calls for action in restoring an environment in which we can live. "There is no escape from the housekeeping duties on earth," he says, and quotes Thoreau. "What is the use of a house, if you haven't got a tolerable planet to put it on?"

Conservation

It is difficult to separate conservation and ecology, especially since the so-called "Third Wave" of conservation *is* ecological. However, for our present purposes, the term will be used in its old-fashioned sense of preservation, regulation, and renewal.

For the youngest readers, *The True Book of Conservation* by Richard Gates gives a surprising amount of information in simple terms. The pictures are only adequate, which is too bad, because children who cannot read all the hard words might be interested in the subject and learn a good deal from excellent pictures. *The First Book of Conservation* (Smith, 1954) though old, is still valuable for the middle grades and some sixth graders. Most of the general, new juvenile works on conservation are a shade too difficult for all but the upper grades.

Man, Earth and Change: The Principles and History of Conservation by Jean Worth, one of the New Conservation Series published by Coward-McCann, is a lucid overview of the field that would be helpful to teachers as well as upper-grade students. A slightly older title is *Conservation and You,* by Hitch and Sorenson, with a very good list of suggested projects tied in with each chapter.

Soil conservation yields three titles, two quite new and the other 12 years old, but written in a simple and interesting style that will make the subject come more alive than it is otherwise likely to. This is Patricia Lauber's *Dust Bowl: The Story of Man on the Great Plains.* Naomi Talley's *To Save the Soil* and Van Dersal's *The Land Renewed,* a revision of the 1946 book, can be used through junior high.

Conservation of the forest is covered in the general books and to some degree in some of the books discussed under Ecology, but a special facet of it is the subject of the Milnes' *Phoenix Forest.* When no fires occur, no new trees can grow, and some foresters have been experimenting with purposeful burning to allow new growth to take place. A dangerous practice, but necessary, according to some, to restore balance, for if all fire is prevented, it will be a case of "save and over-save," and eventually the forest will die out for lack of a new generation. This interesting thesis raises the perennial question, "How much good is good?"

While children may not get too excited about soil conservation, and only mildly so about trees, certainly the plight of animals has instant appeal. *The Last Trumpeters,* by Ross Hutchins, is a simply and movingly written story of a family of trumpeter swans who lived before Columbus. The illustrations by Jerome Connolly have a sweep and beauty to them that is not apparent at first glance, but reveals itself as the story unfolds. The story goes beyond the life of the two swans (who are given their Indian names) to tell of the coming of the Europeans and the consequent destruction of other species. A heart-breaking unsentimental story which should lead to action on the part of the adult who has read it as a child.

For the same middle-grade age (third-fourth, approximately), but less distinguished, is Robert McClung's *Honker: The Story of a Wild Goose,* showing in addition to the life story of geese the work of the National Wildlife Commission.

Studies of vanishing wildlife are numerous, but the best choice for middle-grade readers still seems to be Ivah Green's *Wildlife in Danger.* Information is not up-to-date, of course, especially concerning population counts, and would have to be supplemented with data from encyclopedias or almanacs.

For upper grades and junior high, there are numerous titles of high quality and interest. A sampling of the best includes Stoutenburg's *Animals at Bay: Rare and Rescued American Wildlife,* a book which includes land and aquatic mamals plus the crocodile, but not the whooping crane. (*A Vanishing Thunder* is a companion volume on birds.) Drawings by John Schoenherr have an immediate, personal quality that captures the individuality of each animal.

Children of the Ark: The Rescue of the World's Vanishing Wild Life, by Robert Gray, is by definition more wide-ranging and includes the bontebok and the Nubian ibex as well as the whooping crane and the great auk. Two companion books by George Laycock are *America's Endangered Wildlife* and *Wild Refuge.* The first includes birds (as the Stoutenburg does not), and where subjects are duplicated, as in the case of the sea otter, it is difficult to choose between the two presentations. The Laycock book is a shade more difficult, and has numerous excellent photographs and a fine bibliography which includes magazine articles. *Wild Refuge* tells the story of the National Wildlife Refuges, with a good deal of information about the animals involved, and does to a small degree duplicate the information in *Endangered Wildlife.* It is similar in scope to the much more difficult and detailed book by Robert Murphy, a very recent juvenile version of his *Wild Sanctuaries,* called *A Heritage Restored: America's Wildlife Refuges,* which will be invaluable for reference as well as browsing, if not for reading straight through.

Books on wildlife conservation seem particularly *à propos* for young readers, who identify easily with animals. The saddening knowledge of the actual extinction of species by man may make children more vitally aware of how important it is to institute controls on our environment before it is too late.

Air, Water Pollution

Juvenile books on water control go back much further than those on air control, since water for a long time has been a commodity that needed conserving, pumping, storing, etc., whereas air was just there. But as in so many subject areas, it is hard to find material for younger readers that is clearly and simply written, with good diagrams and excellent illustrations.

At first glance, two series books with the improbable titles of *Let's Go to Stop Water Pollution* and *Let's Go to Stop Air Pollution* (Chester) seem suitable, but despite the large print and direct address (". . . next you go to the filtration plant," etc.) the vocabulary is difficult and the information complicated. The water pollution book has, however, a very good explanation of water purifying devices, though it is hard to imagine anyone over fourth grade condescending to look at it. The air pollution book is not as well done. In one place, the diagram of an automobile engine with a pollution-control device is totally confusing. Otherwise the information is good and can be used with primary children even if they cannot read it all themselves.

Bartlett's *The Clean Brook,* a Let's-Read-and-Find-Out Book, deals mostly with natural pollution and controls, and is suitable for the youngest children. Delia Goetz' *Rivers* uses the Potomac to illustrate concepts of the various types of life existing about its shore and to show how pollution develops. Second and third graders can read it.

The Radlauer *Water for Your Community*, a companion volume to *What is a Community?*, with stylized illustrations in blue and black, with lots of white space on a page, can be used from second to about fourth grade for material on the water cycle, purification, flood control, and pollution and prevention.

For the upper grades, *The First Book of Water* (Smith) contains a lot of sound information and illustrates graphically hydroelectric power, a tree's method of taking water from the soil, and the process of creating heavy water, in addition to some information on pollution control. Helen Bauer's *Water: Riches or Ruin*, covers a good deal of subject matter in a simple, slightly condescending manner. She posed the question in the title over ten years ago, and it has not yet been answered. Carlson and Hanson's *Water Fit to Use* and Halacy's *The Water Crisis* are more difficult, especially the latter one. The Carlson book has better diagrams and will probably be more readily comprehensible to students, but the Halacy is more comprehensive, often divulging quite interesting bits of information, such as Leonardo da Vinci's concern with the hydrologic cycle, or the fact that Kenneth Roberts was an avid dowser.

Clean the Air! Fighting Smoke, Smog, and Smaze Across the Country by Alfred Lewis depicts pollution control devices in present use and is relatively easy to understand.

Pollution of water and air are considered side-by-side in two excellent books. Dorothy Shuttlesworth's *Clean Air—Sparkling Water* consists of three parts. First is a photographic essay of one town through its aroused citizenry to clean up the polluted air and water after an inversion has caused illness and death. A second section is a brief study of cities in America and abroad with their pollution problems, and lastly there is a section on action. Lots of third graders could read most of this, it is entirely suitable for sixth-graders, and it could be used by the teacher in first and second grades, perhaps projecting the photographs in the first section and having the children create the story that goes along with them.

This Vital Air: This Vital Water: Man's Environmental Crisis, by Thomas Aylesworth, covers a large area, including oil pollution, noise pollution, and the problems created by too many people. A final chapter tells of the careers open in environmental control and is slanted toward teenage rather than elementary readers.

Two books on air pollution, both written for young adults but not too difficult for interested fifth graders, are Lucy Kavaler's *Dangerous Air* and *The Air We Live In*, by James Marshall. The latter is in the New Conservation Series and includes more technical details than the Kavaler, which, however, provides more history and more details about the events it describes. Both are excellent choices. If an elementary school librarian were forced to choose, the Kavaler would probably be the more suitable, but it is hard to imagine a junior high library that shouldn't purchase both.

There are of course many many other very good books in the field under discussion, but many of them are for older audiences. Yearbooks, magazines, almanacs, newspapers are obvious sources for recent information.

Many if not most of the preceding books exhort the reader to become involved, to do something. Stories about people who did do something might make readers take this advice more closely to heart. Irene Hunt's *Trail of Apple Blossoms* tells the often-sentimentalized tale of Johnny Appleseed with restrained feeling. Biographies of Teddy Roosevelt, Audubon, and John Muir are natural candidates. A recent book by the Epsteins, *Who Says You Can't?*, consists of seven New Yorker-type profiles of people who successfully bucked established interests for public good. Particularly pertinent here are those of the New Jersey amateur conservationists who took up cudgels for a swamp against a jet airport, of Dr. Frances Kelsey, who fought a drug company for a year but refused to release thalidomide, and of Ralph Nader, whose private life was invaded intolerably by agents of General Motors after he published *Unsafe at Any Speed*, but whose activities have caused legislative changes.

For Teachers

In a subject area as new as environmental control, it is up to the school librarian to provide adult material for the teachers. The following six titles cover the various aspects of pollution control and could form a nucleus around which to build a larger adult collection if necessary.

The Third Wave ... America's New Conservation is the 1967 Conservation Yearbook (#3) of the U. S. Department of the Interior. Stressing the ecological approach and loaded with excellent color photographs, it is an inexpensive source ($2 in paperback) of information and inspiration. Its use would not be confined to teachers. John Perry's *Our Polluted World: Can Man Survive?*, variously classified as juvenile or adult, provides good coverage for the teacher who may want a broad overview of the field before delving into its complicated by-ways. And Stewart Udall's recent *1976: Agenda for the Future* retraces and updates much of the material in his 1963 well-known *Quiet Crisis*, (which, happily, is not so quiet anymore).

Dr. Paul Ehrlich's *Population Bomb*

is a cry for action by the individual. *The Dirty Animal* by Henry Still is comprehensive both in its coverage of facts and its concept of "complete sanitation," as well as its consideration of the complicated social factors underlying decisions concerning our environment, factors perhaps outside the child's comprehension or interest, but certainly ones that should be understood by anyone who is teaching the subject.

And last but not least, whether you live in Bangor, Maine, or Los Angeles, California, William Bronson's *How to Kill a Golden State* is horrifyingly pertinent. *Science Books* (Dec., 1968) calls this an "angry pictorial essay" which is a necessary exception to their rule against including works that might be considered diatribes. Well, this is a diatribe if there ever was one, and its photographs of pollution, both physical and esthetic, in California could be the basis of many a lively discussion among youngsters, hopefully leading to some determination to change things when they're old enough. (Oddly enough, in at least one library, which shall be nameless, this book is classified as Travel.)

There are, of course, many other possible choices for the teachers' shelf —one can hardly turn around these days without bumping into a new book about the environmental crisis—but these six will provide most of the necessary information on the subject and can hardly fail to deliver a great deal of impact.

Following is a list of books mentioned in the preceding pages (with a few exceptions where old favorites were mentioned in a conversational manner). The list is not intended as any final statement on what should be included, but rather is presented as a working guide to the busy librarian who suddenly finds himself flooded with books on a relatively new subject. It is obvious from the list that there is a real need for easy, factual material to meet the needs of our youngest readers. Such material should be largely graphic, perhaps. At the risk of seeming repetitious, it would not hurt if publishers were prodded into providing illustrations and charts in books intended for reading by six-, seven-, and eight-year olds that are at *least* as good as those in the books they publish for the next age group.

Hopefully, the readers of the books on the following list will bequeath to their children a world where Mike Mulligan makes sense, where pop bottles are returned for reuse rather than pitched on the neighbor's lawn (or in the neighboring community's dump), and where the Little House won't need to find a place to move to every generation. Hopefully, these books and others like them will have done their part in making possible a world where the Little House can stay in the same place and watch the sun . . . and moon . . . and stars.

BIBLIOGRAPHY

Picture Books

Burton, Virginia Lee. *The Little House.* Houghton, 1942.
————. *Mike Mulligan and His Steam Shovel.* Houghton, 1939.
Carrick, Carol. *Swamp Spring.* Macmillan, 1969.
Freschet, Berniece. *The Old Bullfrog.* Scribners, 1968.
Jackson, Jacqueline. *Chicken Ten Thousand.* Little, 1968.
Miles, Miska. *Nobody's Cat.* Little, 1969.
Moore, Lilian. *Just Right.* Parents Magazine Pr., 1968.
Peet, Bill. *Farewell to Shady Glade.* Houghton, 1966.
Schoenherr, John. *The Barn.* Little, 1968.
Stone, A. Harris. *The Last Free Bird.* Prentice-Hall, 1967.

Fiction

Anderson, Lonzo. *Zeb.* Knopf, 1966.
Binzen, Bill. *Miguel's Mountain.* Coward, 1968.

Clymer, Eleanor. *A Big Pile of Dirt.* Holt, 1968.
George, Jean. *My Side of the Mountain.* Dutton, 1959.
Holman, Felice. *The Blackmail Machine.* Macmillan, 1968.
Hunt, Irene. *Trail of Apple Blossoms.* Follett, 1968.
Keith, Eros. *A Small Lot.* Bradbury Pr., 1968.
Krumgold, Joseph. *Henry 3.* Atheneum, 1969.
Montgomery, Rutherford. *Kildee House.* Doubleday, 1949.
O'Dell, Scott. *Island of the Blue Dolphins.* Houghton, 1960.
Selden, George. *Tucker's Countryside.* Farrar, 1969.
Taylor, Theodore. *The Cay.* Doubleday, 1969.

Viereck, Phillip. *The Summer I Was Lost.* Day, 1965.
Wagner, Jane. *J. T.* Van Nostrand Reinhold, 1970.
Wier, Ester. *Action at Paradise Marsh.* Stackpole, 1968.

Ecology

Baker, Jeffrey J. W. *Patterns of Nature.* Doubleday, 1967.
Baker, Laura Nelson. *A Tree Called Moses.* Atheneum, 1966.
Billington, Elizabeth T. *Understanding Ecology.* Warne, 1968.
Brandhorst, Carl T. and Robert Sylvester. *The Tale of Whitefoot.* Simon and Schuster, 1968.
Busch, Phyllis S. *Once There Was a Tree: The Story of a Tree, a Changing Home for Plants and Animals.* World, 1968.
Carson, Rachel. *The Sea Around Us* (Special Edition for Young Readers). Golden Pr., 1958.
Darling, Lois and Louis. *A Place in the Sun: Ecology and the Living World.* Morrow, 1968.
Earle, Olive. *Strange Companions in Nature.* Morrow, 1966.
Farb, Peter. *Ecology.* Time-Life, 1963.
————. *The Land and Wildlife of North America.* Time-Life, 1964.
Goetz, Delia. *Swamps.* Morrow, 1961.
Hirsch, S. Carl. *The Living Community: A Venture into Ecology.* Viking, 1966.
Holland, John, ed. *The Way It Is.* Harcourt, 1969.

Milne, Lorus and Margery. *Because of a Tree*. Atheneum, 1963.
Radlauer, Edward and Ruth. *What Is a Community?* Elk Grove Pr., 1967.
Ress, Etta Schneider, ed. *The Community of Living Things*. 5 vols. Creative Educational Society: Minn., 1967.
Schwartz, Alvin. *Old Cities and New Towns*. Dutton, 1968.
Selsam, Millicent. *Birth of a Forest*. Harper, 1964.
Shuttlesworth, Dorothy. *Natural Partnerships: The Story of Symbiosis*. Doubleday, 1969.
Smith, Frances C. *The First Book of Swamps and Marshes*. Watts, 1969.
Weiner, Sandra. *It's Wings That Make Birds Fly: The Story of a Boy*. Pantheon, 1969.

Conservation

Gates, Richard. *The True Book of Conservation*. Childrens, 1959.
Goetz, Delia. *Rivers*. Morrow, 1969.
Gray, Robert. *Children of the Ark: The Rescue of the World's Vanishing Wild Life*. Norton, 1968.
Green, Ivah. *Wildlife in Danger*. Coward, 1960.
Hitch, Allen S. and Marian Sorenson. *Conservation and You*. Van Nostrand and Reinhold, 1964.
Hutchins, Ross E. *The Last Trumpeters*. Rand McNally, 1967.
Lauber, Patricia. *Dust Bowl: The Story of Man on the Great Plains*. Coward, 1958.
Laycock, George. *America's Endangered Wildlife*. Norton, 1968.
————. *Wild Refuge*. Doubleday, 1969.
McClung, Robert M. *Honker, the Story of a Wild Goose*. Morrow, 1965.

Milne, Lorus and Margery. *The Phoenix Forest*. Atheneum, 1968.
Murphy, Robert. *A Heritage Restored: America's Wildlife Refuges*. Dutton, 1969.
Smith, Frances C. *The First Book of Conservation*. Watts, 1954.
Stoutenburg, Adrien. *Animals at Bay: Rare and Rescued American Wildlife*. Doubleday, 1968.
————. *A Vanishing Thunder*. Doubleday, 1967.
Talley, Naomi. *To Save the Soil*. Dial, 1965.

Van Dersal, William R. *The Land Renewed*. Walck, 1968.
Worth, Jean. *Man, Earth and Change*. Coward, 1968.

Air, Water Pollution

Aylesworth, Thomas G. *This Vital Air: This Vital Water—Man's Environmental Crisis*. Rand McNally, 1968.
Bartlett, Margaret F. *The Clean Brook*. Crowell, 1960.
Bauer, Helen. *Water: Riches or Ruin*. Doubleday, 1959.
Carlson, Carl Walter, and Bernice V. Hanson. *Water Fit to Use*. John Day, 1966.
Chester, Michael. *Let's Go to Stop Air Pollution*. Putnam, 1968.
————. *Let's Go to Stop Water Pollution*. Putnam, 1969.
Goetz, Delia. *Rivers*. Morrow, 1969.
Halacy, D. S. *The Water Crisis*. Dutton, 1966.
Kavaler, Lucy. *Dangerous Air*. John Day, 1967.
Lewis, Alfred. *Clean the Air! Fighting Smoke, Smog, and Smaze Across the Country*. McGraw, 1965.
Marshall, James. *The Air We Live in—Air Pollution: What We Must Do About It*. Coward, 1969.
Radlauer, Edward and Ruth. *Water for Your Community*. Elk Grove Press, 1968.
Shuttlesworth, Dorothy E. *Clean Air—Sparkling Water: The Fight Against Pollution*. Doubleday, 1968.

Action

Douglas, William O. *Muir of the Mountains*. Houghton, 1961.
Epstein, Beryl and Samuel. *Who Says You Can't?* Coward, 1969.
Judson, Clara Ingram. *Theodore Roosevelt, Fighting Patriot*. Follett, 1953.
Kieran, Margaret and John. *John James Audubon*. Random, 1954.

For the Teachers' Shelf

Bronson, William. *How to Kill a Golden State*. Doubleday, 1968.
Ehrlich, Paul. *The Population Bomb*. Sierra Club, 1968.
Perry, John. *Our Polluted World: Can Man Survive?* Watts, 1967.

Still, Henry. *The Dirty Animal.* Hawthorn, 1967.

Udall, Stewart L. *1976: Agenda for Tomorrow.* Harcourt, 1968.

U. S. Dept. of the Interior. "The Third Wave . . . America's New Conservation," *Conservation Yearbook No 3* U. S. Govt. Printing Office, 1967.

A Ride Across the Mystic Bridge or Occult Books: What, Why, and Who Needs Them?

Georgess McHargue

UNTIL RECENTLY, members of witch covens, village wise women, gypsy fortune-tellers, and the kings whose touch was believed to cure skin disease got their instructions from local tradition and not from a visit to the local library. Even after the invention of the printing press, occult *books* were most likely to be found in the courtier's private library, the discreet back room at the bookseller's, the locked study belonging to the respectable Victorian Member of Parliament or merchant of provisions, or more rarely, the collection of the self-avowed magus or the suitably disapproving churchman. Especially in the earlier years, roughly 1450 to 1650, it was as unlikely for the actual practitioner of any of the occult arts (except perhaps alchemy) to read or possess a book on the subject as it would have been for the man behind the ox-drawn plow to be familiar with Virgil's *Georgics*. This is obvious. There were no public libraries, very few books, and even fewer who could read them. Further, many of the titles we would now classify as occult covered subjects that were not merely "hidden," as the root of the word implies, but actually forbidden to western readers by the Church. This prohibition extended beyond the worship of the Devil (more properly called Satanism) and the fertility cults of witchcraft (with which

Satanism is persistently confused) to many unrelated practices such as attempting to divine the future (a knowledge reserved for angels) or to summon the spirits of the dead. In the Judeo-Christian world, laws against such activities were at least as ancient as the reign of King Saul, who, in employing the so-called Witch of Endor (actually a medium) to communicate with the spirit of the prophet Samuel, was breaking his own ordinance, made at the express commandment of God.

It was natural, therefore, that most early books on these topics, as well as the rare surviving copies of ancient manuscripts, had a somewhat underground existence. From occult books they became cult books, prized and sought after by a very small fraternity of collectors, believers, and unconventional scholars. They thus acquired a highly romantic aura of danger and value.

At a later date, the forbidden nature of occult books led them to be associated, perhaps unconsciously, with another type of proscribed literature, the sex book. Though there was no necessary connection between the two subjects, they sometimes appealed to the same collectors, were sold in the same sort of shops, and were attacked in the same righteous breath by censors.

154

By the 19th Century, a general image of the Occult Book had become lodged in the popular mind, influenced largely by the fiction of such writers as Poe, Hawthorne, Le Fanu, Horace Walpole, and the other exponents of the gothic. The ultimate occult book, in this view, was a grimoire, a tome dealing with black magic, especially as it was applied to making pacts with the Devil for the sorcerer's personal advantage. Written in strange tongues or mysterious symbols on parchment or vellum and bound in leather, silver, or the (reputed) skins of dragons or human infants, the grimoires of popular fiction were Faustian volumes which might confer on the reader health, wealth, immortality, and sexual irresistibility, but only at the terrible risk of eternal damnation.

The Occult Book Cult

This evolutionary summary of the image of occult books in western Europe reflects a fact well known to both historians and practicing magicians: in accounting for present conditions, what is important is not so much the *actual* facts as what are *believed to be* the facts. (Thus the person who is convinced he has been put under the evil eye will often become physically ill.) It can hardly be doubted that the current interest in occult books is being influenced by earlier attitudes, as they still affect both readers (favorably, one must assume) and professional book-people such as reviewers and librarians (unfavorably, at least in some cases). In other words, this apparent flood of new titles retailing "Sixteen Ways to Know the Future by Examining the Lumps on a Cucumber" or "My Previous Life as Lincoln's Doctor's Dog" are, to some extent, coasting on public relations done in our grandparents' day, although with effects ranging from fascination to multifarious.

Now, in roundabout fashion, we have arrived at the point of acknowledging that there exists something called "the occult book explosion," an event that has inevitably begun to make itself felt in juvenile publishing following the adult trend. This is not a proposition we intend to prove here, if anyone is inclined to dispute it. Let us say only that personal experience has shown a rapid rise in publishers' interest over the last few years and that a lightning-like survey of the review pages of *SLJ* confirmed the fact that from a mere trickle in 1967, books reviewed in the category have increased to well over a dozen in each of the last two years (excluding collections of ghost stories and other weird tales).

What then, if anything, is the import of all this? Should there be occult books for young readers and if so, what kind? Are they, like food, fresh air, and even French grammar, both useful and harmful depending on circumstances, and if so, which books are which?

"Occult" Defined

First of all, what *is* an occult book? Or, to be more precise, what is *in* all those books stocked by occult bookstores? The distinction must be made because the word "occult" is hopelessly vague and even an assist from the dictionary gives us only "mysterious," "secret," "hidden," and "supernatural" as synonyms. Under those terms the general reader might well classify the works of James Joyce, the poetry of Wallace Stevens or T. S. Eliot, all mathematics texts, most government files, and even the books of Agatha Christie and her colleagues as "occult."

The fact is that the occult now includes a sweeping variety of subjects, some of which are hardly related at all to the classical occult, in the sense of black magic. As it is used today, the term occult seems to cover five main subject headings, although there are many areas of overlap.

First come books on prediction. All sorts of systems that purport to tell the future or to read character are included here: palmistry, astrology, the Tarot, numerology, the ouija and planchette, crystal gazing and other forms of scrying, the prophecies of Nostradamus, phrenology, the *I Ching*, the *Kabbala*, and many ob-

scure omancies such as hydromancy, or-
nithomancy, and even onychomancy,
which is done by examining the reflections of the sun on the fingernails.

Next there are works on the history
and practice of magic, as performed either by primitive peoples today, by the
ancients, or in the remarkably eclectic
system of thought current among al-
chemists and learned men of medieval
Europe and sometimes referred to as the
Great Art.

Third, and obviously related to the
above topic, is religion, since one man's
faith is another's superstition. Here we
find material primarily concerned with
religions outside the Judeo-Christian tradition (exceptions are the more obscure
early heresies), with preference for the
transcendental or mystical beliefs of the
orient. Scientology, spiritualism, theoso-
phy and other philosophies and mytholo-
gies are also included, as are physical
aids to enlightenment such as diet, drugs,
meditation, and exercises of the Yoga or
self-defense type (the latter only when
used as a spiritual discipline).

After these come what might be called
occult histories—world views that are
more or less minority reports on human,
planetary, or universal events of the past.
Under this heading are found books of
the "hollow earth" school, accounts of
lost continents such as Atlantis, Mu, and
Lemuria, the "cosmic catastrophe" view
of ancient history headed by Immanuel
Velikovsky, speculations about the lost
tribe of Israel, the Yeti, the Big-foot, and
the Loch Ness monster, various nonre-
ligious predictions of the end of the
world, and the UFO books, especially
those in which influence from other
worlds is seen as responsible for events
on earth.

The fifth topic is psi, a broad term covering all the phenomena relating to psychic powers, from ESP through psychokinesis, poltergeisting, out-of-body
experiences, materialization, precognition, psychic healing, spirit return,
ghosts, water and metal divining, and
many others. The range is from the most
credulous accounts of personal experi-

ence to the rigorously controlled and analyzed experiments and observations of
J. B. Rhine, Ian Stevenson, and other in-
vestigators.

Finally, there are matters peripheral to
these five headings, such as abnormal
psychology, hypnotism, vegetarianism,
world folklore, straight archaeology and
anthropology, biofeedback, and acupunc-
ture.

Taken all together, this is certainly a
fine kettle of fish, a bouillabaisse from
the table of Shakespeare's Weird Sisters.
Why in the world would any sensible person devote more than ten seconds to such
a mishmash? When the semantics is
stripped away, all these topics have one
characteristic in common: they are in
some sense the rejected hypotheses of our
culture, unpopular opinions about the nature of our minds and of the world we live
in.

The Occult in History

Many of the beliefs we now classify as
occult are simply ideas whose time has
past. Yet they have left their traces on every surface of modern life. Attend a performance of *Faust*, reread *The Tempest*,
visit Delphi or Stonehenge, delve into
the history of the court of Louis XIV
or Scotland under the Stuarts, read
Fowles's *The Magus* or Tolkien's *The
Lord of the Rings*. Think, too, about the
origins of such words as "nightmare,"
"pixillate," "bugaboo," "glamor," "her-
metic," "sinister," and "scapegoat."
Then try to tell yourself that the history
of occult thought is irrelevant to present-
day experience.

The position of the historian is that of
an outsider, cataloging and interpreting
in the hope of adding to the sum of human knowledge. This has its own re-
wards, but it is not at all the sole, or perhaps even the principal attraction of
occult studies. The occult holds out the
alluring possibility of finds that possess
more than historical value. Like golden
fibulae tossed out among potsherds, there
are certain areas of occult that *may* turn
out to be deserving of serious consideration.

Just what those areas are is, of course, a matter of opinion. It would imply some obvious contradictions to accept *all* the propositions classified as occult, so that some must be rejected even by the believer, to say nothing of the person who merely tries to keep an open mind. For myself, the topics that hold out the most hope of eventual verification are those concerned with delimiting more exactly the powers of the mind, such as telepathy, precognition, and psychokinesis. Furthermore, I consider the existence of life in other solar systems (though not necessarily in the form of little men in shiny silver saucers) to be a near mathematical certainty. I think it very possible that there is some large, previously unknown creature living in Loch Ness and the other lochs of Scotland and Ireland, and I am convinced that we have a great deal to learn about the power of the mind over the body, both conscious and unconscious. On the other hand, I am not a believer in astrology, and I am unconvinced of the existence of a "soul" that either transmigrates from body to body or returns from the dead to communicate through mediums. So much for the size and shape of the limb onto which I am personally willing to venture.

The point of this confession of faith and the lack thereof is not to make pronouncements about the relative validity of various occult beliefs, since the one thing nearly every reader will agree on is that I have gone either too far or not far enough. Its only legitimate use is to put the reader on notice as to the degree of the writer's involvement with the subject, because the question of objectivity becomes so extremely important as soon as one ceases to speak exclusively as a historian.

Yet objective though we may be in one sense, in another we are less so. It seems that the phrase most noticeably lacking in nonfiction writing for children is "we don't know." Textbooks and reading books alike are filled with comfortable certainties that tell, at best, an incomplete story: "George Washington was the Father of his country." "The

desert is a very hot place." "Richard III murdered the little Princes in the Tower." All these statements are generally accepted as true, although each is open to debate, qualification, or further explanation. To be sure there are exceptional books that give the child any sense of the *gaps* in our knowledge of the universe; but they are few.

This discussion points out an important possible function of occult books for young readers. A *known* fact is at best only a steppingstone to another fact, previously unknown; at worst it is a stumbling block on a list to be memorized. Unfortunately, our educational system often produces adults who view known facts as merit badges while anything unknown is a threat, a possible failing mark on a phantom examination. The best way to kill curiosity is to make it humiliating for students to admit that *they* don't know, and impossible for them to imagine that *we* don't know. Thus occult books, like another despised branch of literature, science fiction, can be mental can openers. If the can in question turns out to be a can of worms, so much the better. No one learns to judge between the false and the true without having had experience of both.

Modern Canutes

We have seen, in a brief and unsystematic way, what is generally meant by occult books and why it may be unwise to reject the whole gallimaufry as either useless or merely trashy. Yet the bald fact is that "we"—writers, educators, editors, librarians—can no more turn back the occult tide than King Canute could command the waves of the English sea. (And the reasons why an Anglo-Saxon ruler believed himself to have power over the waters are to be sought—where else?—in the history of occult thought.) We are not going to be able to dam the occult flood for three reasons. First, it's already here. Second, it is natural and inevitable for kids to want to know about whatever interests their elders, and right now that's the occult; we have already passed that time-lag point after which the juvenile readership starts demanding to catch up with the adult. Last, and perhaps most compelling, occult books are fun. They are exciting and sometimes a little bit scary, and only the most arteriosclerotic mi id is so rigid as to find those emotions altogether painful. Witches are fun, werewolves are fun. Mysteries, mummies, and magicians are fun, like all things that allow us to pretend they are more dangerous than they are. So the popularity of occult books is goii g to run its course regardless, and the only useful question to ask about it is not, "What is to be done about it?" but "Why has it happened and how can we understand it better?"

Of course, questions beginning with *why* are among the slipperiest fish in the language, as children are all too adept at demonstrating. Nevertheless, we can certainly make some reasonable suggestions.

A Sense of Loss

It is not necessary to have recourse to catch-phrases like "counterculture" or "alienation" to perceive that there are many individuals today who find something seriously lacking in the civilization that has shaped their lives. In a recent newspaper interview, Captain Edgar Mitchell, the astronaut who conducted psychic experiments while on a moon mission, had this to say about increasing interest in psi phenomena: "I think it is a fear on the part of people that they're losing identity and that the course of world history is not conducive to ultimate survival. They're concerned about it. I see this fear of deepening planetary crisis. People are just damned concerned and they're looking for answers. The mind, the spirit, is just one area they're looking." (*Freedom: the Independent Journal Published by the Church of Scientology*, December-February).

To some extent, of course, this same pattern has held true for centuries. The witch cults of medieval Europe appealed principally to the powerless, the

individualists, the outcast, and those who had no other socially sanctioned outlet for their energies (the prime example of the latter being women). Today, however, discontent has grown deeper, not only because of the increasingly technological direction taken by western culture but because more people have time to spare from the bare business of survival and because they are freer to express their doubts. One will not, for example, be burned at the stake for reading the *Grand Grimoire*.

For many, the symptom that requires an antidote is materialism, so that it is the otherworldliness or nonworldliness of Buddhism, Hinduism, Taoism, or other eastern religions that beckons. Or it may be the machine, especially the computer, that is seen as the principal evil, and then the cure is often sought in the psychic and magical. The seductive thing about magic is that it restores to individuals the sense that they have some direct control of their lives. (How often have you wanted to turn an obstructive bureaucrat into a toad or a typewriter ribbon?)

The negative side of occult belief is that it can produce a narrow anti-intellectualism that is just as doctrinaire, petty, and repressive as the conditions it claims to be reacting against. Still, as has been said of politics, "The trouble with any good cause is the company one is forced to keep." Certainly there are loud-mouthed, opinionated, irrational astrologists, Krishna people, or Tarot enthusiasts. But then there are the Republicans, Democrats, Dolphins fans, car nuts, bird lovers, bridge players. . .

A more moderate view of occultism would take it to be, not a studied attempt to overthrow all rationalism and orderly thought, but a needed corrective for a culture that has come to honor things and the manipulation or possession of things above human values and intuition. It will not do for us to overlook the fact that magic is in itself a coherent system of thought, shaped by its own internal logic and capable of great flexibility, precision, and communicative power. In this it is parallel to, though utterly different in structure from the system of thought we use every day and which (sometimes without much justification) we name rational. Magical thought describes a universe, or one of the universes, termed by Carlos Castaneda's Don Juan "a separate reality." To view this universe, no matter how briefly and imperfectly, is to be forced to abandon the sort of psychological provincialism that insists on believing its own propositions to be the only possible ones. Anthropologists of recent decades were made to learn this lesson in a hard school, having found that all their carefully preserved field notes presented an excellent reflection of the minds of western anthropologists but bore almost no relation to the realities of life as perceived by members of other (often magical) cultures.

Because the operations of ancient or primitive magic are not predictable and orderly in the manner of a chemistry experiment, the mistake is often made of thinking magic is arbitrary and irrational. It would be more nearly true to describe it as nonrational or pararational. The reason is that the standard of success for a magical operation is not how closely it adheres to some measurable external standard but rather how well the individual magician has combined the symbolic values of the words in the spell or the ingredients in the charm. For example, there are certain chemical procedures that will, when performed with the right equipment and materials under standard physical conditions, invariably produce, say, potassium iodide as an end product, any other result being traceable to an error in technique. The success or failure of the process does not depend on the chemist's name, history, and frame of mind, or whether he or she has fasted before setting to work; neither is it relevant to know the moral purpose for which the potassium iodide is wanted.

On the other hand, although it should be possible to give a detailed explanation of the magical purpose of each ingredient used by Macbeth's three weird ladies in their much-quoted potion, we would first have to know the exact purpose of the brew and also certain details such as the time of year and phase of the moon. Into such an explanation matters like the protein content of eye of newt or the nature of the colloids in toe of frog would not enter (although as rationalists we might speculate on the toxic effects of conine and taxine from the root of hemlock and slips of yew). However it *would* be of the utmost importance that the "toad that under cold stone . . . . sweltered venom sleeping got" should have done so for 31 days and nights as specified, rather than for 30 or 32. We may be sure that if the sisters lived up to their reputation they would not proceed merely by rote, a very low form of magic, fit only for amateurs and outsiders. Probably never again would the conditions be such that the brew could be prepared in an identical manner, so that method and ingredients would have to vary accordingly.

Magic as Art

To have made these statements about magic is to have said that it is truly an art, since all art is concerned with the arrangement of symbols, whether of color, form, sound, words, textures, movement, or a combination. The painter who creates a scene of the Nativity, for example, is working with a rather limited set of visual symbols—mother, father, child, Magi, shepherds, stable, star, angels—which have been combined and recombined in the same basic scene for centuries. The difference in our intellectual and emotional response to a Nativity by Leonardo and one by a fourth-rate Victorian book illustrator is precisely the difference between a good and a bad magical spell. In each case no one but the artist/magician can fully justify or even account for the particular intuition that gave form to the work, nor can a work of the same power be produced solely by application of rational formulas. This last fact is the despair both of aspiring creative artists and sorcerer's apprentices.

Magic not only partakes of the nature of art in general but is closely allied with the specific art of poetry. It is not a coincidence that a magic *spell* and *spell* in the ordinary sense come from a Germanic word root meaning simply to speak or discourse, nor that something en*chant*ed has been placed in the magician's power by virtue of *chant*ing about it. Indeed it might be suggested that the development of words and language was the original magical event in human history, for to *name* a thing is to control it in a very special way, so that the name *stands for* the thing and in a certain sense *is* the thing named. This is one of the two or three universal laws of magic, which are seen to underly the most diverse magical undertakings in every kind of culture. It is likely that the first poetry was pronounced for ritual rather than for artistic purposes. Intuitively we know that magic is additive and that repetition of a name or command makes the magical effect stronger. Thus repetition produces its own rhythms and variations and a simple invocation such as, "Let the game come to the hunter," becomes a hunting chant, a thing of much greater psychological force.

We undertook this short discourse on the nature of magic, and thereby of all occult thought, knowing that we were speaking of times far beyond the reach of recorded history, and open only to speculation. We did so, too, in the hope of showing that there is a dimension in occult studies that goes beyond the question of whether specific occult claims—levitation, precognition, spirit survival, or what have you—should turn out to be "true" in the conventional sense. Magic is a mode of thought that may represent nothing more than a phase in the history of our species. Yet it is certainly with us still, nor is it entirely clear that magical thought, as applied to the quality and forms of life, is merely a superstition to be rooted out, even supposing that could be done.

Serious vs. Solemn

If this profile of the nature of occult thought has succeeded at all, it will have provided a basis for understanding why we now state that a large percentage of books on the occult, both for young readers and for adults, are guilty of failing to take the subject seriously. By "seriously," of course, we do not mean "solemnly." There has been enough portentously solemn writing for both audiences to last several generations. But, by failing to be serious in the sense of recognizing that the subject is not simply quirky or ridiculous, the writer does a disservice to his audience and demonstrates that he or she would have done better to choose another topic. It has been shown to be perfectly possible to write about Hitler without being a Nazi, about Japan without advocating ritual suicide, or about Columbus without sharing his conviction that India lay directly west of Spain. Yet for some reason the prevailing attitude among both writers and public seems to be that one cannot write about the occult without being forever labelled as a new sort of fellow traveler. For this reason qualified researchers often avoid the subject as if they were afraid of catching creeping astrology.

The general disrespect that is felt for the occult contributes, perhaps, to the formation of another unfortunate attitude, this time among those who *do* write about it. We have all seen occult books so sloppily researched and sketchily written that they seem to carry the message, "This stuff is all a fake anyway, so why bother to get the facts straight?" (For a discussion of some of these, see *SLJ*, October 1972, p. 129; *LJ*, October 15, 1972, p. 3471).

Deliberate fakery, as opposed to misguided credulity, is a factor that certainly must be reckoned with in writing about the occult, from the earliest times to last week. The history of the more practical aspects of occultism, such as foretelling the future, reading the past, and communicating with the dead, is riddled with cases of proven (sometimes self-confessed) fraud. This fact *seems* to reinforce the conclusion that all occult claims are bunk, and therefore not worth proper investigation. Logically, however, the existence of fraud is as irrelevant to the validity of occult experience as is the existence of an Elmyr de Hory (the notable art forger) to the greatness of Rembrandt.

Fraud is a fascinating topic in its own right, and nowhere is it seen to better advantage than in the psychic world of the last two or three centuries, where at times the unconscious desire of the public to be fooled was so intense that we can only be amazed that fakes and opportunists were not even more numerous. All of us, not least those who consider themselves hard-headed, have an immense talent for believing what we want to believe. Thus the whole question of belief becomes one of considerable interest, even for the skeptic. Why, for example, does a whole population bow to the persuasions of a Savonarola while another adamantly refuses to believe in vaccination or fluoridation? The fact of belief often makes the difference between history and oblivion, and forms a rather neglected aspect of intellectual history, especially the history of science, which seems often to overemphasize the role played by logic. Fraud is an interesting scholarly sidelight, but certainly not a blanket condemnation of the field.

It would not be fair to imply that the defects in many current occult books are all due to misconceptions about the subject and frivolous treatment by authors. The field in general has been held in such low esteem that tools of research such as specialized bibliographies, indexes, and library collections are few or nonexistent. Of the three major encyclopedias of the occult and related topics in my possession,[1] two are unsystematic and riddled with errors of fact and spelling, while the third is of limited scope, and all are in need of updating.

There is another factor that increases the difficulty of writing good occult books. The occult is a live topic. That is, people seem to hold more passionate opinions on it than on anything except sex and politics. Even from the perspective of one author's very limited experience as a writer and reviewer of occult books, it seems that one cannot publish a word on the subject without exciting the wrath of both opposing camps. Prominent psychic writers leap to denounce the "antipsychic bias" of the same work cited by unbelievers as evidence of rank gullibility. American history or art appreciation simply does not call forth such intense reaction. It is no wonder that some excellent writers have shied away from becoming involved in this kind of circus. We can only hope that increasing interest and a wider market will attract better researchers and encourage both writers and editors to require of themselves the same degree of accuracy and objectivity that would obtain in other fields, and that librarians will not buy bad books simply to fill a demand. Certainly, some aspects of the occult are sensational, some are incredible (from the point of view of the depth of human folly if from no other), some are titillating, and some are marked by fraud ranging from blatant to brilliant. But that may be said of other topics and is really no excuse for simply producing a pastiche of startling instances and reputed happenings in the manner of Ripley's Believe-It-or-Not.

This is not to say that some first-rate juvenile books have not been produced on occult subjects. The topic of UFOs has been well covered, as have those perennial favorites, the Abominable Snowman and haunted houses. There are two or three good books on ghosts and perhaps too many on witchcraft. Magic and lost continents have been given at least a once-over, and there is a good supply of collections of tales, both from folklore and from alleged personal experience which are far too numerous to mention. However, there are many noticeable gaps. In only two or three cases are there enough good books on a topic so that an interested reader can get an informed and, what is more important with a controversial subject, a varied and objective view of, say, secret societies, telekinesis, or the life of Mme. Blavatsky.

Rationalists will have to live with the fact that occult books are here, at least for a while. After all, our society has certainly not lost its appetite for the impossible. It is only that circumstances have conspired to deprive us of a genuine sense of mystery, thus forcing us to pretend to find prodigies in the prosaic. Come, take a little trip in search of the evidence. Just dab a little "Tabu" or "Sortilege" behind your ears and don't forget the Secret deodorant. Put on your best clothes (freshly washed in Miracle White) and your charm bracelet. We'll start out across Boston's Mystic Bridge. Shall we head for Hell's Canyon, Devil's Lake, or the Garden of the Gods? The kids in the back seat are happily drawing with Magic Marker. Later we'll stop for sandwiches made with Wonder Bread and Miracle Whip. For dessert some angelfood. And, if we're lucky, tonight's motel may have beds equipped with Magic Fingers. Now turn on the radio for an analysis of the Apollo flights. What about some music? Are they playing the Beatles "Magical Mystery Tour," or is it just "That Ol' Black Magic?"

RECOMMENDED JUVENILE BOOKS

Aylesworth, Thomas G. *Servants of the Devil.* Addison-Wesley, 1970.
Bowman, John. *The Quest for Atlantis.* Doubleday, 1971.
Cohen, Daniel. *The Natural History of Unnatural Things.* Saturday Review Pr., 1971.
Jennings, Gary. *Black Magic, White Magic.* Dial, 1965.
Kettlekamp, Larry. *Haunted Houses.* Morrow, 1969.
Soule, Gardner. *The Maybe Monsters.* Putnam, 1963.

_____. *The Trail of the Abominable Snowman.* Putnam, 1966.
_____. *UFOs and IFOs: A Factual Report on Flying Saucers.* Putnam, 1967.
White, Dale. *Is Something Up There?* Doubleday, 1968.

ADULT BOOKS FOR YOUNG READERS

Cohen, Daniel. *Myths of the Space Age.* Dodd, 1967.
Hall, Trevor. *New Light on Old Ghosts.* Transatlantic, 1965.
Hughes, Pennethorne. *Witchcraft.* Penguin, 1965.
Hansen, Chadwick. *Witchcraft at Salem.* Braziller, 1969.
Sanderson, Ivan T. *Uninvited Visitors: A Biologist Looks at UFOs.* Cowles, 1967.
Wilson, Colin. *The Occult.* Random, 1971.**

**An excellent, infuriating, and impressive book, by far the best general introduction to the subject for the advanced reader.

REFERENCE

1. Fodor, Nandor. *Encyclopedia of Psychic Science.* University Bks., 1966.
Useful but spotty and not always accurate.
    Robbins, Rossell Hope. *The Encyclopedia of Witchcraft and Demonology.* Crown, 1959.
Excellent but inherently limited in scope.
    Spence, Lewis. *Encyclopedia of Occultism.* University Bks., 1960.
More systematic but often even less comprehensive than Fodor.

From Mad Professors to Brilliant Scientists

Ben Bova

FOR GENERATIONS, librarians and teachers have felt uncomfortable about science fiction. Since the lurid covers of magazines perpetuated the image in the 30's, detractors of the genre have called it pulp literature. Its critics have judged the books by their covers. Silly movies and the haughty sniff of an occasional literary critic confirmed their opinion. Yet kids loved it and kept demanding more: science fiction has been especially popular among preteens and teenagers.

They have discovered that very few science fiction stories picture humankind as a passive species, overwhelmed by all the forces of nature or history. No matter how omnipotent the invaders from the Crab Nebula, no matter how inexorably the glaciers of a new ice age grind down on civilization, no matter how hopeless the condition of our explorers on Mars— the characters battle back, they challenge nature, enemies, and their own short-comings. Sometimes they win, sometimes they lose; but their struggles make exciting stories and tell us more about what it's like to be a human being.

In this sense, science fiction mirrors science itself.

Basically, in its attempt to measure and order the vast universe, science is an utterly humanistic endeavor. It is the work of men who believe that the human mind can *understand* the seemingly infinite chaos of nature. And with understanding comes appreciation. No poet rhapsodizing about a starry sky truly knows the wonders he rhymes about unless he understands something of astrophysics. To be ignorant of science is to be partially blind.

Bridging the "Two Cultures"

Science fiction forms a bridge between the Humanities and Technology bringing to readers a far deeper and keener sense of wonder over the physical universe and man's place in it. The exotic settings and strange creatures in science fiction stories are evidence of man's ability to stretch his imagination beyond the confines of the here-and-now. And where man's imagination can go, ultimately his understanding and appreciation will follow.

Perhaps that is why, year after year, youngsters demand science fiction from librarians, they buy science fiction magazines with a zeal approaching religious faith, and, with the availability of paperbacks, they have made science fiction one of the most profitable *genres* for publishers.

Nevertheless, astute observers continue to wonder what there is in science fiction to attract young readers. As recently as five years ago, a librarian told me, "I don't know what they see in it! I never read any of it myself, of course, but the youngsters are *fascinated* by it!" Never read any of it. Never!

Years ago, librarians bought science fiction books on the strength of reviews or because a publisher had established a science fiction line for which libraries could place standing orders. Teachers were even worse. Teachers of English tended to gag over the words "science fiction"; teachers of science turned red at the mention of it; teachers of social studies, history, and other subjects professed a studied indifference.

The SF Boom

Today the situation is very much reversed. A recent issue of *Social Education*, the professional journal of teachers of social studies, was devoted to science fiction as a means of teaching social values and social change. At the 1972 convention of the National Council of Teachers of English, no less than three seminars were devoted to science fiction topics. Several hundred colleges and universities are now offering courses in science fiction. These courses are often over-subscribed, and students are turned away. Science fiction writers are invited to lecture at auditoria crowded with English majors, science and engineering students, political science majors, historians, ROTC men, and student anti-war activists. No one has yet been able to determine how many high schools and junior highs are now giving courses in science fiction—usually at the demand of students. An organization of teachers and researchers has been formed specifically for SF and is called the Science Fiction Research Associates. In my office at *Analog* magazine, I am asked regularly to assist teachers who are putting together science fiction courses or students who are researching term papers on the subject.

There have been many theories about science fiction's sudden ascent into respectability. Certainly the success of the Apollo program showed many people that "shooting for the moon" was no longer an impossible dream. Our growing concerns with pollution, population, and other problems that stem from science and technology have also helped to turn the spotlight on science fiction.

And, fortunately, kids are finally getting what they've been asking for. One of the favorite aphorisms of today's youth is: "Tomorrow is the first day of the rest of your life." Science fiction is about tomorrow. It deals with the future. It speaks of the changes that will come to our society, to other societies, and to man himself. Its medium is a gigantic canvas that includes all the universe of space and stars, all of time, and the whole universe inside the mind of man.

Science fiction is about the interaction of human beings and some aspects of science or technology, or some aspects of the natural world that do not exist on Earth at this time. This rather broad definition deliberately excludes fantasy tales of sorcery and monsters, as well as "day after tomorrow" stories about how awful New York City will be by the end of the century.

Fantasy vs. Realism

Historians of literature have pointed out that many of the great figures of letters have tried their hands at what might loosely be called science fiction. Indeed, Cyrano de Bergerac began the modern era of science fiction in his tales of journeys to the moon and the sun. Some of his tongue-in-cheek ideas were used by Rostand in his play about Cyrano.

L. Sprague de Camp, a science fiction writer and historian, has pointed out that just about *all* of literature dealt with fantasy and unworldly romance until Cervantes' *Don Quixote* cast literature's first realistic look at the contemporary world.

Most of the writers treated so lovingly in high school literature—Dickens, Defoe, Stevenson, Poe—wrote stories of wild fantasy or science fiction at one time or another. By the latter decades of the 19th Century, English literature was rife with so-called *scientific romances*: popular stories in which scientific discoveries or technological inventions were the key features of the background and plot.

Out of this scene stepped Jules Verne and H. G. Wells, who until rather recently were the only "respectable" writers of science fiction known to most adults.

The Pulp Magazines

On this side of the Atlantic, other forces were at work. By the beginning of the 20th Century, pulp magazines were an important segment of the American publishing industry. Using the cheapest paper and printing available, the "penny dreadfuls" and dime novels were the TV of those years. They were filled with stories that emphasized romance and adventure: in the wild west, on the high seas, in darkest Africa, or remotest Asia.

One enterprising man, Hugo Gernsback, began to include science fiction stories in the pulp magazines he edited. In 1926, he published a new magazine totally devoted to science fiction: *Amazing Stories*. Although it has gone through many changes in ownership and format, *Amazing* is still being published today.

The success of the magazine drew rival publishers into this new field of science fiction. Soon newsstands were flooded with magazines with titles like *Fantastic, Startling, Astounding*, and *Thriller Wonder*. For the most part, they were out-and-out copies of *Amazing*.

And terrible! By modern standards, most of the stories in these science fiction pulps were unbelievably poor. Some were stiff lectures by a character who was labelled "brilliant scientist." His assistant and beautiful daughter held hands while he discoursed endlessly on some arcane discovery or invention. The so-called science was almost always pure nonsense.

At the other end of the scale were the adventure stories that could have been written for any kind of pulp. Indeed, many pulp writers sold virtually identical stories to science fiction, western, detective, and other types of magazines. All

they did was change the cowboy's Stetson to a space helmet, change the sixgun to a raygun, the western plains to the deserts of Mars, and the evil red Indians to the evil red Martians.

This is the kind of awful stuff that still clings to science fiction's reputation like a youthful indiscretion no one can forget. These pulp stories—and the imitations *still* being cranked out in movies and TV shows—are what most adults think of as science fiction.

They're 30-odd years behind the times. They are victims of a culture and a generation gap. For sandwiched in-between the lurid covers of half-nude women about to be eaten by giant lobsters were stories and ideas that thrilled young readers. Not sexually. Despite the racy covers of the 1930's, science fiction was asexual in the sternest Victorian manner. Even today there are older SF fans who complain when sex occasionally invades their favorite literature.

What excited the kids of the early 30's, who are the astronauts of today, was the idea, the scope, the *grandeur* of science fiction. There is no other word that describes the best in this field.

Rocketships to the moon, intelligent races on Mars, time travel, death rays, eternal life, the ability to step through solid walls, to fly like a bird, to read men's minds, and lift mountains with mental power alone—all these concepts appear in science fiction. And they strike some of the deepest chords in the human psyche. Science fiction tells its readers that they can be immortal supermen— gods, if you will. Even though it is only vicarious, readers love it.

Although Gernsback had no intention of doing so, he placed science fiction squarely in the realm of pulp magazines. No other kind of publisher would touch it. Since pulp magazines paid little, science fiction failed to attract the best talents of the 1920's and 1930's. During the later 30's and through the Second World War, most of the pulps died. But some science fiction magazines survived, and, by the end of the war, they were no longer pulps.

Coming Out from Under

This survival was due largely to one man: John W. Campbell, Jr.

Campbell became editor of *Astounding* in 1937; he was a student at MIT and therefore widely versed in modern science. He was also one of the most prolific and successful writers in the SF field. Eventually, he gave up writing in order to devote all his time to editing; in the process, he revolutionized the genre. He insisted on two elements in every story: plausible science and good fiction.

With no pseudo-scientific gimcrackery, writers were free to invent anything as long as no one could prove that known laws of science had been violated. This set up an exciting mental contest between readers and writers: writers were constantly trying to bend the known laws of science and present plausible explanations for present-day impossibilities such as time travel, interstellar flight, invisibility; readers were trying to find the flaws in the scientific background.

Secondly, these straightforward stories were populated by believable characters: the hackneyed mad professor with the beautious daughter went out the window, and real characters began appearing.

Campbell wanted *ideas*, he wanted strong stories, and he got them.

The writers that Campbell developed are now the immortals of the field: Asimov, Heinlein, de Camp, Sturgeon, Anderson, Blish, Dickson.

Over a period of 34 years ending with Campbell's death in 1971, science fiction became a vital force in American letters. Campbell's influence, long dominant within the SF field, is now being felt in the publishing industry as a whole. Science fiction is the last viable market for commercial short fiction; there are other magazines being published today, devoted to fiction, but few people read them. Most of today's best-selling novelists and many serious writers are examining science fiction themes, ideas, and techniques.

Campbell and his writers predicted the world we live in today. They were writing of nuclear weapons and mind-controlling drugs back in the 1930's. They were worrying about the impact of global communications and rising population pressures and our increasing dependence on a very complex, yet very fragile technology, more than a quarter century ago.

In the 1960's, Campbell changed the name of his magazine from *Astounding* to *Analog*. The new title was more in keeping with science fiction's self-image, as a mirror held up to the future, a means of helping us to see all the possibilities of tomorrow. The name change also confirmed what everyone had known for nearly two decades: the old "gee-whiz" days of the pulps were dead.

Meanwhile, the massive impact of social changes, the obvious power of modern technology to accomplish good *and* evil, the imminence of a new millennium only a generation away, the realization that *change* is inescapable, the coining of the term "future shock" were all making science fiction the only literature that spoke to all these needs of young readers. And, while all this was happening, the book publishing industry was sleeping away, largely ignoring science fiction.

It's interesting to note that Isaac Asimov (whose book earnings have added dividends to the annual statements of several publishing houses) could not get a book published in the 1940's. His earliest novels were serialized in *Astounding* and that remained the only vehicle for his work until well into the 50's. No book publisher wanted to consider the *Foundation Trilogy* or a collection of stories about robots. It was unheard of!

A few publishers were perspicacious enough to realize that there was a market for juvenile science fiction books. But even as recently as the early 60's, what passed for juvenile science fiction wouldn't have made the grade in the old pulps. It may have been better written, but the plotting was hamstrung by the publishers' insistence that juvenile novels must have juvenile protagonists. Hence, a stream of books in which Dick and Jane save the universe.

The Paperback Revolution

Gradually this changed. What changed it most was the paperback revolution. When paperbacks began appearing everywhere, science fiction quickly became a staple item; at first, mainly because science fiction writers were hungry and accustomed to working for low rates; then, too, young science fiction fans could afford paperback books and bought them in large numbers.

Finally hardback publishers realized that there were profits in science fiction. By the late 1960's, several houses had developed science fiction lines. One of the oldest and most successful of these is Doubleday's.

Today, no matter whether a hard-back science fiction novel is tabbed "juvenile," "young adult," or "adult," most of its sales are to libraries. In fact, the material inside hard-cover science fiction books does not vary all that much from one age category to another, and the readers of all three categories are apt to be the very same people: youngsters.

Just as the works of Robert Louis Stevenson and Mark Twain appeal to young and old alike, most science fiction can be read for fun and profit by anyone old enough to follow the vocabulary.

My own "juvenile" science fiction novels have been read by corporation presidents and scientists, reviewed and debated by science fiction fans and critics of all ages. And I am very proud of a letter which was written by a nine-year-old, he thanked me for writing a certain novel because it was hard for him to read, and he enjoyed the challenge.

The blurring of distinctions between adult and juvenile science fiction also means that youngsters are reading stories that would have been taboo ten years ago. In the late 1950's, the general rule about juvenile science fiction was: no swearing, no drinking, and no sex. Entire solar systems could be destroyed and billions of people remorselessly wiped out—but no lovemaking!

It was rather ridiculous to have all of space and time for your arena but not be able to mention matters of which most young people are not only aware, but in which they are keenly interested. To keep sex taboo meant keeping pornography a viable business.

Some teachers and librarians still insist on using their own standards of propriety in the selection of books for younger readers. But in doing so, they ignore the fact that youngsters have very different standards—and are usually far more aware and knowledgeable about sex, war, drugs, perversion, and sadism than their self-designated protectors.

Examining Tomorrow

Many of these young men and women like science fiction so much that they try their hand at writing it and send their stories to *Analog*. While most of these are amateurish, of course, it's fascinating to see how they reflect an awareness of today's society and tomorrow's problems—the hopes and fears of the future are spelled out in these stories.

These young people know that they're going to live out their lives in the future. They look at the world around them, and, in their attempts to understand it, to make some sense out of it, they turn to science fiction. They are aware, as few adults are, that science and technology are *both* the problem *and* the answer.

Science fiction does not predict the future. But it helps to draw rough maps of what the future might hold. It illustrates both the opportunities and the dangers that lie ahead.

The way these youngsters perceive themselves and their society is shaped to a considerable extent by what they read. They read science fiction because they are concerned about tomorrow. If they can understand enough about the possibilities that lie ahead, perhaps they can work toward the kind of future they desire.

Until someone actually does invent a time machine, science fiction is the best way we have to examine tomorrow. That's why young people love it, and that's why they read it.

Sexuality in Books for Children

Josette Frank

THERE is nothing new about discussion of sex education for children. Books purporting to tell children the "facts of life"—as it was then polite to call them—began appearing about the turn of the century. They were, for their time, brave books, though their "facts" were largely buried in euphemisms, and they were designed to be read quietly to the young child, seated on mother's lap, at twilight.

What *is* new, however, is the appearance of fiction for the teenager, or younger, dealing candidly (if that isn't an understatement) with the sexual activities of other teenagers. Stories about early sexual experiences, out-of-wedlock pregnancies, abortion vs. adoption, unwanted marriages—the whole gamut—are presented in so-called "young adult" books which reach down in readability to ten-year-olds. Perhaps it is time, now, to pause and consider.

The Child Study Association was, I believe, the first nation-wide organization to discuss with parents the sex education of their children. When I first joined the staff of the Association in 1923, they had already published a pamphlet and conducted parent discussion groups on this then highly prohibited subject. We gave what must have been the first radio talk on sex education—and I well remember our battle with the station censors who deleted from our script the mention of any parts of the body and especially the word "masturbation." We lost that battle but we gave the talk anyway, grateful that they allowed us to mention the word "sex." So much for history! In the intervening years we've learned that sex education involves more than words, more than "facts."

That the Child Study Association especially welcomes books for children which help them understand themselves and their world is evidenced by the fact that, ever since 1942, we have given an annual award to a book dealing with some of the realities children face in growing up. At that time (1942), when war and world holocaust were lapping at their feet, their books were filled with nothing but sweetness and light. The award was intended to emphasize the need for books about realities.

Now that this tide has turned, bringing flotsam and jetsam in books "telling it like it is" we have considered whether this award is now redundant. Yet, exactly because this new free-wheeling literature of realism is so uneven, it now seems urgent to honor those books which, in presenting realities and life problems, offer positive values and leave their young readers with hope and faith in themselves and in others.

Here I should explain that the Children's Book Committee of the Child Study Association, through whose heated weekly discussions many of these books pass, considers the age limit of its selected list as about age 13, since the older teens are already browsing in adult literature. This seems to put many of the so-called "young adult" books over-age for our listing. I confess, though, that sometimes we wonder whether, in deciding that a particular book is beyond our age range, we are merely copping out on a difficult decision.

On this point I want to quote from a paper by Dr. Mary Calderone. Pleading for greater freedom in sex education, she says, "learning about sex, being sexual and feeling sexual can and must be harmonized within the individual. At some time the thoughts, the feelings, the attitudes and the behavior must all come together in a congruent whole." For me the key phrase here is: *At some time.* And this is our dilemma. What time? And for which child? You look at a girl of 13 or 14 and you wonder. How much vicarious sexual experience is she ready for? How much can she take, or *should* she take? How much is too much? If she identifies with the girl in *You Would If You Loved Me* (Avon, 1969) she is led to a very high point of sexual stimulation indeed. What will she do with her feelings thus aroused? Certainly it is reality. It is informative. It is authentic. But what will it do for the young reader? Actually, the girl in this story is a conscious tease. She comes through with her virginity intact and feels very virtuous therefore. But what about the boy? The author fails to make clear the real moral question of relationships here, and the reader is left with a false and confusing set of values.

We know that as adults we have to wrestle with our own hang-ups in viewing young people's reading. But we cling to the hope of offering boys and girls something of positive value in their books. One asks of each book not, will it *damage* the young reader but rather, will it *benefit* him or her, and in what way? "Benefits" may come in many forms: information, emotional satisfaction, escape, expanded horizons, or just plain fun. Since the young cannot read *everything* in the limited time available, we hope the books they do read will be those which "stretch the mind and spirit."

Therefore when, in an otherwise conventional adventure tale, we come suddenly, without warning, to an episode in which a 13-year-old girl teaches a boy the way of what she calls "mating," we wonder how this can profit the young reader. Is it information he or she needs or can use at this point in maturing? Is it an integral part of the story or is it dragged in for titillation? When we give this book, or others like it, to a young teenager, are we, in effect, saying "Try it—you'll like it"?

In the last analysis, the criteria I would apply in the acceptability of books of high sexual content concerns the integrity of their purpose, their authenticity, their moral and social validity, and most important, the resolutions they offer. This is not to call for a so-called "happy ending." Rather it is to ask that the characters—especially those with whom the young reader will identify—come through their experiences, however grim or seamy, with a feeling that somehow he or she will cope. I believe it is not a healthy resolution when the heroine ends up on the human junk pile. The scare technique, I believe, profits the young reader nothing.

In contrast, I think of John Donovan's *I'll Get There—It Better Be Worth the Trip* (Dell, 1971). Here, for all their searing life experiences, there is health in both these boys—and the reader comes away knowing they have matured and learned to cope with their difficulties. Their homosexual experience is real, it is threatening and painful. It is handled with grace and insight. And the boys' own reactions are healthy and reassuring.

I think also of Irene Hunt's gently adolescing heroine in *Up a Road Slowly* (Follett, 1966). When, by chance, she comes upon a couple making love in the bushes—a boy and girl she knows—she steps back both physically and emotionally, with a feeling that she is not ready for this intimate knowledge. So the young reader can also step back from this episode, so delicately handled, reassured that it has left no scar on the girl they have come to care about.

Dr. Mary Calderone remembers from her own childhood a drama in which two adolescents, as she describes them, "took that one last step to each other and touched only their palms together, arms spread wide." And she says "in those two moments I knew with my entire self what sex was all about." I doubt this experience would have been enhanced for the little girl she was then by a blueprint of sexual intercourse.

Reviewers frequently stress the "moral dilemma" faced by the characters in these books, and therefore shared with their readers. I have some question whether the dilemma is not *social* rather than *moral*. We are told that puberty tends to come at an earlier age to girls today. Certainly social sophistication does, too, to both boys and girls. We know there are cultures in which, at the onset of puberty, sexual intercourse is acceptable, even encouraged. But our culture makes no place, no provision for its consequences. We have the sad story of 12- and 13-year-old girls coming to clinics for abortions. We have, too, the painful knowledge of venereal disease appearing in ever younger children.

True, these same children are exposed at all ages to movies, television, paperbacks, and news media setting forth lurid details of sexual activity and aberrations. Our children do not wear blinders. And of course they are curious. Yet in these media, as in the adult books earlier generations foraged in, they are confronted by the sexual behavior of adults. Here are feelings they don't share, people with whom they don't identify. In today's juvenile books it is *children* who are having the sexual experiences, experimenting with sexual behavior. It seems to me that here the impact is more real, more immediate, more compelling.

I confess I am thinking in terms of shielding children from unnecessary, premature, unhealthy sexual stimulation, beyond their present maturity and capacity to manage. Just when and how that capacity arrives cannot be defined for all children. Their exposure to sexual behavior in the omnipresent media most certainly hastens their information and their sophistication. Whether it hastens their *maturity* is an unanswered question. So also is the question of the effect of these sexual exposures on their healthy growth in attitudes and perceptions. This applies to books, and other mass media.

A father recently told me that he had accidentally come upon, in his 12-year-old daughter's bathrobe pocket, several of those so-called "bathroom" joke books—not juveniles, of course. He wasn't surprised, and neither was I. We agreed that she was probably enjoying the very clandestine aspect of it. But we agreed, too, that these are *not* the books her parents will give her.

Rightly or wrongly, I am convinced that there is a difference in impact between a book a child happens upon, or reads surreptitiously (like the forbidden books of my childhood), and one that is received with *commendation* from a parent, teacher or librarian—a so-called "approved" or recommended book. Therefore I feel that we adults—and this includes especially writers and editors—have a grave responsibility in commending books to children's attention, to give them books whose positive value we believe in. I do not consider this censorship. The children are free to read other books too, or to reject our suggestions.

But I dare to believe that children—even young teenagers—are impressed by the approval of adults whom they respect, and by the values they stress. Maybe the wish is father to the thought. Maybe I am whistling in the dark!

Certainly I do not have the answers to the serious questions I have raised here. But I am sure we should give them thought. The sexual maturing of the young in our culture today isn't all that simple.

Sexuality in Books for Children

Barbara Wersba

IT OCCURS to me that what we're talking about is political. We're talking about the control of one group of people by another group of people: namely, children by adults. We are not merely discussing what children should read about sex, but what they should *do* about sex—and the fascism implied by this is a bit mind-boggling. Yet somehow children tolerate us and go on doing the same things generation after generation: which is, reading those "forbidden" books, and indulging in sexual activity—and surviving.

I would like to see more sex in children's books—starting with picture books and going right up to the young adult novels—but I would like to see it treated a different way. I have a friend who sat down with his 9-year-old son recently, and because he felt anxious about the child, proceeded to tell him all about sexual intercourse, abortion, venereal disease, contraception, and homosexuality. After an hour, this tiny child turned to his father and said, "Oh, Daddy, I know all about *that* because we get it in school. What I really wanted to know was—is it terrific?" Now, the one thing we don't seem to be able to tell children is, is it terrific? Or is it awful? Or can it be both? Is it beautiful? Is it degrading? Is it ridiculous? What I'm looking for here is

what Dr. Mary Calderone so perfectly described as The Mystery. That's what is absent in our children's books, because it is absent in our adult books—especially in this decade. I think it's typical of our culture that we have leapt directly from Puritanism into pornography; pornography being the meshing and interworking of parts rather than people. What we rarely find in American fiction is the meshing and interworking of minds. Sex in human beings is psychological, not genital. Sex in human beings either succeeds or fails because of mental response. Sex in human beings is emotional. People respond to one another because of what is in their heads—and hearts.

However, if you examine the sales figures to see what books are selling on this subject, you will find that they are called *The Sensuous Man*, *The Sensuous Woman*—and at the bottom of the barrel is Dr. Reuben's shabby work, *Everything You Always Wanted To Know About Sex*. I find these books alarming because Americans are very sexually naive, and many people take such information literally. In *The Sensuous Woman*, written by "J", who will not give her name for good reason, she tells the female reader that she (the reader) is probably an ugly upright piano who, through fine tuning, could become a Steinway grand. Dr.

Reuben's book describes the human body as a complex electrical system, which shortcircuits occasionally. He describes master switches and explosions and fuse problems. The most shocking thing about these books is not the sexual information they impart—but the fact that they are discussing human beings in terms of pianos and electricity. And the fact that these books go into dozens and dozens of printings—all the while talking about parts rather than people—is terrifying to me.

The next thing I want to say is that the so-called New Liberalism in children's books just isn't there. I think what *is* there is the Old Morality disguised as the New Sex. In the old books, the boy and girl would go for a soda after a movie; in the new books, they smoke a little pot and go to bed. It's all very contemporary and a few four-letter words are tossed in. But when you examine these books closely, you find that the morality is still the same; that a judgemental quality pervades. Those who might have been homosexual, of course, go straight; those who were pregnant are sorry; those who were promiscuous are guilty; and if an adult has been attracted to a child, heaven help him. Recently, to my great fascination, I read a young adult novel in which a child seduces an adult. The adult is not at fault, and the child very much needs contact with him. I was tremendously impressed with this book until the last page—when (gratuitously) the author kills her adult character. I thought, "My God, what a price to pay for one orgasm." This writer, whether she knows it or not, has killed her adult character to conform to the Old Morality. But her book will be considered representative of the New Sex.

Children's books only reflect adult books—and adult books only reflect the culture. And as a culture we are still profoundly Puritanical. Our sexual revolution has emerged as a kind of ghastly pragmatism, a do-it-yourself car repair manual. We're very practical, we Americans, we believe in fixing things. If the car won't work, take it back to the shop. If your body won't work, read *The Sensuous Woman*. The pragmatism involved in all this assumes that bodies can be fixed the way cars and vacuum cleaners can be fixed. They cannot, because sex is still a mystery—like God.

I believe that it is up to the children's writer to take a chance and delve deeply into the subject of sex—even if it gets him into trouble. Because children today are not the children we were. They have television. They have seen Lee Harvey Oswald die before their eyes. They have seen murder in Vietnam. I connect Vietnam with this because I find it very strange that I eat dinner while I watch the news: gazing at wholesale slaughter while eating a good meal. There is something in me that is obviously dehumanized—and this, in turn, connects with the dehumanization of our sexual attitudes. There's something terribly tired—or perhaps it's dead—in us, because if we were alive, we would watch the television news and weep. We would consider what we were doing to our children with this disguised sexual Puritanism, and we would grieve for them because *our* lives were spoiled by sexual Puritanism. What we need to explore is not outer space, but inner space. And it is up to the artists and writers to do this.

I was thinking before I came here today that the book I most enjoyed as a child was *Wuthering Heights*, and the film I most enjoyed was *Wuthering Heights*. And it also occurred to me that there is more sex in *Wuthering Heights* than in *Portnoy's Complaint*. *Portnoy's Complaint*, which was well described by one critic as the *Moby Dick* of masturbation, also deals with how to fix the parts of the car, how to repair the vacuum cleaner. *Wuthering Heights*, by contrast, is an old-fashioned book—and to me, a hundred times more erotic. So you can see that I am not asking for graphic explicitness in children's books, but for depth and truth. I think the 19th Century Romantics knew things about sex that we don't. They knew that it implied distance and strangeness; that compatibility and closeness killed eroticism. People in 19th Century literature always had immense difficulties to overcome, miles to cross, social barriers to leap. In this way their books are not only romantic, but erotic— and better than ours.

Perhaps the real fault with our culture is that we lack reverence for life; that we are more concerned with things than people; and that The American Dream has murdered our sensibilities with its insistence on material happiness. Sexual happiness—human happiness—these are areas yet to be explored.

The Maturation of the Junior Novel: From Gestation to the Pill

Lou Willett Stanek

IN 1880 Henry James complained that English and American novels were addressed to young, unmarried ladies to whom half of life was a sealed book. This sexual omission, he thought, was a good thing for virgins and boys, but bad for the novel. By 1930 James, who said this tightly closed window should be opened, but didn't open it himself and found George Sand's sense of delicacy defective, would probably have been shocked to learn how far the window had been raised. Not only had sex become a subject, but books such as Dreiser's *An American Tragedy* (World, 1925) and Faulkner's *The Sound and the Fury* (Random, 1929) characterized young, unmarried, pregnant ladies. In the novels of the 1920's premarital intercourse between adolescents was more likely to take place among the relatively uneducated people than among middle-class, college or college-bound young people, but these novels represented a transition between the unquestioning condemnation of premarital intercourse and pregnancy found in novels of the genteel tradition, in James' time, and the almost casual treatment of these problems in later novels.[1]

Perhaps it was because serious literature had become more realistic that educators were at first so pleased with the emergence of the junior or adolescent novel in the early Thirties. These books were written to a specific audience (virgins and boys), its parameters loosely defined between the ages of 12 to 16. The protagonist was usually a year or two older, 17 to 18. Personal problems such as grades, shyness, fears, family problems, career concerns, and no sex beyond a first kiss were the subjects. They were immediately popular with the young.

Although these books presented and reaffirmed middle class values almost as strongly as the Sunday sermon, the initial adult enthusiasm for the junior novel began to wane when it became apparent that it had settled into a firm pattern. For 40 years parents, teachers, psychologists, and librarians have debated its value, but each year the percentage of school and library book budgets for the junior novel has increased. It would seem that the question no longer is *Should* young teens read these books. They are reading them and will probably continue with or without our sanction. I feel that it would be more reasonable to accept the fact that a book is not necessarily worthless because it is structured by a formula. The formula may have artistic merit and the individual books should be judged on how skillfully the elements of the formula are executed. Another question is: does the formula lend itself to the reflection of a

174

changing adolescent culture? Such an approach should not only give us a critical tool for the novels but also insights into the adolescent culture and its development.

John Cawelti has defined a formula in literature as a conventional system for structuring cultural products.[2] Since 1933 when Longmans, Green and Co. (the first publisher to use the term junior novel) published the immediately popular, *Let the Hurricane Roar*, by Rose Wilder Lane,[3] that conventional system for the junior novel has remained relatively consistent:

1) After the introduction of the protagonist, the problem is dramatized by a brief episode, and then explicitly stated by an intrusion of the omniscient author.

2) Although the protagonist has managed to function adequately up to a point, now some event destroys the precarious equilibrium and precipitates a crisis.

3) The protagonist reacts with increasing frustration, refusing to heed the advice of wiser characters, and instead of approaching the solution of the problem, seemingly getting further and further away from it.

4) Just as a point of absolute hopelessness seems to have been reached, an accident, coincidence, or the sudden intervention of a "transcendent" character bring illumination and insight to the beleaguered protagonist.

5) The problem is solved by the protagonist and appropriate action is taken.[4]

Just as adults who creep through snarled expressway traffic like to read stories of cowboys who ride freely on the open range, teenagers having trouble establishing their identity vicariously enjoy reading about students, who with a little effort, became school paper editor or student government president. Similarly, the manager of a chaotic business escapes into a mystery where the detective always solves the crime and restores order, while his gawky, adolescent child devours stories of awkward colts transformed into Prom Queens and agile football quarterbacks.

This formula works well for both author and reader as long as the student's main problems are how to get a date and what to do about acne, but young people's concerns have changed drastically in the past ten years. Nat Hentoff, successful author and educator, predicts that the young can no longer be conned by a simplistic daydream of an updated interracial Horatio Alger myth:

Many of the young ... are "up tight" in their worlds. Because of poverty or vacuous affluence, because of the very real possibility of being killed in Vietnam in a grotesquely immoral war not of their making, because of the racism that is still pervasive in this country ... books specifically for twelve-and-over in the years to come—and I would not be certain this category will long survive—are going to be much more complex, more shocking to librarians though not to the young, and much more openly—and healthy erotic than "books for young readers" have ever been before.[5]

In 1966 Nat Hentoff made the same plea for the junior novel as James had for the serious novel in 1890. Just as Joyce, Faulkner, Dreiser, et. al., responded in the early part of the century, in the past few years, authors writing for adolescents have been making attempts to treat previously taboo subjects and to avoid the condescending adult attitude. This discussion will limit its scope to well-known junior novels about premarital pregnancy, but there are now books dealing with homosexuality, "ripping off," use of drugs, and other antiestablishment behaviors. In the past ten years the teenage protagonist has moved a long way from Mildred Pace's Clara Barton or Rosamond du Jardin's Tobey Hayden, but she is still conveyed by the same formula.

The adolescent and his sexual drive presents as much difficulty for the author of junior novels as it always has for society. There appears to be two major conflicts. First, the author is writing to young people, but adult librarians, parents, and teachers must approve the work before it can get into the library, school, home, or into the running for a book award. The adults want the book to perform a community service and the kid wants to know how to deal with his problem. Since cultural conditions do not allow for satisfactory sexual experiences in adolescence, this is a difficult subject to execute. Secondly, the junior novel formula promises that the problem will be solved. Fans of the formula do not want the author to tamper with it, but this leaves the author with the dilemma of solving the problem without evoking more anxiety than is reasonable and without betraying society.

Felsen's *Two and the Town* (Scribners, 1952), Zoa Sherburne's *Too Bad about the Haines Girl* (Morrow, 1967), Ann Head's *Mr. and Mrs. Bo Jo Jones* (Signet, 1968) and Paul Zindels *My Darling, My Hamburger* (Bantam, 1969), examined in this study, strive valiantly for a compromise.

All adhere to the formula with only slight variations. Similarly, all of these authors place their emphasis upon the consequences after the teenagers have experimented with sex and either ignore or briefly treat the feelings and frustrations before the act. By glossing over an important aspect of the problem, these authors have failed to deal as deeply and sincerely with the problem as it merits, but this lack of honesty is not because of the formula; it does not limit the breadth of the problem to be explored.

The artistic merit, or lack of it, in these books results from the author's choice of viewpoint, sympathetic rendering of the protagonist, and the development of his or her relations with the minor characters. Setting plays little part. All of these situations could have happened in any small town in any part of middle America and there is little emphasis on the larger community. The protagonist's world is primarily home and school. The plot is determined by the formula and the subject. The only differences are whose story it is and the authors' decision to deal with the immediate or long term consequences of teenage pregnancy.

Perhaps the weakest element in all of the books is the contrivance of the cause. In two of the novels, alcohol was responsible, one the hysteria of a championship football game, and the fourth was parental lack of faith and trust in a good girl. These books show little awareness of the nature of the sexual conflict and Dr. Goldings, child psychiatrist, contends that there is an unwarranted and perhaps dangerous oversimplification in most of the presentations.[7]

In studying adolescents' response to literature, James Squire found the most distressing distortion and misconceptions to be the reliance on familiar and stereotyped patterns of thinking. One of the most frequent stock responses is that adolescents are not responsible for their own actions.[8] One wonders if a steady diet of these books could not reinforce this misconception.

The introduction of the earliest treatment, Felsen's, *Two and the Town*, would please any formula fan. Handsome, popular football captain Buff Cody—who dates pretty, popular cheerleader Carol Edwards is involved in the hysteria of the school and town over the championship game. Still in this feverish excitement they lose the game, Buff and Carol quibble, and he seeks comfort from quiet, scholarly Elaine Truro who has always admired him from afar. The excitement and disappointment cause them "to make a mistake." Elaine is pregnant. Everything from this point is downhill. Felsen who was able to describe so well the tension on the football field and the whole town's involvement in the championship is unable to adequately portray the feelings of either Buff or Elaine as they confront their difficulties.

Felsen follows the conventional ideas Martinec found interrelated to the formula.[9] Adults can't help: they mean well but are ineffectual. Buff and Elaine's parents with unrealistic acceptance and tolerance give them a wedding, honeymoon, house, furniture, and job for Buff; but this doesn't help. The young couple is miserable. Their misery is the result of another stock idea, they are isolated from the group. The other members of the team have abandoned Buff. Just as the formula promises, when a point of absolute hopelessness is reached (Buff has left Elaine and the baby to join the Marines and be one of the gang again) a transcendent character, a fellow Marine, who is happily married and proud of his children, brings illumination and insight to the beleaguered protagonist. This is much too quickly accomplished through the contrivance of a family photograph. Buff sees his mistake and luckily goes home with a medical discharge.

Felsen has done little either for the teenager and his problem other than acknowledge it, or for the novel. His purpose was not an attempt to develop healthier attitudes toward sexual tension, but to capitalize on its social derivations. His technique is similar too, but not as masterful as Camus' portrayal of the murder scene in *The Stranger* (Knopf, 1946) when the reader is made to feel that the sun, not Meursault, caused the gun to fire. Here the football game excitement caused the baby. Felson's minor characters are ficelles, and the protagonist is unsympathetic.

Two and the Town is Buff's story, and this is the most serious error of the novel. All of the others are more successfully told from the girl's perspective. This is a "girl in trouble" theme, and the double standard still operates. Felson's failure is not his close adherence to the formula, but his having missed the dramatic center of his tale.

Zoa Sherburne's *Too Bad about the Haines Girl* is technically much better handled than the Felsen book. The plot is developed through Melinda Haines' consciousness, and Sherburne's sympathy for the adolescent character is apparent. There is a deeper plunge into human feeling in this novel. This is accomplished not only by the personal anguish Melinda shares with the reader, but her considerations on how her pregnancy will affect her sympathetically drawn parents, two younger sisters, and close friend, Suky. The minor characters are skillfully drawn through Melinda's perception. This development of the minor characters inten-

sifies the impact of the problem. Sherburne uses the formula, but is not bound by it, and perhaps that is what saves her book from being sentimental and simplistic.

Following the pattern, the crisis comes when Melinda is elected Queen of the Valentine Ball, which forces her to reveal her secret to her parents. Melinda supercedes other youthful protagonists in not placing too much emphasis on her lost opportunity to be queen. She is more wisely concerned about her lost opportunity to choose a husband, go to college, set an example for her siblings, and live up to the trust her parents have in her. She also understands and is sympathetic to her boyfriend Jeff's lost opportunities.

Sherburne chooses invention over convention when she does not suggest a solution other than Melinda's confession to her parents. Using Poe's technique of leaving much to the imagination of the reader is effective rather than a "cop out" in this situation. She has planted all of the seeds that lead to great compromise for both Melinda and Jeff. To have colored in the outline would have been wasteful.

Although the technique is more artistic than Felsen's, the subject of youthful sex drives is no better handled. This time the punch at a high school dance was spiked and both Jeff and Melinda are ashamed of their action.

July Greher and Bo Jo Jones, unlucky lovers in Ann Head's *Mr. and Mrs. Bo Jo Jones* (an adult book widely recommended for and read by younger readers), are such believable characters that it is unfortunate she does not allow them to present the cause for their problem more openly, but this time it was champagne, ironically, drunk to celebrate Bo Jo's winning of an athletic scholarship to college. However, there are two interesting deviations from the usual treatment. Although July never really admits to enjoying their sexual activity before marriage, it is not presented as the one-time-mistake as in the earlier books. July says that they were sorry they had done it and promised each other that it wouldn't happen again, but found that they couldn't make a relationship go backward. In later scenes, after their marriage, their lovemaking is treated in as mature a fashion as befits adult fiction, whereas tracing the development of the sex theme in a junior novel is comparable to the long drawn out Tiparello commercial; the researcher awaits the book that finally admits a teenager could have a strong sexual urge without an outside stimulant.

Head uses two technical devices, quite commonplace to adult fiction but usually avoided in the junior novel. July tells her own story, and it is more effective than the omniscient author because she does not use the moralizing tone that writers of these books usually can't seem to avoid. Secondly, it is told in flashback, the detached autobiographical style of *Catcher in the Rye* (Bantam, 1970) and *A Separate Peace* (Dell, 1960).

Having the protagonist look back in time on the problem after it has been worked out removes much of the immediate anxiety and tension and focuses on problems that do not seem as important when the protagonist discovers her problem, but are more lasting. July is a member of a dignified, educated, old-moneyed family who has class and dignity; Bo Jo's family are working class who lack taste, but are expecting Bo Jo's success and education to give them social mobility. Classical music, poetry, and quiet simplicity are July's taste and style. Bo Jo is an inarticulate football hero with bad table manners. Perhaps the distinctions are too black and white, but the emphasis on the long term implications gives teenage readers a more realistic picture of this aspect of human experience than junior novel counterparts.

Paul Zindel, Pulitzer Prize winner for drama and author of *Miss Reardon Drinks a Little* and *The Effects of Gamma Rays on Man-in-the-Moon Marigolds* (Harper, 1971), has attempted to use his stage techniques within the formulaic construction with some interesting results. He presents four characters in the introduction section of *My*

Darling, My Hamburger and it is difficult to determine whose story it is to be. Maggie is the traditional protagonist of the early junior novels. She is self-conscious, awkward, lacking in style, and on the fringe of the gang. In contrast her friend Liz is pretty, sure of herself, and dating Sean, a handsome "in-guy." Sean is presented in contrast to his friend Dennis who is a male version of all Maggie's problems. The omniscient narrator alternates among the four viewpoints, always presenting two scenes and sometimes four simultaneously. For example, one of the first incidents is a double date arranged by Liz and Sean. The scene opens in the viewpoint of Dennis, revealing his discomfort and his reaction to Maggie; it then cuts to Maggie's consciousness creating an ironic situation impossible to reveal through a single viewpoint. The rest of the scene is a series of contrasts between Dennis and Maggie uncomfortably aware of each other in the back seat of the car and in the movie compared to smooth Sean and Liz who handle the situation and each other with ease.

Zindel is experimenting within the formula, but his inventions cause him to sacrifice content for technique. All of the elements of the conventional junior novel are present. Maggie and Dennis have the usual problem of overcoming shyness and awkwardness and developing self-confidence. (Whether the problem is Maggie's or Dennis' does not interfere with the development because they simply represent the male/female version of the same problem). There is a crisis which drives them farther from the solution of their problem and from each other. Liz and Sean, at first directly and later indirectly, play the role of the transcendent character who gives advice and brings illumination and insight. In the end Maggie, wiser and more sure of herself, walks gracefully across the stage for her diploma, and she and Dennis get together and are comfortable.

The problem with the plot and this analysis of it is twofold. First the crisis situation is bigger than all the rest of the book. Liz gets pregnant and involves Maggie in the problem and the abortion which she uses as a solution. This is an overly dramatic device to help Maggie overcome her immaturity. The second problem is that the reader doesn't realize it is Maggie or Maggie and Dennis' story until the last chapter. Since Liz's viewpoint is given equal exposure and her problem is the more difficult, the reader is tricked into thinking Maggie is the transcendent character who will help Liz. But after a melodramatic incident involving the girls in evening dresses going off on prom night to acquire an abortion from a sleezy character whose initials, not credentials, spell D.R., Liz fades from the plot. Ironically, dressed in white, she begins to hemorrhage in the back seat of the car, and Maggie—against Liz's wishes—rings Liz's parents' doorbell for help. Liz appears no more.

This is as serious a tampering with an accepted formula as a detective who does not plant the proper clues for the murderer in a thriller. The last chapter, which is totally Maggie's doesn't help. Even though Maggie sums it all up thinking, "Inside, though she knew she had come a long way since she had worn cockeyed eyebrows and pleated dresses... With one glance she had seen the million things Liz had somehow taught her... They (Sean and Liz) should have known what they were risking..." The reader is left asking, "But what happened/is happening to Liz? How did she resolve her problem?"

Even though he has seriously tampered with the formula, Zindel manages to reinforce the major ideas related to the formula. The most strongly underlined is that adults can't help you much; teachers and parents fail miserably in every incident. Irony is his tool. The book opens with the female gym teacher telling Liz, Maggie, and their class that the way to stop a guy who wants to go all the way is to suggest going to get a hamburger. When Dennis is destroyed because Maggie has broken a date to the prom, his parents spend the dinner hour talking about the correct way for him to handle

the kitchen garbage. While Liz is debating suicide, abortion, or forcing Sean to marry her, her mother gives her long lectures on smiling and being sweeter to her stepfather at the dinner table. And the most ironic of all is the A+ Sean's English teacher gives him on a theme called, "The Circus of Blackness," the gruesome story of a young couple in a circus doing a ritualistic murder of their child in front of an audience. The theme was written the night after Sean tells Liz he can't marry her and gives her a dozen long stemmed white roses and two hundred dollars for an abortion. The teacher's comment: "A+, you have a remarkable imagination."

For all of his inventions in multiple point of view, structure, and powerful use of irony, Zindel handles the subject of youthful sex drives almost as unrealistically as his predecessors. Sean is presented as a normal, healthy boy who is attempting to convince the unyielding Liz. The night she acquiesces, it is not alcohol or left-over football game excitement, but the lack of understanding and trust her parents have in her.

In 1972, the adoration of childish innocence is still with us. The American Dream with its vision of youth, hope, and the open road (that leads to college) has waned only slightly, at least in the hearts of the adult novelists who write junior fiction. It has taken 20 years for sex to become a subject and when it does, it is amazing how easily it fits into the conventional moral patterns. These premarital pregnancy books were not only still written for virgins and boys but also written in a didactic tone warning virgins to retain their state until after marriage. I do not suggest that authors advocate premarital sex for teenagers, but neither do I believe that these narrow views of the situation will in anyway control, limit, or help with the problem.

All four of the novels examined in this study suggested the following: 1) If you do not conform to the code, you will be ostracized by your peers and won't be able to go to college. 2) Friends will desert you, but parents will stand by you.

However, they will be hurt, disappointed, disillusioned, or angry and they won't understand. 3) Your mate will be too immature and scared to give you support or strength. 4) No matter how attractive, popular, talented, or socially secure, this tragedy could happen to you. 5) Early marriage is not idyllic. 6) Life will be a compromise at best for both the boy and girl.

If these novels fail either artistically or in their purpose, the failure cannot really be attributed to their formulistic nature. Felsen fails by missing the dramatic center, Zindel identifies his protagonist too late, Head and Sherburne distort the cause of the action. None of these shortcomings are due to the formula and the pattern is a useful means of comparing artistic technique. The conflict is between the artist and his art, society and the subject.

Written in the heat of a sexual revolution in our society, books of this nature, which ignore sexual desire, contraception (especially the pill and teenagers confusion with it), and, in most cases, abortion, do not deal with reality. They simply exploit a time of change. A book dealing with premarital pregnancy can be as old fashioned as the cliché how-to-get-a-date-for-the-prom story.

The writer who really treats premarital pregnancy will deal with all facets of the issue. He or she will be sympathetic, but will present the real conflicts, look at all of the alternatives, portray actual emotions. He or she will tell the whole truth, not just pieces which support the existing social values he or she wishes to reinforce. I do not feel that the books in this study reflect the changing adolescent culture. These are old ideas against a new backdrop.

REFERENCES

1. Witham, Tasker W. *The Adolescent in the American Novel, 1920-1960.* Ungar, 1964.
2. Cawelti, John G. "The Concept of Formula in the Study of Popular Culture," *Journal of Popular Culture,* p. 386.
3. Magaliff, Cecile. *The Junior Novel.* Kennikat Pr., 1964, p. 10.

4. Martinec, Barbara. "Popular—But Not Just a Part of the Crowd: Implications of Formula Fiction for Teenagers," *English Journal,* March 1971, p. 341-342.
5. Hentoff, Nat. "Getting Inside Jazz Country," *Horn Book Magazine,* October 1966, p. 532.
6. Sanders, Jacquelyn. "Psychological Significance of Children's Literature," in Sarah Fenwick, *A Critical Approach to Children's Literature.* Univ. of Chicago Pr., 1967, p. 17.
7. Goldings, Carmen R., M.D. "Some New Trends in Children's Literature from the Perspective of the Child Psychiatrist," *Journal of American Academy of Child Psychiatry,* July 1968, p. 392.
8. Squire, James R. *The Response of Adolescents while Reading Four Short Stories.* National Council of Teachers of English Research Report, No. 2, 1964.
9. Martinec, p. 344.

BIBLIOGRAPHY

Burton, Dwight L. *Literature Study in the High School.* Holt, 1960.
Cawelti, John G. "The Concept of Formula in the Study of Popular Literature," *Journal of Popular Culture,* 111:3. p. 381-390.
——————. "Prolegomena to the Western," *Studies in Public Communication,* Autumn 1962. p. 57-70.
——————. "Recent Trends in Popular Culture," *American Studies and International Newsletter,* Winter 1971. p. 23-37.
Felsen, Henry Gregor. *Two and the Town.* Morrow, 1967.
Goldings, Carmen R., M.D. "Some New Trends in Children's Literature from the Perspective of the Child Psychiatrists," *Journal of American Academy of Child Psychiatry,* July 1968. p. 377-395.
Head, Ann. *Mr. and Mrs. Bo Jo Jones.* Signet, 1968.
Hentoff, Nat. "Getting Inside Jazz Country," *Horn Book Magazine,* October 1966. p. 528-532.
Magaliff, Cecilie. *The Junior Novel.* Kennikat Pr., 1964.
Martinec, Barbara. "Popular—But Not Just a Part of the Crowd: Implications of Formula Fiction for Teenagers," *English Journal,* March 1971. p. 341-342.

Patterson, Emma L. "The Junior Novels and How They Grew," *English Journal*, October 1956. p. 381–387.

Sanders, Jacquelyn. "Psychological Significance of Children's Literature," *A Critical Approach to Children's Literature*, ed. by Sarah Fenwick. Univ. of Chicago Pr., 1967. p. 15–22.

Sherburne, Zoa. *Too Bad about the Haines Girl*. Morrow, 1967.

Squires, James R. *The Responses of Adolescents While Reading Four Short Stories.* National Council of Teachers of English Research Report, No. 2, 1964.

Thomison, Dennis. *Readings About Adolescent Literature.* Scarecrow, 1970.

Witham, Tasker W. *The Adolescent in the American Novel 1920-1960.* Ungar, 1964.

Zindel, Paul. *My Darling, My Hamburger.* Bantam, 1971.

V
Past, Present, and Future

Children's Books in Translation: Facts and Beliefs

Mary Ørvig

THE FARM in southern Sweden once owned by Dag Hammarskjöld was the scene in 1966 of a meeting between publishers, critics, and translators from different European countries to discuss the prospects of the representatives of minor languages obtaining a hearing in major cultural contexts. Those present agreed that literary prejudice is quite common in large language areas and that people do not feel any the worse for it. There was also unanimity on many other things, including the numerous national limitations of higher literary studies in the majority of countries. There is a striking lack of concrete literary knowledge concerning a series of language areas. Another problem of cultural communication lies in ignorance of foreign environments and lack of any desire to rectify that ignorance. All were agreed, however, on the important fact that a first-class book can be untranslatable because it is on a wave length that another country's receivers cannot pick up. This is probably part of the reason for so many failures which in the eyes of the country of origin are quite inexplicable.

In this context, one of the leading critics in Sweden, Ingemar Wizelius, has an instructive tale to tell in the introduction to a survey of Swedish literature abroad. A professor of literature related how an English colleague who had called on him caught sight of the seven volumes of Schück and Warburg's history of Swedish literature on the bookshelves and saw fit to ask what this mammoth work was about. On being told he was silent for a moment and then asked: "But what is it about, *really?*" Mr. Wizelius remarks that in asking what Schück and Warburg was really about, the English professor of literature had given the international status of Swedish literary output in a nutshell.

As to children's books, one is amazed to see over and over again how readily and effortlessly one tends to generalize about the internationality of them on the strength of some classical novels which have become children's reading and a few works whose writers have had no difficulty in negotiating the international frontiers with all that this implies. Although we owe Paul Hazard a great deal, it was he, in his famous *Books, Children and Men* (Horn Bk., 1932), who first expressed some of the ideas and phrases which are almost invariably reiterated on the majority of international occasions. For example:

Yes, children's books keep alive a sense of nationality: but they also keep alive a sense of humanity. They describe their native land lovingly, but they also describe faraway lands where unknown brothers live. They understand the essential quality of their own race, but each of them is a messenger that goes beyond mountains and rivers, beyond the seas, to the very ends of the world in search of new friendships. Every country gives and every country receives—innumerable are the exchanges—and so it comes about that in our first impressionable years the universal republic of childhood is born.

Paul Hazard's book was, after all, published in Europe between two world wars, at a time when internationalism had very little concrete background. Again, after World War II his book touched us deeply because of the isolation enforced by the long years of war. Nowadays perhaps Hazard is important, above all, as a comparative literary historian and one of the first critics to place children's books in their comparative historical context. 'One of his greatest works, La Crise de Conscience Européenne (1935), was devoted to the study of major literary currents in the collective consciousness and cast light on a number of interesting literary facts.

The sentence, "every country gives and every country receives," often comes to mind. Now that the western world has opened its eyes to the fact that there are countries in many parts of the globe without a body of children's literature of their own, perhaps it is time to discard a few illusions, painful as the process may be. Thus, is not internationality after all based on a mutual give and take? For indeed, reciprocity and, consequently, true internationalism are quite small and there are many linguistic and cultural frontiers which are extremely hard to cross. Or, how seriously have we really tried?

The distribution channels of books provide an interesting subject which in the nature of things is bound up with such circumstances as war, peace, political constellations, copyright questions, and monetary relationships. Economic laws and situations play a very important part in this context. Nor should one forget the great influence of ancient cultural links on the translation scene.

There can be no doubt that many new initiatives are needed on the translation side, especially within children's literature, but also the cultural sector as such. Children's books are mostly regarded as an isolated phenomenon in the cultural exchange of different countries, which of course is as wrong as wrong could be. Some concrete problems related to the book publishing may perhaps be illustrated by the comparatively small Swedish language area, comprising some eight million people. The volume of publication in Sweden is unusually high in relation to the number of people who understand the language. If one considers the number of titles published, Swedish book publication per capita is more or less on a level with Great Britain, even though that country has the whole world for its reading public while Sweden's is less than the population of greater London. In conditions like these, book publication frequently becomes something akin to gambling. The profile of children's book publication in Sweden in 1970 was as follows: we brought out 637 titles (227 of them new editions), including 179 new Swedish titles and 175 new foreign titles, which will give almost an even balance between original works and translations. Of these translations, 212 were from English, 18 from German, 11 from Danish, nine from Norwegian and one from Czech.

Day by day it is becoming increasingly obvious that the comparatively generous and ambitious scale of book publishing which we are used to in Sweden can no longer be accommodated within the framework of a stringent market economy. Publishers have to concentrate more and more on established authors and reliable types of books. This creates difficulties for new writers and it means also that many important translations fail to materialize, especially as regards the books on the difficult wave lengths which need to be published regularly for many years in order to break down the resistance of the reading public, above all, books from the eastern bloc and from other new areas where children's books are gaining ground.

Certain of the circumstances relating to book consumption and the conditions of Swedish literature led to the appointment in 1968 of a Commission to consider the forms of public support to literature. The experts concerned within this commission, who have been given very wide terms of reference, are to study the need for measures at the consumption, production, and distribution levels to strengthen the status of literature in Sweden's cultural life. Confronted by the difficult economic situation within the book market, many Swedish publishers have shown a remarkable unanimity in calling for state subvention, indeed they have pointed to the need for this form of assistance, which is already enjoyed in Sweden by the theatre, the cinema, the film industry, and music. Government support to authors was channelled through the Swedish Authors' Fund set up already in 1954, when library royalties were introduced. The Fund exists to handle the royalties paid out of the public funds to the authors of books used by public libraries. The Swedish Riksdag determines the allocation to be made to the Fund each year. For the budget year 1971-1972, a royalty of 15 öre was fixed for each external loan, the royalty on reference copies being 60 öre. Royalties are paid for translations at four öre per external loan and 16 öre per reference copy. Altogether the Fund has received nine million 307.000 kronor for the budget year 1971-1972.

The above illustrate how a small country tries to surmount the crisis of its book trade so as to avoid individual isolation and the dangers of provincialism. Whether we regard books from a commercial, individual, cultural, or even social angle, we need to know more about the factors governing people's reading interests and their use of different kinds of literature. This in turn begs the question—for small language areas at least—how are translations controlled? Are the translation movements which so obviously exist really controlled at all? Children's books provide a good starting point for such an inquiry.

When the Swedish scholar, Göte Klingberg, first coined the term "children's literature regions" in a lecture given at a Unesco seminar in Denmark in 1970 on the subject of "Literature for Children and Young People as a Means of Promotion of International Understanding," he said,

Four countries were studied, Sweden, Austria, West, and East Germany. It became apparent that Sweden, Austria, and West Germany belonged to the same children's literature region characterized by a predominant import from the English language area (that is from Great Britain and the U.S.); in Sweden, 70-77 percent (in two different samplings); in Austria, 57 percent; in West Germany, 57 percent; and further by an import of a smaller number of French, Dutch, and Scandinavian books, an interchange of books in German and Swedish, but also by the very small imports from other countries, such as the Slavonic language area. East Germany belongs to another children's book area, as Dr. Klaus Doderer has shown in his report from the research institution in Frankfurt. East Germany imports from the English language areas were listed to 17 percent, on the other hand, 51 percent of the books were translations from Slavonic languages and, in addition, 12 percent came from Hungary.

What is the answer? Is it a simple question of foreign politics? It goes without saying that we in Sweden belong to the Anglo-American translation area, which, however, did not start after World War II, but probably already in the 1870's.

At the Swedish Institute for Children's Books, one of the most frequent questions asked by students at library schools and teachers' colleges is: "Why this Anglo-American domination of the translation side, why not a little more from Eastern Europe and other parts of the world?" In reply, a reference is usually made to unsolved copyright problems and financial situations. The important part played by old, established cultural links in the translation context is not to be discounted, as can be seen from a visit to the Frankfurt book fair, even though the eastern countries usually put in as much of an appearance as they can manage. A great deal of information is required to make the discussion of these and kindred topics more specific and less emotional. Nonetheless, one may ask why the children's book publishers of the west do not in their turn try to visit the Leipzig book fair in East Germany, which among other things could be their gateway into the eastern book sector.

In her interesting paper *Children's Literature and Libraries around the World*, Marguerite Bagshaw has shown a real concern over the important issues:

> There is much talk today of the mutual exchange of ideas and cultures from one country to another. In actual practice there seems to be little reciprocal sharing as far as cultures are concerned from East to West... How can we engender closer international contacts?

Mildred L. Batchelder, an authority on children's books and libraries in several European countries, was also one of the first to raise the problems of translation. In her article, published in *ALA Bulletin* (1963), "Learning about Children's Books in Translation," she touches upon many important matters, for instance:

> Tailoring children's books to their new country takes various forms. When a book comes through an English translation to an American edition, additional adjustments are made to make it conform to our national taste and style. I question whether all such changes are necessary to accommodate English editions to America, or for that matter, American editions to England.

Miss Batchelder also found "that characters are removed, incidents are taken out." "Perhaps," she concludes, "the cutting and changes were for economic reasons."

One valuable research project on children's books would be to compare original texts with translations and adaptations. It would be a good idea to start with a title published in several countries, so as to expose what is termed adjustment or discreet or overt cutting. In translations from Swedish to English and German, for instance, one may frequently find:

1) overemphasis of the basic plot, often at the expense of the real essence of the book;
2) the different climates of humor are always difficult, therefore, one often finds the elimination of all but the most elementary or slapstick humor;
3) a playing down of sensibility which often by Anglo-American standards is typically European or too profound;
4) a constant tendency to smooth things over;
5) an emasculation of content, due to an aversion to intellectual contents or conclusions in children's books.

Often the reason is to be found quite simply in the translator's ignorance, not so much of words and grammatical structure as of the images behind them. One would also like to stress that differences are every bit as important as similarities when describing foreign environments. There is a dangerous tendency for differences or customs and morals to be degraded to quaint details for tourists. Yet it is a salutary experience to learn early in life that in certain parts of the world men can weep without losing their dignity or embrace each other without causing any embarrassment.

If, as Marguerite Bagshaw wrote, there is to be more reciprocal sharing between different countries through the medium of translation, we must learn more about the conditions and ways of the translation process. We should use the tools at our disposal, such as the international organizations, to find out how literature operates in different countries, for example, starting with those belonging to IBBY. This organization should pay far more attention to translators. We need to learn more about the literary process, production, distribution, and consumption. Many of the Hans Christian Andersen prize-winners, for instance, have run into difficulties on the translation market. Let us find out why: are the books untranslatable because, as mentioned earlier, they are attuned to wave lengths which the receivers of other countries cannot pick up? Let us find out the facts about this. Without wishing to cause any serious ructions, it may be suggested that the reason for important children's books being refused—in spite of the Andersen Medal—is an important factor for our knowledge of untranslatable books.

It is remarkable that so little scope has been given to the conditions and ways of translations in all these top level international research projects and discussions. The distribution channels of children's books and the part played by translations within children's literature of different countries are neglected fields of research. Most of the work has still to be done. We who are concerned with children's books, nationally and internationally, must study more in detail the practical results in the field of translations in different countries. Then we will have greater opportunities to make concrete observations and perhaps enter some new paths. Coprinting seemed to be an excellent instrument as far as translation was concerned, but this supposition has often been given the lie. The original idea has often been lost sight of, and a coprinted book in several languages can provide a manual of national tabus in the children's book sector, and not, as was really intended, a children's book that has broken down barriers.

The isolation of children's books must concern us all. This isolation must simply be overcome, even at the sacrifice of a few well-loved tribal deities. Children's literature must be more consciously integrated in the whole pattern of cultural life. Analyses are needed of events in the field of criticism, not only our specialized journals but popular periodicals and the daily press. The coverage given by press critics should not be determined by personal preference or the cultural and literary interests of the chief editor. Let it be said aloud and repeatedly that no serious cultural observation can exist without an interest in children's books. Children's books are everybody's business, for we all spend a quarter of our lives being children and growing up.

Translations are often said to be more important to small countries than to big ones. But national and cultural isolation is not necessarily the exclusive fate of small countries. Big countries also need to know what is important at the other side of the border, what people laugh at and what makes them cry. There are many doors which need to be opened in order to help our understanding. To popularize translations of children's books from new and different language areas is a question of breaking down all sorts of inhibitions and attitudes of which the book world is so rich. As always one has to start with the young. Translation is the strongest link in an international chain which is constantly in need of amplification and reinforcement.

BIBLIOGRAPHY

Amos, Flora Ross. "Early Theories of Translation," *Columbia University Studies in English and Comparative Literature.* New York, 1920.

Arnold, Matthew. *On Translating Homer: Three Lectures Given at Oxford.* London: Longman, 1861.

Bagshaw, Marguerite. "Children's Literature and Libraries Around the World," *International Library Review*, No. 1, 1969, p. 119-129.

Batchelder, Mildred. "Children's Books in Translation," *ALA Bulletin*, January 1966, p. 33-42.

Bates, Ernest Stuart. *Intertraffic, Studies in Translation.* London: Jonathan Cape, 1943.

————. *Modern Translation.* London: Oxford Univ. Pr., 1936.

Belloc, Hilaire. *On Translation . . . The Taylorian Lecture.* Oxford: Clarendon Pr., 1931.

Bredsdorff, Aase. "On the Problem of a Small

Country Concerning the Translations of Children's Books," in Lisa-Christina Persson (ed.), *Translations of Children's Books.* Sweden: Bibliotekstjänst, 1962.

Cauer, Paul. *Die Kunst des Ubersetzens: Ein Hilfsbuch für den Lateinischen und Griechischen Unterricht.* Berlin, 1914.

Escarpit, Robert. *La révolution du livre.* Paris: Presses Universitaire de France, 1965.

————. *Sociologie de la littérature.* Paris: Presses Universitaire de France, 1968.

Hazard, Paul. *Books, Children, and Men.* Boston: The Horn Bk., 1944.

————. *La crise de conscience européene, 1680-1735.* Paris: Boivin et Cie, 1935.

Klingberg, Göte. "To Write for Children and Young People—The Problem of Adaptation." In *Literature for Children and Young People as a Means of Promotion of International Understanding.* Contributions made to the seminar at Skarildshus, September 1970. Copenhagen: Danish Unesco Schools Project, 1971. p. 15-24.

Korlén, Gustav. "Konstruktive Ubersetzungskritik als Aufgabe der Schwedischen Universitätsgermanistik." In Babel. *International Journal of Translation.* Paris, 1966. p. 26-31.

Larbaud, Valery. *Sous l'invocation de Saint Jérome.* Paris, 1946.

Lundqvist, Ake. *Hög tid att diskutera bokkrisen.* Stockholm, 1971.

Macandrew, Ronald Maxwell. *Translation from Spanish.* London: Black, 1936.

Matthiessen, Francis Otto. *Translation: an Elizabethan Art.* Cambridge: Harvard Univ. Pr., 1931.

Nottebohm, Brigitte. *Zur deutschsprachigen Jugendbuch produktion des Jahres 1968.* Frankfurt/Main: Institut für Jugendbuchforschung der Johann Wolfgang Goethe Universität, 1971.

Nowak, Lilian. *Bokläsaren: En översiket över nordisk forskning efter 1945 med an-*

noterad bibliografi. Stockholm: Sveriges radio förlag, 1971.

Painter, Helen W. "Translations of Traditional and Modern Material." In Helen Huus (ed.), *Evaluating Books for Children and Young People.* Delaware: International Reading Assn., 1971. p. 36-56.

Phillimore, John Swinnerton. *Some Remarks on Translation and Translators.* London: English Assn., 1919.

Ritchie, Robert Lindsay Graeme & James Middleton Moore. *Translation from the French.* Cambridge: University Pr., 1918.

Savory, Theodore. *The Art of Translation.* London: Jonathan Cape, 1957.

Scherf, Walter, ed. *The Best of the Best.* New York: Bowker, 1971.

Schildt, Margareta. "The Translation of Children's Books from the Viewpoint of a Swedish Children's Book Editor." In Lisa-Christina Persson (ed.), *Translations of Children's Books.* Sweden: Bibliotekstjänst, 1962, p. 21-36.

The State and Culture in Sweden. Stockholm: Swedish Institute and Swedish National Commission for Unesco, 1970.

Stein, Ruth. "Launching the New Literate," *SLJ,* November 1966, p. 51-53.

Sutherland, Zena. "Suffering in Translation." *Saturday Review,* May 15, 1971.

Fakta om Forfattarfonden. Stockholm: Sveriges Forfattarfond, 1971.

Tolman, Herbert Cushing. *The Art of Translating.* Boston: Sanborn, 1901.

Tytler, Alexander Fraser, Lord Woodhouselee. *Essay on the Principle of Translation.* London, 1791.

Vallquist, Gunnel. "Små Stämmor i stora världen." In *Svenska Dagbladet.* Stockholm. May 17, 1966.

Whibley, Charles. "Translators." In Sir Adolphus W. Ward and A. R. Waller, *The Cambridge History of English Literature.* England: Cambridge Univ. Pr., 1919-1930.

Wizelius, Ingemar. "Svensk litteratur utomlands." In *Modersmålslärarnas förenings årsskrift 1968/69.* Sweden, 1969. p. 30-44.

Concerned Criticism or Casual Cop-outs?

Patricia Schuman

CONSIDER the plight of parents and adult relatives or friends who wish to buy books for their favorite children. Let us assume that they are neither teachers nor librarians themselves, that they know little about their communities' library information services and that they do not have a fully-stocked general book store at hand. What do they face in their children's book buying? Over 35,000 books for children are in print. Over 2000 new books for children were published in 1971.

An adult's most visible sources of information are probably the newspapers and general magazines that pay review attention to children's books in special issues each Spring and Fall. If they read these before buying what do they find out about current children's books? To answer this first question, I compared the Fall children's book issues of the following periodicals:

New York Times "Children's Book" section (November 8, 48p.)
New York Review of Books (Dec. 2, 2½p.)
Book World (November 6, 15p.)
Christian Science Monitor (November 11, 6p.)
Saturday Review (November 13, 5p.)
Commonweal (November 19, 12p.)
Scientific American (December, 10p.)

My perusal of these revealed a few prevalent patterns, but provoked many more questions.

General Observations

A combined total of only 350 titles out of the possible 1000+ published this Fall were reviewed and another 150 received brief mention. The longer articles and full reviews tended to discuss the latest books by established authors and well-known illustrators. Reviews of fiction and picture books outnumbered nonfiction by better than 2:1. Picture books alone accounted for over one third of all the titles reviewed. Books written especially for teenagers got nodding attention in the least amount of space. Of the books covered, only 13 percent of the titles were reviewed by more than one of the periodicals.

The unabridged *Random House Dictionary of the English Language* states that the words review and criticism imply "carefully examining something, making a judgment, and putting the judgment into (usually) written form."

Unfortunately, there is little to indicate careful examination and judgment in the reviews offered to the general public by the popular reviewing media. Over 90 percent of all books mentioned received favorable reviews or, more frequently, short descriptive annotations. No doubt titles were probably pre-selected by the review editors because of limited space, but isn't it just as important to forewarn adults about shoddy—or even "fair" titles, as well as to point out the good ones—and to offer them some clue as to the judgmental and/or weeding process involved?

The uninitiated adult might also wonder about the expertise of the reviewers published. Are they really experts in the field, or just dabbling? Sometimes it's hard to tell. The *Christian Science Monitor* did not even bother to identify its reviewers beyond giving their names, though it did so for adult reviewers in the same issue, and in several cases *Children's Book World* neglected to provide any reviewer identification. The majority of reviewers identified were children's book authors, a smattering of adult authors, and a few editors and teachers. Only a few reviewers had any connection at all with children's library service.

The sparse negative criticism went from almost nonexistent in the *Saturday Review*, to a literary essay in the *New York Review of Books*, and some outright panning in the *New York Times* "Children's Books."

Round-ups—Advice or Summaries?

Commonweal, *Saturday Review*, *Scientific American*, and the *New York Review of Books* all employed the "round-up" technique in their fall obeisance to the children's book field, with a few variations. The *Saturday Review*'s Zena Sutherland offered ten to 20 line annotations with zingy last sentences—"Deft little drawings enrich a sweet little story." The only critical comment to be found among the 24 titles listed is the one for Edward Connally's *Deer Run* (Scribners): "It isn't a great first novel, but it's a good one, despite Connally's tendency to paint the commune white and the community black."

For the most part Sutherland covers familiar authors, but the age spread is fairly representative, and there is an obvious, if only partially successful, attempt to cover a wide range of topics.

"Turning on Parent Power," the short introductory essay to *SR*'s section by Sophie Silverberg, director of advertising and promotion for children's books at Thomas Y. Crowell, is of particular interest to adults. She offers some advice to parents and other interested adults who are frustrated both because they can't find what they want in local bookstores and because they want to learn more about current children's books, suggesting Books for Children groups along the line of the English model.

"The root of the problem," she says, "is probably that too many bookstores rely today on self-service supermarket techniques, and, especially in the case of children's books, the average customer lacks the necessary confidence to make the right choice. Because it's so easy to pick the familiar classic, many bookstores have learned to concentrate on the tried and true."

Commonweal's children's section was up two pages this year for a total of twelve and included two longer articles in addition to its standard "Selected List." Elizabeth Minot Graves (children's book editor, Garrard Publishing Company) offered a glowing roundup review of 20 titles on the occult in "Year of the Witch." "The authors of this seasons books about magical happenings seemed to have gained magic from their very subject matter itself," says she, "and have written with great skill, sensitivity and distinction. These books are more than just entertainment: They will set children to thinking." (At least in the case of occult books, reviewers in other publications did take issue with Graves.)

Michael J. Ballard follows with an essay highly favorable to the paperback trend in juvenile publishing, offering an overview of who is doing what, for how much, and why, and a "Paperback Sampler" listing 40 "popular" children's books. Ballard is identified in *Com-*

monweal's blurb as covering "cultural developments for the United States Information Agency."

The 123-title "Selected List," selected by Elizabeth Minot Graves, does not list any paperback titles. They are arranged under 18 categories, e.g., Christmas, religion, teenage novel, and storybooks for ages nine to 12. Most books have two or three-line annotations, though some don't have any at all. This year she added two additional categories to her list: "drugs" (two titles) and "for adults—books about children's literature" (three titles).

Minot provides an almost equal balance of fiction and nonfiction, though picture and elementary age titles predominate. There is a smattering of "relevant books"—ecology, the black experience, women's liberation, but this list, as are most others, is still culturally biased. (A fact which may be either a fault of the selector or the publishing industry.) The closest one can come to nonwestern thought in her religion section in this list is an African version of the story of David and Goliath. The six titles under world history include one each on monsters of the middle ages, Russia, the Sahara, Taiwan, anarchism, and the dynamics of dress.

The *New York Review of Books* came through this year with a limited roundup of children's books. It is an essay review of 16 titles written by Janet A. Smith, identified as the editor of *The Looking Glass Book of Verse* and an edition of Robert Louis Stevenson poems. She concentrates heavily on fiction and picture books and includes one title about children's literature. Age levels for the titles were not specified. Smith's tone is generally favorable, but she does include some unfavorable critical comments on a few titles and a fair amount of background detail, though less than usually found in *NYRB* adult book reviews. "I wouldn't buy the book for a child," says Smith, commenting on Anne Sexton's *Transformations* (Houghton, 1971) (which may or may not be considered a "children's book," depending on how one

classifies a modern verse version of fairy tales—with a dash of Freud thrown in), "but I would much rather a child came across it than many a cute, crude, and gaudy horror of a fairy book." Just what does that comment tell parents about children's reading?

In balance, *Scientific American's* ten-page "Books About Science for the Younger Reader: An Annual Christmas Survey" is the best of the roundups, albeit more specialized. Written by Philip and Phylis Morrison (unidentified—at least on the advance proof pages) it covers 45 books in detailed reviews, varying in length from 20 lines to several columns. Though titles were obviously pre-selected for quality, the reviews point up both assets and faults. The Morrisons say that many of this year's books, "judging by their length, visual design, and presentation, were marketed for readers between eight and ten years old," but make a particular effort to note when titles are appropriate for their age groups. They cover eight subject areas: general, biology, specific forms of life, field guides, man, perception, physics, earth and skies, and mathematics, and have included such "adult" titles as *The Whole Earth Catalog.*

Newspaper Reviews

The six pages allocated to children's books by the *Christian Science Monitor* is whittled down to three and one-half by advertisements. As previously mentioned, reviewers of children's and young adult titles are not identified, though reviewers of adult books in the same issue are. About 95 titles are covered, with a three to one fiction to nonfiction ratio, the usual heavy emphasis on picture and elementary age books, some at the junior high level, and a few young adult titles.

Carolyn Klingston's lead article, "It's Hard to Fly a Kite," is probably one of the most valuable of the essay reviews published in the special children's books supplements and sections, with its emphasis on reality in books for children. She asks: "Should children have rats and garbage as well as pleasant scenes in books? If squalor and grime are the furniture of one's life, the question is unnecessary."

"What is more important is to ask what the authors of children's books have to say and if the picture is honest."

Klingston discusses 13 titles for children she considers realistic, and offers the parent some pointed insights: "Interesting customs—are no longer the central themes of books about Spanish-speaking Americans;" and "the picture story, a medium familiar in young children's books, is being used for their older brothers and sisters." She includes a fair range of age levels and a few paperbacks.

Unfortunately, Klingston fails to confront any of the current questions raised about the fact that many of the books she cites about minority groups were written by white, middle class, Anglo-Saxon adult authors.

CSM covers over 75 other titles in 16 additional shorter essay reviews, following freely much the same categorical and age spread of the other children's supplements. These range from Neil Millar's syrupy "Leapin' Buffalizards: Verse and Worse" ("The whole book squirms with humor. Perhaps Miss Watson has mixed her colors with gigglejuice, which accounts for some rather blotchy washes. But the washes are never wishy, the blotches never bitchy.") to June Goodwin's more lucid and critical "Sitting Lightly on the Whimsy Scale." Unfortunately, Goodwin, as did several other reviewers of children's books in this and other children's sections, found it necessary to rely on a *deus ex machina*, in this case the "next best thing" to a child—a pregnant sister-in-law—as a literary reviewing device.

Then there are Melvin Maddocks' discussion of ". . . a few of the season's books for young jocks that came close to winning the Big Game of literature," and Nancy Garden's "Romance and Realism" look at books for eight to 12. Unfortunately, she asks, "Why must books for eight to 12-year-old's fall

clearly into 'boy' and 'girl' categories," then proceeds to recommend them, though she does commend one title for "girls with more on their minds than future housekeeping and maternity."

The moralizing in Patience M. Canham's "Left Alone in the Wilderness," a review of *A Wild Thing* by Jean Renvoize (Little, Brown, 1971), and John Donovan's *Wild in the Woods* (Harper, 1971) becomes a bit much. "Do I recommend these books for teenagers? Yes, with reservations. Essentially honest as I think they are, these books tell only part of the whole human condition." Janet Farley Smith offers a look at what she considers the good black biographies (seven) in "Some Who Overcame" and in "Make My Trouble Go Away" she points out to parents why their children should read books about drug addicts. Guernsey Le Pelley's "For the Screamy Younger Set" offers a slightly more critical view than Graves of books for younger children.

Children's Book World's 15-page section is about half the size of last fall's section, and is down about six pages from last spring. Eight-and-one half pages are advertisements. A lead article by *CBW* editor Polly Goodwin concentrates on "Answer to Inflation: Children's Paperbacks," covering much the same ground as Ballard, though she mentions some 30 titles in her text and two bibliographies of paperbacks for children, and says: "The next important step is to see that bookstores and libraries stock and display children's paperbacks so they can easily be found, bought, and enjoyed."

Parents can then turn to some 12 other conglomerate reviews of another 70-odd titles, including "Tried and True," a review of 11 picture books by Michael Ballard, this time identified as "a freelance critic whose five-year old son serves as an unpaid consultant."

"If you find a 'Welcome Home' sign in your favorite bookstore draped above the juvenile picture books, don't be surprised," Ballard tells us. "It merely signifies the return this year of such popular authors and illustrators as Martha

Alexander, Ezra Jack Keats, Tomi Ungerer, Charlotte Zolotow, William Steig, and the ubiquitous Dr. Seuss." Two other articles, "A Magical Tour," six "new stories by recognized craftsmen in the field," reviewed by Virginia Haviland, head of the children's section, Library of Congress, and "Favorite Characters Return," a review of six titles by Polly Goodwin, take a similar established author approach.

On the whole, the quality of *CBW*'s reviews vary. Some are completely favorable, some critical, others are gratuitous. (Jane Yolen on Jeanne Hardendorff's *Witches, Wit, and a Werewolf:* ". . . it seems silly to waste her professional story-telling art on these trifles." Coverage leans very heavily on the fiction side and includes only a few young adult titles. Authors of reviews are often scantily identified, and in some cases, not identified at all. Some reviews include age levels, other do not. The topics covered include nature, ecology, horror and suspense, art, books for beginning readers, and fiction for ten to 14-year-olds.

Last, but not least, is the *New York Times* "Children's Book Section," down eight pages from last year, but still the season's largest at 48 pages, even subtracting 27 pages for advertisements. There were only two roundup- reviews—as compared to six last November, and essay reviews were also missing. Joan Bodger Mercer, consultant to publishers and libraries, and supervisor of seven day care centers in Toronto, reviews eight picture books, good and bad, in her roundup. "A Ghoulash of Ghouls," by Richard Elman, "raised by witches in Brooklyn, and . . . the author of *An Education in Blood*," supposedly covers 13 titles, but he liked one so much he devotes half his space to describing it, then discusses two he doesn't like briefly—without mentioning their titles—pans a few others, and recommends a few. The other titles are never mentioned. His essay does offer fascinating facts and observations about witchcraft and trends in publishing, but it

might have been helpful to offer criticism on each, rather than panning jointly—without reference to specific titles—a majority of the titles reviewed.

Some 12 other titles received detailed treatment in reviews, six fell between the elementary and junior high range, three were picture books, and three were young adult; two were nonfiction.

Three young adult titles were reviewed by Benjamin De Mott, author of *Surviving the '70s*, who really didn't like any of them particularly and gives his detailed reasons why. (Though the books were by Nat Hentoff, Maia Wojciechowska, and John Neufield, the *Times* was the only review to mention them.) Selma G. Lanes, author of *Down the Rabbit Hole*, discusses thoroughly the good and bad points of picture books by adult authors Ionesco, Barthelme, and Delessert—"One hit, one miss, and one near disaster." Toni Cade Bambara, editor of *Tales and Stories for Black Folks*, devotes a page worth of favorable review—with plenty of logical backup—to a collection on the third world and a book on being young and black in Africa. Other reviewers include Sarah Webster Fabio, a specialist in black literature, John Hersey (*Hiroshima*, et al.), Susan Sheehan, a staff writer on the *New Yorker*, and Ingeborg Boudreau, a faculty member of the Pratt School of Library Information Science, all of whom provide detailed, in-depth reviews.

Among other regular features of the *Times* are "Best Illustrated Books," with a sample illustration from each of the ten; "Outstanding Books of the Year," 33 titles arranged by age level, with quotes from previously published *Times* reviews; and "You've Read the Paperback—Will You Buy the Hardcover?" by Douglas Mount, a former editor of *Publisher's Weekly*. The latter is more detailed than both the Ballard and Goodwin paperback pieces, and though favorable towards the trend, criticizes the industry for proceeding with the sort of boneheaded caution that characterizes the rest of publishing; i.e., "among the current crop there is a disturbing number of very dated titles—from the '30s and '40s—of questionable value to the child of the '70s." Mount briefly, but critically, reviews about 15 paperback titles for children and teenagers.

" 'So You Are Another Alice' " and "Lad as a WASP in Dog's Clothing" are two other features the *Times* chose to publish in its children's section. The first, written by Morton N. Cohen, who is preparing an edition of Lewis Carroll's letters, is an interesting historical piece, but has little new to say. The second piece on the Albert Payson Terhune "Lad" stories by Gaddis Smith, a professor of history at Yale, is long and rambling, but may possibly score a point with "now nostalgic grandparents who fail to see the racial intolerance and other prejudices implicit in the stories," and "supply the demand to keep his books in print." Frankly, though, some of the features cut out from last year, such as the roundup of teen-age novels, or a roundup of books on drugs, might have served the parent better.

General Conclusions

The *Times* best seller list, leading off with Roald Dahl's *Charlie and the Chocolate Factory* (Knopf, 1964) and following with *Richard Scarry's Best Word Book Ever* (Golden Pr., 1963); *The Trumpet of the Swan*, E.B. White (Harper, 1970); *Charlotte's Web*, E.B. White (Harper, 1952); *The Velveteen Rabbit*, Margery Williams (Doubleday, 1958); *The Little Prince*, Antoine de Saint-Exupéry (Harcourt, 1943); *The First Four Years*, Laura Ingalls Wilder (Harper, 1971); *Winnie-the-Pooh*, A.A. Milne (Dutton, 1926); *The Giving Tree*, Shel Silverstein (Harper, 1964); and *The Tale of Peter Rabbit*, Beatrix Potter (Warne, 1902) confirms our worst fears. The only ones even published in this decade are *Trumpet of the Swan* and *The First Four Years*, both by extremely well established children's authors.

If these books are indeed the bestsellers, current children's books are *not* something most parents know anything

about. There may be a plethora of quality "classics," but children of the '70s desperately need to be more aware of relevant, contemporary literature. Most of the children's supplements are guilty of the "highly recommended" syndrome, but librarians, in their booklists, are too. We, as well as the editors of children's book sections, might take a cue from the general consumer movement, which is calling for advice and warnings, as well as recommendations. Parents need to know which books they probably shouldn't buy, too. They might also find helpful reviews of books *about* children's literature and information as to good bibliographies available. At present, the message that comes through loud and clear, to quote from John Hersey's review in the *Times*, is of a "spate of flat, safe, bland, commercially prudent books for children. . ."

As far as balance is concerned, perhaps in this "media-age" children get their facts from other sources than books, but in this age of burgeoning information and misinformation, the lack of attention paid to current nonfiction titles is a glaring gap. Also, as the war and post-war babies reach adulthood, isn't it about time the general review media started paying attention to young adult literature and adult literature for young adults? It seems to be a well-kept library secret. What about subject coverage? Very few books on drugs, sex, alternative life styles, or even science fiction were even considered worthy of mention.

And then there is the question of the final consumer—the child. "Children's Liberation" is something we haven't heard much about yet, but groups like the Summerhill Collective and other's concerned with alternative education are beginning to talk and write about it. Though the notion may seem ludicrous at first, the fact is that children and young people *are* the single, largest segment of modern society subject to stringent controls by others—legally, educationally, physically, and morally. Whole industries and institutions, including children's publishing, reviewing, and library service, have been built on this premise. The general review media might do well to encourage capable children to review—or at least to solicit their input, rather than rely on one or two reviewers' use of their own children as "unpaid, unofficial" consultants.

Librarians also have a role to play. We are the market for over 80 percent of the new children's books published. One of our self-assumed professional goals is to inform our clientele about books for children. Why, then, aren't librarians who are children's book specialists sought out as a source of informed reviewers for the general press? Will their letters extending or protesting review coverage in these periodicals be published? Will the letters even be written?

Children's Literature as a Scholarly Resource: The Need for a National Plan

James Fraser

"CHILDREN'S BOOKS . . . not only . . . have as much scholarly and bibliographical interest as books in other fields, but more than any class of literature they reflect the minds of the generation that produced them. Hence no better guide to the history and development of any country can be found than its juvenile literature."—A. S. W. Rosenbach, 1933.

When considered more than a generation later, the late Dr. Rosenbach's observation has failed to stimulate any North American research library into the initiation of a broadly conceived, systematic sampling of domestic and foreign children's literature in its many forms. Carolyn Field's recent *Subject Collections in Children's Literature* [2] would seem to controvert this statement. But a closer examination of this guide clearly demonstrates that the traditional preoccupation with *the book* is still with us and that as far as collecting twentieth century materials is concerned, the predominant emphasis is on the "quality children's book," its authors and illustrators, at the expense of what Rosenbach implied, i.e. the total children's literature: good, bad, and in its various forms.

This enthusiasm for accumulating and preserving the "quality" books is not difficult to understand and certainly such materials are of importance to the librarian, some educators and publishers, as well as the scholar interested in samplings of the best of a given country's children's literature production. But if the needs of the sociologist, the cultural historian, and other social scientists are to be met, a re-evaluation of collecting emphases is going to be necessary and some form of national coordination established.

Part of our problem may be heritage, for when institutional collecting of children's literature gathered momentum in this country in the period between World Wars I and II, the book and the periodical were the primary forms in which this literature appeared. During this same period, however, the comic book, the children's phonorecord, the mass market children's book, the mass produced family game, and the radio program for children became part of the experience of the majority of literate children in the United States and Canada. Librarians in those years (and the situation is somewhat the same today) frequently collected the children's ephemera of the previous generation or century at the expense of the current production. Consequently, the social scientist with interests in the total literary environment of the post World War I child in the United States or any other literate society, will have difficulty finding systematic samplings, let alone comprehensive collections of the media cited above and in addition collections of religious publications for children, if Field and Ash[3] provide any indication of such resources.

In another area, the librarians involved in developing the major national programs for the acquisition of foreign library materials have, for one reason or another, all but ignored the importance of children's literature as a scholarly resource, a neglect difficult to explain in light of the sizeable body of literature of the past generation dealing with the role of children's media in the formation of cultural values. In the late 1930's and throughout the 40's, articles were appearing in popular periodicals and professional journals with such titles as "Nationalism in Children's Literature," "Sadism in the Nursery," "Experimentation with Children's Books in Russia," "Children's Books with Fangs," and the like, calling attention to the overt abuses, in some cases, of children's literature. This was the period in which the Co-operative Acquisitions Project for Wartime Publications and the Farmington Plan were being formulated and established, yet children's literature was not considered of sufficient import as a social document to merit inclusion in either of these plans. The attitude toward children's literature including textbooks is clearly stated in the *Farmington Plan Handbook* of 1953 and reiterated in the 1961 revision:[4]

> Publications of certain kinds were believed to be numerous, expensive, and of relatively little research value; this explains the exclusion of books primarily of interest for format, juvenile literature, newspapers, textbooks, reprints . . . and translations from one modern language into another.

Admittedly, the overwhelming bibliographical problems of the immediate post World War II period gave little time for reflection or debate on the categories of material to be included in large scale acquisition programs. Areas of common agreement needed to be decided upon quickly and most librarians could agree on the acquisition of foreign scholarly monographs and *belles lettres*. However, in 1958 when the effectiveness of the Farmington Plan was being evaluated[5] by Vosper, Talmadge and others, none of the survey participants suggested a reconsideration of the exclusion policy on children's literature.

Two foreign acquisition programs developed in the 1950's, and in operation since the early 1960's are the Latin American Co-operative Acquisitions Program (LACAP) and the Public Law 480 Program. The LACAP, a commercial venture administered by Stechert-Hafner & Co., is designed to provide participating libraries with a regular flow of current publications from Latin American countries. This undertaking has strengthened immeasurably North American holdings from this area but children's literature in any form and textbooks are excluded.

The Public Law 480 Program is a federally administered program through which selected United States research libraries are able to receive for token payment books and periodicals from Israel, India, Indonesia, Pakistan, Ceylon, Nepal, Yugoslavia, and the United Arab Republic. Although children's literature is officially excluded from the program,[6] the flexibility of the program has permitted inclusion in the shipments of some children's books having "literary or artistic merit." The director of the Israeli office of the Program, Harry Strittman, has had the foresight to go even further than this by selecting a broad representation of the year's children's book production of Israel and has, as well, regularly sent a selection of children's periodicals. Unfortunately, children's materials were dropped from the Israeli Program in January 1969 because of a shortage of funds.[7]

Children's books are currently being cataloged within the network of the National Program for Acquisitions and Cataloging but here again, as is the case with children's books coming in through the Public Law 480 Program, the titles selected for cataloging seem to be those which are distinguished for their literary merit or their distinctive illustrations, a situation which brings us right back to the basic problem: the social scientist making use of children's literature as a social document needs a much broader sampling of materials than those selected solely for their sophisticated graphics and outstanding literary qualities.

But with all of the problems implied above, there is, however, much over which to be optimistic, for we are seeing the elements coming into existence which are necessary for the development of a national plan for the acquisition and control of children's media resources. In 1963, the Library of Congress established a Children's Book Section under the direction of Virginia Haviland in order to give primary attention to the needs of the teacher, librarian, publisher, author, and illustrator of children's books.[8] Over 130 other institutional collections of varying size currently exist in the United States and Canada. In 1967, the United States Committee for Unicef called Anne Pellowski to develop an Information Center for Children's Cultures. This pioneering venture has an important sampling of children's media from most of the publishing countries of the world although its purpose is not, as its title implies, to become a repository for comprehensive collections. 1968-69 saw the publication of two much-needed reference works necessary to any preliminary planning of a national-international effort in this field: Anne Pellowski's international bibliographical guide, *The World of Children's Literature*[9] and Carolyn Field's *Subject Collections in Children's Literature,* cited above. Such undertakings as these are, hopefully, only the beginning.

The next step, now that a guide to domestic collections has been published, might be a formal inquiry into institutional interest in sharing the responsibility for maintaining research collections of representative samplings of the total domestic and foreign children's media production. Logically following such an inquiry would be the development of a national plan for the systematic acquisition, cataloging, and reporting of these media, a plan which might take into consideration the feasibility of utilizing existing frameworks such as have already been mentioned, e.g. Public Law 480 Program, LACAP, National Program for Acquisitions and Cataloging.[10] For if our existing collections are to be developed purposefully and for a wider scholarly audience, a coherent national plan must be forthcoming.

REFERENCES

1. Rosenbach, Abraham S. W. *Early American Children's Books.* Portland, Me.: Southworth Press, 1933. pp. xxvi-xxvii.

2. Field, Carolyn W., ed. *Subject Collections in Children's Literature.* New York: Bowker, 1969.

3. Ash, Lee, ed. *Subject Collections,* 3rd ed. New York: Bowker, 1967.

4. Williams, Edwin E. ed. *Farmington Plan Handbook*, revised ed. Ithaca, N.Y.: Association of Research Libraries, 1961. p. 14.

5. Association of Research Libraries. *Farmington Plan Survey: Final Report.* Directed by Robert Vosper and Robert Talmadge. Chicago: Association of Research Libraries, 1959.

6. Williamson, William L. ed. *Impact of the P.L. 480 Program on Overseas*

Acquisitions by American Libraries. Madison: University of Wisconsin Library School, 1967. p. 11.

7. *Public Law 480 Newsletter,* Feb. 1969, no. 16, p. 3.

8. Haviland, Virginia, ed. *Children's Literature: A Guide to Reference Sources.* Washington: Library of Congress, 1966. p. vii.

9. Pellowski, Anne, comp. *World of Children's Literature.* New York: Bowker, 1968.

10. Involvement of foreign research institutions, e.g. Swedish Institute for Children's Books (Stockholm), Children and Youth Book Section of the Deutsche Staatsbibliothek (Berlin), Institute for Youth Book Research of the Johann Wolfgang Goethe University (Frankfurt am Main), International Institute for Children's . . . Literature (Vienna), International Youth Library (Munich), Centro Didattico Nazionale (Florence), in an international network of bibliographical exchange in this area is also worthy of consideration in the formulation of this national plan.

List of
Contributors

BEN BOVA is a science and science fiction writer and is editor of *Analog Science Fiction Magazine.* "From Mad Professors to Brilliant Scientists: the Evolution of a Genre" originally appeared in the May 1973 issue of *School Library Journal.* Copyright © 1973 by Ben Bova, all rights reserved.

DOROTHY BRODERICK is Associate Professor at the Dalhousie University School of Library Science, Halifax, Canada. Her latest book is *The Image of the Black in Children's Fiction* (R. R. Bowker Company, 1973). "Censorship—Reevaluated" originally appeared in the November 1971 issue of *School Library Journal*; "Moral Values and Children's Literature" originally appeared in the December 1971 and January 1972 issues of *School Library Journal.*

LEONA DANIELS is a library media specialist, Grand Island Middle School, Tonawanda, New York. "The 34th Man —How Well is Jewish Minority Culture Represented in Children's Fiction?" originally appeared in the February 1970 issue of *School Library Journal.*

MAVIS WORMLEY DAVIS is Resource Teacher of Library Media for the elementary schools of New Rochelle, New York. "Black Images in Children's Literature: Revised Editions Needed"

originally appeared in the January 1972 issue of *School Library Journal.*

SHEILA EGOFF is a professor in the School of Librarianship at the University of British Columbia, Vancouver, Canada. "If That Don't Do No Good, That Won't Do No Harm: the Uses and Dangers of Mediocrity in Children's Reading" originally appeared in the October 1972 issue of *School Library Journal.*

FEMINISTS ON CHILDREN'S MEDIA was formed in 1970 and has published "Little Miss Muffet Fights Back," a bibliography of non-sexist children's books. "A Feminist Look at Children's Books" originally appeared in the January 1971 issue of *School Library Journal.*

JOSETTE FRANK is Director for Children's Books and Mass Media, Child Study Association of America/Wel-Met, New York. "Sexuality in Books for Children" originally appeared in the February 1973 issue of *School Library Journal.*

JAMES FRASER is Library Director at the Madison, New Jersey, Campus of Fairleigh Dickinson University. "Children's Literature as a Scholarly Resource: the Need for a National Plan" originally appeared in the December 15, 1969 issue of *Library Journal.*

203

DR. KENNETH GOODMAN is the Director of Reading Miscue Research, Wayne State University, Detroit, Michigan. "Up-tight Ain't Right!" originally appeared in the October 1972 issue of *School Library Journal*.

JAMES A. HARVEY is Executive Secretary of the Illinois Library Association, and former Assistant Director of the American Library Association Office for Intellectual Freedom. "Acting for the Children?" originally appeared in the February 1973 issue of *School Library Journal*.

GERTRUDE B. HERMAN is Associate Professor at the Library School of the University of Wisconsin, Madison. "Africana: Folklore Collections for Children's originally appeared in the May 1972 issue of *School Library Journal*.

KATHERINE M. HEYLMAN is a librarian at Sunview Elementary School, Lyndhurst, Ohio. "The Little House Syndrome vs. Mike Mulligan and Mary Anne" originally appeared in the April 1970 issue of *School Library Journal*; "No Bargains for Frances: Children's Trade Books and Consumer Education" originally appeared in the October 1971 issue of *School Library Journal*.

MARGARET HIGGS is a recent graduate of Purdue University, Lafayette, Indiana, and is co-author with John Stewig of "Girls Grow Up to Be Mommies: A Study of Sexism in Children's Literature" which originally appeared in the January 1973 issue of *School Library Journal*.

JUNE JORDAN is a Black poet and writer who is the author of two books written in Black English, *His Own Where* (Thomas Y. Crowell Company, 1971) and *Dry Victories* (Holt, Rinehart and Winston, Inc., 1972). "Black English— The Politics of Translation" originally appeared in the May 1973 issue of *School Library Journal*. Reprinted by permission of the Julian Bach Literary Agency, Inc., New York.

ANN KALKHOFF is a children's librarian for the Brooklyn Public Library, and president and editor of *Children's Book Review Service*. "Innocent Children or Innocent Librarians" originally appeared in the October 1972 issue of *School Library Journal*.

ELAINE KONIGSBURG is an author of children's books, including *From the Mixed-Up Files of Mrs. Basil E. Frankweiler*, winner of the 1968 Newbery Award. "The Double Image—Language as the Perimeter of Culture" originally appeared in the February 1970 issue of *School Library Journal*.

ALAN LEVINE is director of the New York Civil Liberties Union's Student Rights Project and author of *The Rights of Students: the Basic ACLU Guide to the Rights of Public School Students* (Avon Books, 1973). "Impressionable Minds—Forbidden Subjects" originally appeared in the February 1973 issue of *School Library Journal*.

GEORGESS MCHARGUE is a writer and reviewer. Her books on the occult include *Facts, Frauds and Phantasms: A Survey of the Spiritualistic Movement* (Doubleday, 1972). "A Ride Across the Mystic Bridge or Occult Books: What, Why, and Who Needs Them?" originally appeared in the May 1973 issue of *School Library Journal*. Copyright © 1973 by Georgess McHargue, all rights reserved.

FRANK MCLAUGHLIN is editor of *Media and Methods* and Assistant Professor at Fairleigh Dickinson University, Teaneck, New Jersey. "Kids, Kulture and Us" originally appeared in the October 1972 issue of *School Library Journal*.

REY MICKINOCK is a librarian in the Belgrade Public Schools in Minnesota and a member of the Ojibway Nation. "The Plight of the Native American" originally appeared in the September 1971 issue of *School Library Journal*.

ELI M. OBOLER is University Librarian, Idaho State University, Pocatello, and chairman of the Idaho Library Association Intellectual Freedom Committee. "The Grand Illusion" originally appeared in the March 1968 issue of *School Library Journal*.

MARY ØRVIG is the Director of the Swedish Institute for Children's Books in Stockholm. "Children's Books in Translation: Facts and Beliefs" originally appeared in the November 1972 issue of *School Library Journal*.

PATRICIA SCHUMAN is a former Associate Editor of *School Library Journal* and is currently Library/Education/Information Resources Editor, Book Editorial Department, R. R. Bowker Company. "Concerned Criticism or Casual Copouts?" originally appeared in the January 1972 issue of *School Library Journal*.

LOU WILLETT STANEK is the Assistant Director of the English MAT Program at the University of Chicago, Illinois. "The Maturation of the Junior Novel: From Gestation to the Pill" originally appeared in the December 1972 issue of *School Library Journal*.

JOHN STEWIG is Associate Professor of Curriculum and Instruction in the School of Education, University of Wisconsin, Milwaukee. He is co-author with Margaret Higgs of "Girls Grow Up to Be Mommies: A Study of Sexism in Children's Literature."

PEGGY SULLIVAN directs the Office for Library Personnel Resources of the American Library Association, and is the author of *Problems in School Media Management* (R. R. Bowker Company, 1971). "Victim of Success? A Closer Look at the Newbery Award" originally appeared in the May 1972 issue of *School Library Journal*.

BARBARA WERSBA is the author of 10 children's books and a regular reviewer for the *New York Times*. "Sexuality in Books for Children" originally appeared in the February 1973 issue of *School Library Journal*.

"THE COURTS AND THE CHILD: SCHOOL BUREAUCRACY VS. THE FIRST AMENDMENT" originally appeared in the January 1970 issue of *School Library Journal*.

Index